THE AFRICAN IMAGINATION

THE AFRICAN IMAGINATION

Literature in
Africa & the Black Diaspora

F. Abiola Irele

OXFORD
UNIVERSITY PRESS

2001

OXFORD
UNIVERSITY PRESS

Oxford   New York
Athens   Auckland   Bangkok   Bogotá   Buenos Aires   Cape Town
Chennai   Dar es Salaam   Delhi   Florence   Hong Kong   Istanbul   Karachi
Kolkata   Kuala Lumpur   Madrid   Melbourne   Mexico City   Mumbai   Nairobi
Paris   São Paulo   Shanghai   Singapore   Taipei   Tokyo   Toronto   Warsaw

and associated companies in
Berlin   Ibadan

Published by Oxford University Press, Inc.
198 Madison Avenue, New York, New York 10016

Oxford is a registered trademark of Oxford University Press.

Library of Congress Cataloging-in-Publication Data
Irele, Abiola.
The African imagination : literature in Africa and the black diaspora /
F. Abiola Irele.
   p. cm.
Includes bibliographical references and index.
ISBN 0-19-508618-X; ISBN 0-19-508619-8 (paper)
1. African literature—History and criticism.   2. Literature and society—Africa.
3. African diaspora.   I. Title.
PL8010 .I74   2001
809'.896—dc21   00-052417

9 8 7 6 5 4 3 2 1

Printed in the United States of America
on acid-free paper

For

Mma Ette

and the girls
Tinu, Aya, & Idia

Preface

During my undergraduate days in the late 1950s at University College, Ibadan (as it was then known), a major annual event on campus was the performance of a musical work in the Western repertoire, in a production that was undertaken as a collaborative effort by students, faculty, and other amateur musicians recruited from the city, the latter often providing a crucial component of the cast. Indeed, the choice of Mozart's *The Magic Flute* for 1958 was determined by the happy fact that the wife of an English officer in the military garrison stationed at Ibadan during that year—Nigeria was still a colony of Britain at the time—was a trained soprano with the vocal capability to take on the demanding role of Queen of the Night. As it happened, I was assigned the role of Monostatos, the lascivious Moor in her service who torments the hapless heroine, Pamina, until he is finally cast off with his evil mistress into the night by Sarastro, the high priest of Osiris.

It appears that, from comments by friends and other observers who saw the production over the three nights that it ran, I played Monostatos with considerable relish. It certainly did not occur to me at the time to approach the role with any kind of circumspection, for it was not until years afterward that I came to be fully aware of the stereotyped and demeaning image of the black man that the role represented. So essential is this image to the Western imagination as it informs the simple moralism of the libretto for which Mozart supplied the music—a feature that also subserves in a curious way what we must now recognize as a fascist ethos—that even the great Swedish director Ingmar Bergman has his actor/singer play the lurid element of the role to the hilt, as it were, in the famous film he made of Mozart's opera.

I have recalled here the peculiar circumstances of my ambiguous involvement with Mozart's masterpiece because the episode seems to me significant in at least two ways. The first and immediate point has to do with the fact that the less appealing aspects of Mozart's opera reveal themselves only after reflection, for the overwhelming impression the work conveys is that of a profound aesthetic experience, sustained by the incomparable beauty of the music, its sublimity even, in terms of the Western convention of which it is of course one of the greatest instances. It thus illustrates the insidious and sometimes terrifying power of certain works of art to obscure with their very brilliance the moral zones they impinge upon. The outstanding example of this phenomenon in literature is perhaps Céline's *Voyage au bout de la nuit*, in which the aesthetic value generated by the sheer virtuosity of the writing becomes inseparable from the nature and extratextual import of the vituperations the work proffers. Second, and to be more particular, the episode places in sharp relief the fundamental irony of colonial education, whose ideological premises obliged its agents to have recourse to texts, images, and other modes of discourse and representation that devalue the humanity of their dark-skinned wards, as part of the effort to establish the cultural and moral authority of the colonizing race. But, as Albert Memmi has pointed out, the initial phase of submission and acquiescence on the part of the colonial subject who undergoes this form of education is invariably succeeded by a violent reaction against the systematic assault upon consciousness and sensibility that it is ultimately recognized to entail (Memmi, 1957).

The problematic relation between the aesthetic and the ethical suggested by these remarks has been examined by Michael Echeruo in the African context, with specific reference to Joseph Conrad's *The Nigger of the Narcissus*. If I have read him properly, Echeruo clearly identifies the bigotry behind Conrad's shadowy and ultimately sinister depiction of the black character in his tale as a shaping element of the work, but he goes on to interpret this factor as the driving force of a creative impetus conducive to the production of great art (Echeruo, 1978). Chinua Achebe for his part is less accommodating, for he finds Conrad's other tale, *Heart of Darkness*, so offensive that he is unable to concede the aesthetic and moral significance claimed for it by its numerous advocates. We know that he was stirred to literary creation himself by the realization that his own humanity as an individual was called into question by the negative representation of Africa that he encountered in Conrad's novella and in the work of other European writers who have located their imaginings in his continent of origin. For him, these works provide the clearest indication of the compelling need for Europe to cast Africa as the polar opposite of itself, in order to enforce its self-affirmation as the unique source of human and spiritual values. Africa has thus been projected in the West both imaginatively and conceptually as what he calls "the place of negation" (Achebe, 1988).[1]

Achebe's imaginative and ideological challenge of Western representations of Africa in his own work clarifies admirably the mental process that has attended the emergence of African literature in modern times. African responses to the pressures of colonial domination have found a privileged mode of expression in imaginative literature, which has not only registered the epochal significance of the encounter with Europe and its objective implications for African societies and cultures, but even more important, the complex relation of African experience to the norms and precepts commonly associated with the modern West, and ultimately their determination of the directions of African thought and expression. In this respect, African literature may be said to derive an immediate interest from the testimony it offers of the preoccupation of our writers with the conflicts and dilemmas involved in the tradition/modernity dialectic. This observation is based on the simple premise that, as with many other societies and cultures in the so-called third world, the impact of Western civilization on Africa has occasioned a discontinuity in forms of life throughout the continent. It points to the observation that the African experience of a modernity associated with a Western paradigm is fraught with tensions at every level of the communal existence and individual apprehension (Poirier, 1994; Gyekye, 1997). Modern African literature, in particular the literature expressed in the European languages, can be interpreted as a dramatization of and meditation upon the problems of existence posed by this situation.

The historical experience in all its ramifications thus serves as a constant reference for the African imagination; this has a consequence for any form of criticism concerned with our literature. It is impossible, in the particular circumstances of its development, to ignore the specific historical and sociological references of African imaginative expression in the European languages, for these references have determined the genesis and evolution of the literature. The thematic approach is thus fundamental to the inspiration of African literature: as with the themes by which all forms of literary expression are mediated, the external references constitute the points of articulation that enable a primary mode of entry into the literature in question.

The essays that constitute this volume explore the immediate correlation in African literature between life and expression on the continent, within the thematic and methodological perspective outlined above. It hardly needs to be stated that a thematic approach does not imply a simple subordination of the textual and aesthetic values evinced by the literature to purely historical and sociological considerations. I hope it will be clear that while these essays acknowledge the primacy of content, they do not neglect the necessary constraints of form that arise from the processes of signification central to the shaping and direction of imaginative discourse. I have endeavored to take full account of the "rhetorical strategies" that African writers have deployed in formulating their themes. In short, the critical activity here is intended not as a single-minded exposition of themes and the pursuit of judgments and affirmations that can only be summarily determined, but as a reaching through form to the complexities of experience of which the literary text is a mediation.

It is inevitable that in the effort to explore and to articulate the correlation of lived situation to imaginative expression in Africa, the problems that are evoked and the questions that are raised should sometimes be formulated at a certain level of abstraction. The reference to tradition as one of the terms indicative of the conflicts enacted in African literature may suggest a rigid dichotomy, and may be interpreted to imply a static, ahistoric conception of precolonial Africa placed over and against a modern dispensation inaugurated by the Western encounter. Moreover, although as a dominant theme the dilemma of modernity can be said to provide a privileged perspective on African literature, one has to be mindful of the risk of setting it up as a restrictive concept either for a consideration of the development of the literature itself, or for an appraisal of the cultural reality of Africa in the contemporary world, its complex aggregation of oppositional and subversive responses to modernity, and the creative appropriations of the same in areas as diverse as religion, the arts, and even the economy. Above all, the temptation to approach Africa as a vast, undifferentiated entity is an ever present one. But while it is true that one cannot avoid some generalization in any proposition that is concerned with the broad range of expressions represented by the corpus with which I am concerned in this book, it goes without saying that the critical activity called into play must cultivate a sense of context that can only emerge from an attentive focus on texts as indicators of meaning, an activity in which the specificities of reference necessarily enter into the effort of elucidation.

It will be apparent that the guiding principle of the readings offered here derives from a tradition of literary criticism conceived not merely as an exercise in the elucidation of meaning in the text but in the clarification of tone and inference. In the prevailing atmosphere of literary scholarship, this conception has come to be considered as a conservative one. However, it has not been satisfactorily demonstrated, in my opinion, that structuralist and deconstuctionist approaches are necessarily the most productive in rendering a proper sense of literary texts in their fullness of being, involving a proper conjoining of form and reference. Jonathan Culler has emphasized the intellectual appeal of structuralist criticism, which opened the way to current trends, as arising from a dissatisfaction with earlier practice, considered as amounting to no more than an exercise in paraphrase, and a compelling need for a more rigorous approach, distinguished by its focus on the text as a signifying system, as a form of code (Culler, 1975). However, Edward Said has deplored the absence of a sense of history or of social fact in the New New Criticism that has resulted from this exclusive preoccupation with text.[2] The scorn with which earlier practices are sometimes regarded seems to me therefore rather misplaced. No one who has experienced the penetrating reading by F. R. Leavis of T. S. Eliot's *Four Quartets* in his late work, *The Living Principle*, will be inclined to look down upon or speak with disdain of "Lit. Crit." Leavis was widely regarded as the greatest modern critic in the English language, and we cannot all achieve the acuteness of insight and the vigor of statement that he brought to his criticism, but his work has an exemplary value for the conduct of literary analysis as a serious engagement with texts in their significant connection with life and values.[3]

I have attempted to recover some of the impulse that animates this earlier practice of criticism in the essays that constitute this volume. In their focus upon a collective experience, they represent a continuation of the effort begun in a previous collection, *The African Experience in Literature and Ideology*. While a common intent runs through the two volumes, I believe it is of some interest to point out certain developments that have a bearing on the composition of the essays in the present volume. In contrast to the essays collected in *The African Experience*, those presented here, with a single exception, have been written during a period in which I have been removed from my habitual environment, a condition that has involved a physical and mental distance from the primary audience that I assumed I was addressing during an earlier phase of my professional career in Africa: an audience constituted by the local community of students and scholars. That phase was marked by an effort to formulate lines of approach to what was then an entirely new academic field, so that the dominant preoccupation at the time was with the definition of African literature as a distinctive area of expression, along with its promotion not merely as an academic discipline but also as a form of cultural activity. In this perspective, the literary criticism that developed as an extension of one's academic teaching was expected to fulfill a double function: to contribute to the formation in the African context of what Stanley Fish has called "an interpretive community" (Fish, 1980), and in this way to establish for the literature a form of validation.

It is not clear to what extent the assumptions and hopes I've evoked were based on an illusion, but it is now obvious to me that it is no longer possible to entertain them in a situation where the profession of scholar-critic is pursued in exile. For where before I could envisage African literature as central, or at least potentially so, to an evolving national community to which I felt bound despite the vicissitudes that attended its fortunes, I am now obliged to work with the acute awareness that this literature is largely marginal to the interests of the scholarly and intellectual community within which I presently operate. This raises the issue of the situation of African literature in the Western academy, a situation that requires to be commented upon insofar as it has a bearing on the possible reception of these essays.

The flourishing of literature by Africans writing in the European languages is one of the significant cultural events of our time, and the African achievement in literature in the past half century or so is underscored by the emergence of African literature as an academic subject.[4] Yet it has continued to be considered a very narrow area of studies and of specialization in Western universities. Because the subject was at first treated as a subcategory of the general field of African Studies, it suffered a certain distortion of its true academic significance. African literary forms—whether oral or written—were featured in early studies more as secondary documents, providing material for other disciplines, such as linguistics and sociology, rather than as literary artifacts in their own right, and it was only gradually that they came to be approached from a proper literary perspective. Even then, African literature has hardly been accorded more than a very minor status in the curriculum of most Western institutions. In American universities, the subject can be found distributed among various departments, according to the circumstances that have attended its introduction into each institution. This has created a somewhat ambiguous situation for African literature in the American academy.

It is true that, apart from cultural and historical reasons that worked against its ready acceptance, the considerable coverage of the field embraced by the term "African literature" itself, with the internal diversity implied by its various definitions, has militated against the kind of neat departmental arrangement that has been found serviceable for the traditional areas of literary study such as those related to English and the continental European languages. With African literature, which encompasses at least three areas—the oral tradition, written literatures in the indigenous African languages, and in the European languages—it has often been unclear whether the language of expression or the area of reference of the literature should determine the departmental affiliation of the subject. The problem is further complicated by the thematic and historical connections between literary expression in Africa, the Caribbean, and Black America. Part of the difficulty in finding a proper home, so to speak, for African literature thus derives from the fact that the definition of its boundaries and consequently its status as a discipline have remained problematic. But while these factors have their importance, it seems fair to observe that the ambiguous institutional and academic status of African literature in the American university system has to do essentially with the marginal interest that non-Western literatures in general and African literature in particular have had for "mainstream" scholarship.

In recent years, however, this situation has begun to change, as a result of developments within the Western academy itself that may well turn out to have positive implications for these literatures, including the African. In the past few years we have witnessed a profound transformation of literary studies in the West, with unsettling effects on the traditional conception of literature and the academic organization of its study. It is hardly a simplification to observe that literature has come to be regarded less as a purely aesthetic phenomenon, enjoying an ideal status in an autonomous realm, than as essentially a mode of discourse that, for all its particular character, shares with other modes of discourse a common ground in social experience and cultural practice (Hodge, 1990). Moreover, the explosion of theory that has marked literary scholarship in recent times has been closely related to a reappraisal of the entire field of literary creation and has thus provoked a challenge of the established canon. A concomitant of this process has been the effort of revaluation of what has been called "minority discourses," especially with regard to their literary aspects, which derive from particular forms of experience related to issues of race, ethnicity, and gender.[5]

Thus, while current movements in literary scholarship and critical theory have been marked by an often inordinate display of scholasticism,[6] they have undoubtedly promoted a lively climate of debate in which the so-called noncanonical literatures are being increasingly invoked as a reference for alternative approaches to questions of literary expression and critical discourse. What is more, at the moment, there is a noticeable trend toward establishing a connection between poststructuralist "deconstruction" of Western systems of thought and institutions as reflected in their dominant discourses and the postcolonial emergence of an expanding and vibrant Third World literature (Ashcroft et al. 1989). The result of these developments can be described as a widening of the horizons of literary studies in a process that is bringing these literatures into clearer view, if not into a new prominence, with consequences for literary theory and criticism. As Said has formulated the matter, "In a sense . . . there has been a reemergence of comparative literature, if by using that term we do not restrict the phenomenon either to philology or to the thematic study of works in their original languages. For, indeed, the new comparative style is metacritical, transnational, intertextual" (Said, 1980, viii). I believe I can claim to have worked instinctively, as it were, with the conception of literature and criticism enunciated by Said's remarks.

This book will probably be ranged under the rubric of "postcolonial studies," but I hope this convenient label will not obscure its wider connections. For example, I have not hesitated, where necessary, to stress the dynamic imparted by Western texts to our literatures, an important factor in the historical circumstances of their emergence and modes of existence. This is a factor whose formal character is best conveyed by the term "Euro-African intertextuality," a term that must be understood as denoting not a validating norm but rather an enabling principle in the development of modern African literature (Irele, 2000). More circumscribed is that other context indicated by the title essay, in which I propose the notion of an African imagination as a general perspective for apprehending in a single vision the various dimensions of Black expression. The essays that follow may be said to enlarge in varying degrees upon this notion. Given the historical and thematic connections between forms of imaginative expression and intellectual movements in Africa and the Black Diaspora in the Caribbean and North America, a fundamental concern here is to chart the directions of modern expression in Africa and the Black Diaspora, as embodied both in the imaginative and the ideological writings, within the general perspective of an intellectual history that reflects African and Black responses to the encounter with the West.

But apart from exploring the relations that connect the different areas of Black literature, a major burden of these essays derives from the need to formulate a theory of African literature in a comparative perspective, stressing its significance as reflecting a truly heterogeneous and diversified experience of literary form. This has, paradoxically enough, required an insistence on the distinctive features of African literature: in other words, its differentiation in formal and cultural terms. The centrality of orality to the African imagination, the original dimension it confers on African forms of expression, has provided the principal means for demonstrating not merely the distinctive character of African literary genres but also their comparative interest. For this reason, I have had to consider the question of orality in the development of my argument in the title essay, and to confront it directly, so to speak, in the succeeding essay entitled "Orality, Literacy, and African Literature" (chapter 2). I have also found myself having to return to the question in some of the other essays, for example in my reading of *The Fortunes of Wangrin* in chapter 5, in which I discern a form of counterpoint between orality and literacy as the informing principle and driving force of Hampaté Bâ's textual practice. The primary objective in all these forays into theory has been to try and shed some light on a phenomenon that is manifestly an important cultural feature in Africa, in order to facilitate reflection on the fundamental questions it raises for literary scholarship.

There can be no doubt about the necessity for this reflection. It has sometimes been asserted that the insistence in African scholarship on the primacy of orality in traditional African cultures and forms of discourse has been motivated by purely ideological considerations. A notable instance of this view is provided by Eileen Julien who, in a well-known study, proceeds to set up what will strike many as a straw man against whom to direct her challenge of what she considers a racialized conception of oral communication (Julien, 1992). Taking his cue directly from Julien, J. M. Coetzee has gone further and adopted a sneering tone that turns this straw man into pure caricature, when he suggests an association between African theories of orality and a vulgar conception of black masculinity (Coetzee, 1999). While it is clear to anyone with an inside experience of orality that these views are somewhat incomplete, as with Julien, and totally inadequate, as in the case of Coetzee, one cannot presume to dispel the misconceptions they foster without a demonstration in scholarly terms of orality as a defining feature and significant modality of African expression. And when one learns, as I have, that an African-American university professor had no inkling of the immediate derivation of the Brer Rabbit stories from the African folktale tradition, which he apparently confuses with Aesop's fables, the immensity of the task of information that needs to be undertaken in this area emerges in all its scope and urgency.

The seminal work of Kwabena Nketia on the funeral dirges of the Akan people (1958), Isidore Okpewho on the oral epic in Africa (1979), Daniel Kunene on Sotho heroic poetry (1986), and Karin Barber on *oriki* or lineage poetry among the Yoruba (1991)—to cite just these examples— has demonstrated that documentation and analysis of oral forms can serve as steps toward the elaboration of concepts that enable a proper understanding of the dynamics of oral literature.[7] It is my conviction that such an understanding can only support the contention that literacy obscures the nature of narrative and poetic forms in their pure phenomenality, unmediated by writing. For the issue that orality raises for literary scholarship is metacritical, one that goes to the very heart of the status, modes of existence, and cultural significance of speech acts when they assume an imaginative and symbolic function.

This observation prompts a final question concerning the place of "theory" in the study of African literature. The question may be understood in either the narrow sense of an examination of the relevance of current theories to the particular circumstances of African literature, or in the wider sense of the potential for the expansion of the conceptual field of literary theory itself through a consideration of the specific forms and functions of this literature in relation to the Western. The parallel immediately suggests itself here of the impact of the folk tradition on the Russian formalists in the elaboration of their methodological and theoretical studies. The point that needs to be stressed is that the distinctive situation of African literature as a comprehensive field that embraces several conventions of imaginative expression and brings into view different traditions of literary valuation constitutes what one might call a strategic position for gaining a more inclusive perspective on the general phenomenon of literature than is afforded by the established Western canon. For while the postulate of a universal, undifferentiated experience of literature does not appear to be tenable, it is nonetheless useful, if only from a theoretical and methodological perspective, to examine the lines of convergence that relate various literary traditions to one another despite the differences of language, conventions, and historical development. Literary scholarship thus stands to benefit from bringing African literature firmly within its purview.

The recognition of orality as a valid expressive medium can be seen from this point of view to be a responsibility that is incumbent upon African literary scholars to promote. But this does not by any means imply a repudiation of literacy, which has served us well in our confrontation with the vicissitudes of history and especially in the imaginative engagement with the dilemma of modernity.[8] Given the circumstances of their composition, this aspect of the African experience has provided the inevitable focus of the essays in this volume. They may be thought perhaps to reflect an unusually strong awareness of the function of literature in Africa as a mode of self representation. This may be imputed to the recognition they express of this literature as the channel of an internal discourse of which Africans remain the undisputed subjects. It has been my purpose to examine African literature as a form of discourse whose suggestive force derives from its recourse to image and metaphor, but in which the symbolic mode by which it seeks to organize experience entails, to borrow Gerard Graff's term, a "propositional" aspect (Graff, 1980). For the conception of literary scholarship that underlies and sustains these essays has derived from a continuous engagement with African and Black historical experience as refracted through the prism of literary texts, with all the affective and symbolic charge implied by this form of representation. In the event, literary criticism has come to represent for me a special mode of intellectual endeavor: although grounded in an intuitive response to imaginative texts, it also represents a form of active participation in the process of reflection generated and sustained by these texts upon the existential problems that enter into what Ali Mazrui has described as "the African condition" (Mazrui, 1980).

Beyond the theoretical and methodological concerns evoked above, I have been at pains, then, to present the imaginative phenomenon in Africa in its referential function, that is, as a central component of the symbolic field of awareness and, hence, as a regulatory factor of the communal experience in Africa. For the literary/aesthetic cannot be divorced from the climate of reflection and discourse arising out of the comprehensive context of an African experience that extends from the precolonial to the present postcolonial situation. The term "African Literature" is thus to be taken here in a wider sense than is denoted by the usual reference to imaginative expression. As in other contexts, literature here not only communicates a structure of feeling but also reflects a climate of thought. The essays in this book are intended to register this irreducible character of the literary phenomenon as it applies to the African world. In their specific orientation, they seek to place literature within the total framework of life and expression so as to connect it to other forms of the social production of meaning in contemporary Africa.

Acknowledgments

The field of scholarship is now so extensive that it is no longer possible for any single individual to pretend to mastery of even a small part of it. For this reason, every published work has to be considered the outcome of a collaborative effort, either explicitly solicited and welcomed, or recognized as implicit in the informal system of exchanges and conversations that are a part of the collegiate culture the academy has a vocation to promote and sustain. I have been especially fortunate in the collegiate company into which I have been thrust, especially since my expatriation in 1987. While I cannot possibly name all those who have in one way or the other contributed to this volume, it gives me great pleasure to identify at least some of them.

I must begin with Henry Louis Gates, Jr., to whom I owe the idea for bringing together in a volume a selection of my essays scattered in various journals; for this, and for his constant support in other spheres, I owe him a wealth of thanks. Other friends and colleagues from whose ideas and suggestions, freely and generously provided, I have benefited over the years include Kwame Anthony Appiah, John Conteh-Morgan, Tim Cribb, Irène D'Almeida, Joan Dayan, Biodun Jeyifo, Simon Gikandi, Eileen Julien, Sylvie Kandé, Bernth Lindfors, Lupenga Mphande, Francesca Mirizzi, Isaac Mowoe, Tanure Ojaide, Ato Quayson, Alain Ricard, Elaine Savory, Sarah Suleri (now Firestone), Nouréini Tidjani-Serpos, and Olabiyi Yai. The publication of this volume brings back memories, impossible for me to forget, of the wonderful intellectual companionship that I enjoyed with my two late friends and colleagues, Richard Bjornson and Josaphat Kubayanda.

It is usual for an author to feel a sense of obligation to the institutional libraries that have supported his or her research. Never is any mention made of the bookshops from which some of the books that went into this research were procured, yet they are important to all our scholarly work. I have every reason to express my appreciation on this account to Paul Watkins and his staff at the SBX Bookshop in Columbus, Ohio— Kara Kostiuk, Lee Badger, Mike Rau, Darryl Price—for the courtesy and promptness with which they have always attended to my book orders. They helped in no small way to ease for me the tension and near desperation of keeping up with the flood of publications in literary studies and related fields.

Once again, I owe Ruthmarie Mitsch a special debt of gratitude. She proved as usual a most diligent first reader and editor; she went over the text with a fine comb, so to speak, and compiled the general bibliography. I'm also grateful to Karen Leibowitz and Stacey Hamilton at Oxford University Press for their forbearance while seeing the work through the production process.

To all these named individuals, and to so many others whom it is impossible for me to list here, I wish to express the warmest thanks.

Finally, a word about the text. With the exception of chapter 7, which is an expanded version of a paper first delivered as a lecture in Lomé, and subsequently as a conference paper in Bordeaux, the essays in this volume have been reprinted with only minor revisions in the form in which they first appeared. The credits are as follows:

"The African Imagination." *Research in African Literatures* 21, no. 1 (1990): 47–67.

"Orality, Literacy, and African Literature," in *Semper Aliquid Novi: Papers in Honour of Albert Gérard*, ed. Janos Riesz and Alain Ricard, 251–63. Tübingen: Gunter Narr Verlag, 1989.

"African Letters: The Making of a Tradition." *Yale Journal of Criticism* 5, no. 1 (Fall 1991): 69–100. Revised and expanded version of the keynote address delivered at the conference on "Tradition and Transition in African Letters" organized by the Common Wealth of Letters at Yale University, April 19–21, 1990.

"Dimensions of African Discourse." *College Literature* 19, no. 3 (Oct. 1992), and 20, no. 1 (Feb. 1993): 45–59. Reprinted in Kostas Myrsiades and Jerry McGuire, eds., *Order and Partialities: Theory, Pedagogy* and the *"Postcolonial,"* 15–34. Albany: State University of New York Press, 1995.

"Study in Ambiguity: Amadou Hampaté Bâ's *The Fortunes of Wangrin.*" First published as "Wangrin: A Study in Ambiguity," introduction to Amadou Hampaté Bâ, *The Fortunes of Wangrin (L'Etrange destin de Wangrin)*, iii–xvi. Trans. Aina Pavolini Taylor. Ibadan: New Horn Press, 1988.

"Narrative, History, and the African Imagination: Ahmadou Kourouma's *Monnè, outrages et défis.*" First published as "Narrative, History and the African Imagination." *Narrative* 1, no. 2 (Spring 1993): 156–72.

"The Crisis of Cultural Memory in Chinua Achebe's *Things Fall Apart.*" First published as *"Le monde s'effondre* de Chinua Achebe: Structure et Signification," in *Littérature africaine et enseignement,* ed. Jacques Corzani and Alain Ricard, 171–86. Bordeaux: Presses Universitaires de Bordeaux, 1985.

"Return of the Native: Edward Kamau Brathwaite's *Masks." World Literature Today* 68, no. 4 (Autumn 1994): 719–25.

"A National Voice: The Poetry and Plays of John Pepper Clark-Bekederemo." First published as introduction to *John Pepper Clark-Bekederemo: Collected Poems and Plays,* vii–1. Washington, D.C.: Howard University Press, 1991.

"Parables of the African Condition: The New Realism in African Fiction." *Journal of African and Comparative Literature* 1 (Mar. 1981): 69–91.

My thanks go to the editors and managers of the various journals for permission to reprint these essays in this volume.

Contents

THE AFRICAN IMAGINATION

The African Imagination

Ever since the advent of African literature in the late 1950s and early 1960s, critics have been occupied with providing an account of its distinctive features and arriving at a definition of its specific nature. Most notable among these critics was Janheinz Jahn, who proposed the term "neo-African literature" to cover the specific corpus of writings produced by Blacks in the modern age and in the European languages, on both sides of the Atlantic; these writings were distinguished by a fundamental unity not only of reference but also of vision (Jahn, 1961, 1966). His approach consisted of positing a structure of mind common to members of the black race, an informing principle of a collective vision of the world. This vision was presumed to be discoverable in specific modes of traditional African thought as expounded by scholars such as Placide Tempels, Marcel Griaule, and Alexis Kagame. For Jahn, this structure of mind and this collective vision are manifested in one form or another in the imaginative expression of Black writers, both Africans and those of African descent. Jahn's approach, which derives from the essentialist tenets of the Negritude movement, is summed up in his use of the concept *nommo* as the operative factor of neo-Africanism in literature: the word is conceived as a living principle, an active force to be deployed in the writer's confrontation with experience.

In the United States, a similar preoccupation can be discerned in the effort of the Black Aesthetics movement to identify and account for a specific African-American literary tradition distinguished from the so-called mainstream of the national (white) literary expression (Gayle, 1971). While the quasi-mystic dimension of Jahn's account is absent from the formulations of the writers and critics associated with this movement, their effort was also bent toward the clarification of the distinctive quality of African-American literature, in their case by reference to the profound implication of this literature in the Black experience, in terms therefore inherent in its history and framework of elaboration. In both cases, the larger question of a Black identity provides the background for these efforts, the presumption being that such an identity would find its clearest and most profound expression in works of the imagination produced by Black writers.

The title of this book may suggest that my aim is identical to the efforts I have evoked above and so may give rise to undue expectations. It is, however, not my intention to propose a model of the structure of a racial imaginative faculty nor to demonstrate the impress of a Black identity upon the imagination. I would like more modestly to explore what seems to me a coherent field of self-expression by Black writers in relation not only to a collective experience but also to certain cultural determinants that have given a special dimension to that experience and therefore to have imparted to Black expression a particular tonality. My position does not of course rule out the possibility that such an exploration may well offer an opening for the elaboration of a distinctive Black aesthetics nor indeed, through the analysis of the dominant modalities of the literary works of Black writers, for the elucidation of the particular structure of mind fashioned by their cultural environment.[1] These are not, however, my immediate concerns here. My aim, rather, is more modest: to explore the terrain of African literature in the widest acceptance of the term and to arrive at a sense of its possible boundaries, that is, in its immediate reference to literary expression on the African continent and in what may be perceived to be the extension of this expression in the New World. In other words, I am exploring a field invested with a particular body of imaginative discourse, marked by both a convergence of themes and a common preoccupation with the modes of address of a new self-formulation. I would like my use of the term *African imagination* to be taken therefore as referring to a conjunction of impulses that have been given a unified expression in a body of literary texts.[2] From these impulses, grounded both in common experience and in common cultural references, Black texts have come to assume a particular significance that is worth attempting to elucidate.

The exploratory approach I am adopting has been prompted by the fact that the term *African literature* (to which we can directly relate what I have called the African imagination) carries with it a particular ambiguity of reference in its present and common usage. In the first place, our use of the term is posited upon a disjunction between language and literature. Ordinarily, we assume an organic and intimate association between the two. The association between language and literature can be said to be "natural" insofar as language constitutes the grounding structure of all literary expression, so that the unity of a body of literature is most readily perceived in terms of its language of expression rather than by any other criterion. For historical reasons with which we are familiar, the term African literature does not obey this convention. The corpus is in fact multilingual. The variety of languages covered by the term can be appreciated by a consideration of the range of literatures in Africa. These literatures fall into three broad categories: the traditional oral literature, the new written literature in the African languages (these two closely bound by their common basis in the various indigenous languages), and, finally, the written literature in languages not indigenous to Africa, in particular the three European languages of English, French, and Portuguese. It should be noted here that Arabic, though possibly the most widely employed non-indigenous language in Africa south of the Sahara, is usually excluded from our use of the term.

What I have called the disjunction between language and literature in our understanding of the term African literature has often been perceived as unnatural. It was at the root of the controversy that raged in the 1960s concerning the proper application of the term *African* to the new literature in the European languages, a controversy inaugurated by Obi Wali in his now famous article, "The Dead End of African Literature" (Wali, 1963). Despite this initial controversy, which surfaced at the dawn of the reception of African literature in the early 1960s, categorization according to languages indigenous to the continent has not yet become so compelling as to inhibit the use of the term African literature in the comprehensive continental sense in which it has become customary to do so. The reason seems to be that the ethnic dimension suggested by the appeal to indigenous languages does not appear to have received recognition as a determinant in the contemporary political, social, and cultural experience of the continent. In short, the notion of Africa as a unified geopolitical concept serves as the primary validation for the continued application of a term whose all-inclusive character does not seem to impair its efficacy of reference.

This situation leads to the other important association disregarded in our use of the term: the connection between literature and nation, which is understood as a community of people bound by ethnicity, language, and culture. The notion that literature is the collective expression of a people in this sense, of their heritage as a constituted national community, is of course an eminently modern one. Since the 1970s, there has been a movement in African literary studies toward the recognition of national literatures in the new African states, such as Cameroonian, Senegalese, Beninois literatures, and so on (Kadima-Nzuji, 1984; Huannou, 1989; Bjornson, 1991). But while there has undoubtedly emerged a definite sense of corporate identity, often marked by clear thematic and formal progressions, in some of the literatures expressed in the European languages, because of the common interests and involvements that have arisen out of what one might call the "territorial imperative," it remains an incontrovertible fact that the European-language literatures in Africa, for which a national status is being canvassed in each of the states where they have been produced, are not yet generally experienced as having attained such a status, largely because the languages in which they are expressed have at best only an official acceptance. They are neither indigenous to the societies and the cultures on which they have been imposed nor are they national in any real sense of the word. This must limit the claims to national significance of any of these literatures, however abundant the corpus or coherent the internal configurations.

The present position, then, is that literature in Africa does not quite function in the limited national range suggested by the conventional association between literature and nation save in a few exceptional cases, the most prominent being that of Somalia. Given the decidedly multi-ethnic and multilinguistic character of African states as presently constituted and the circumstances of the emergence of modern literature in Africa—along with the development of literary studies related to Africa— it has not been felt to be either appropriate or functionally valid to employ this micro level of definition or categorization of works. Today they are grouped together in the general corpus designated by the term African literature.

Clearly, Africa is not a nation in the ordinary sense of the term: without a common language and common institutions, the idea of an African "nation" with a recognizable political personality founded upon a common heritage of history and culture is an "invention" (Ranger, 1983). Objectively, then, where African literature as presently understood is concerned, there is no real correspondence founded upon conventional associations between literature and language on one hand or literature and nation on the other. Often, therefore, one feels a lack of congruence between the term African literature and the object to which it is applied. However, when considered from the point of view of reference to a framework of experience, the term acquires a pertinence that cannot be denied. African literature exists and has meaning primarily in the context of a recognizable corpus of texts and works by Africans, situated in relation to a global experience that embraces both the precolonial and the modern frames of reference. The significance of this continuous scheme for the notion of an African imagination will, I hope, become apparent later in this volume.

The point is that, for historical reasons that include important developments in the New World, *Africa* has emerged as an operative concept, which can be applied to an entire area of existence and historical experience. It is essential to bear in mind that this notion, starting as an ideological construction, has developed beyond this contingent factor to assume the significance of objective fact: there is today the sense of an African belonging that commands the vision of an entire people regarding their place in the world. The term is thus closely bound up with the emergence in Africa itself of a self-focused consciousness of which literature has been an essential medium of expression. The use of the term African literature therefore presupposes an attention to the complex of determinations that have endowed the term *African* with real meaning, with a special significance for us as Black people. But precisely because of the developments in the New World and their consequences for our notion of Africa, the term African literature itself can be restricting, since it excludes a dimension of experience that brought it into being in the first place. Moreover, we have seen the difficulties thrown up by its application to the African corpus itself. For this reason, it may be preferable to employ a term that is both more embracing and more flexible in its definitions. The notion of an African *imagination* corresponds to this wider scope of expression of Africans and people of African descent, which arises out of these historical circumstances.

In what follows, I shall attempt a pragmatic survey of the field that is covered by this extended term, taking into account the total framework of the imaginative expression that it represents: the areas of articulation and levels of representation and creation in relation to Africa, whether as an immediate reference or as a mode of connection to what has come increasingly to be accepted in the New World as an ethnic and cultural resource. I would like in short to consider the image of Africa as the figure of an engagement with the world in and through language from a comprehensive historical, ethnic, and cultural perspective.

Despite the disproportionate attention paid to literature by Africans in the European languages, the primary area of what I have called the African imagination is represented by the body of literature produced by, within, and for the traditional societies and indigenous cultures of Africa. This literature forms an essential part of what is generally considered the oral tradition of Africa, though it does not entirely account for it. Furthermore, it is a literature that is fully contemporary—still being produced, in various forms, updated in its themes and references, and, what is more significant, integrating influences from the written conventions adapted from the literate tradition of Europe. It is also beginning to employ new technological means of production and performance as the audiovisual media create a revolution in the oral tradition: records, cassettes, films, and videos have been pressed into service in several African countries for the transmission of the traditional literature in its original oral/aural form of expression.

What the preceding remarks indicate is that, although the traditional literature of Africa in its original form is being increasingly marginalized, it has retained an undoubted vigor. What is more, its practitioners display a sharp sense of context, which has enabled them to maintain it as a cultural form, open nonetheless to change and adaptation. Its appropriation of modern, Western-derived forms has a peculiar interest therefore as an indication not merely of what Ruth Finnegan has called an "overlap" between the oral and the written in traditional societies in the modern world (Finnegan, 1982) but also of the strategy involved in what Soyinka has called the "survival patterns" of traditional culture in Africa (Soyinka, 1988a, 90–203). Soyinka's point has to do especially with the creative accommodation to cultural change of traditional forms of drama. When we consider the impact of radio and television on the production and transmission of traditional literature, the striking fact that we encounter is the interaction, if not fusion, of the three phases (or levels) of orality distinguished by Walter Ong—the primary, residual, and secondary (Ong, 1982). Despite this interaction, we recognize in the oral literature a fundamental and indeed organic aspect of the African imagination. For all their undoubted diversity, the manifestations of the imagination in our traditional societies have one common denominator: they rely primarily on an oral mode of realization. It is this that accounts for the pervasiveness of the spoken word in traditional African cultures.

This observation has implications for our conception of literature and our values of interpretation. With regard to the oral literature of Africa, I recall the scheme of three levels of orality that I have proposed elsewhere (Irele, 1981, 1990). There is, first, the level of ordinary communication with a purely denotative use of language, as in simple factual statements and commands. At a second level, we have the forms of orality associated with the rhetorical uses of language, forms that are not necessarily reserved for special situations but are ever-present in traditional African discourse through the use of proverbs and aphorisms, which regularly channel communication in African cultures and therefore provide what one might call a "formulaic" framework for speech acts, discursive modes, and indeed the structure of thought. As the Yoruba metaproverb puts it: *Owe l'esin oro* (Proverbs are the horses of discourse). Finally, we have the strictly literary level, which is concerned with and reserved for the purely imaginative uses of language.

In reality, these three levels exist along a continuum, for it is difficult to draw a sharp line between denotative and connotative uses of language in oral communities. It is useful nonetheless to make the distinction for clarity and to facilitate analysis. In any event, it is the last level or category that interests us, for it is here that we encounter what must be accepted in many African societies as a consecrated body of texts.

The notion of *text* itself needs to be clarified here. Not only must we conceive of this as a sequence—whether extended or not—of structured enunciations, which form therefore a pattern of discourse, but we must also consider the nature of those specimens in the oral tradition that are endowed with the same character of literariness as written texts. In other words, where we are dealing with imaginative creations, we must expect to see a preponderant recourse to those aspects of discourse that signal this character of literariness: metaphors, tropes, and other figures of speech that create a second order of language with constitutive elements—*words*—foregrounded, organized in highly stylized ways, and subjected therefore to artifice so as to carry a special charge of meaning. In other words, a literary text, whether oral or written, is language *intensified*.

Two points arise from the foregoing. First, the conventional dichotomy established for prose and poetry loses much of its relevance with oral literature; the idea of the "prose-poem" becomes inoperative and inappropriate in an oral context. Thus, orality invites us to a revision of notions about genre and generic conventions. Second, the view of the literary text I have advanced provides an occasion for challenging the conventional Western view of textuality and consequently of literature as linear and spatial, which is based on the exclusive model of writing. Orality operates with a different scale and category of apprehension, the temporal, but this does not by any means preclude its possibility for generating texts endowed with the same level of interest and significance as those produced in writing.[3]

In the ordinary sense of the word, therefore, we have here literature, understood as imaginative expression, at the third level of orality I have distinguished. We have a coherent body of texts that constitute not merely a repertoire with established conventions for composition, performance, and transmission, as in the case of the Akan dirges studied by Nketia (1958) or the family praise names *(oríki)* of the Yoruba (Barber, 1991), but also, quite often, a *canon* in the strict sense of the word; that is, a body of texts that have been fixed and set apart, reified as it were, as monuments of a collective sensibility and imagination, expressive of a structure of feeling itself determined by a profound correspondence between experience and imagination. Examples of canonical texts in this sense abound in Africa; they include the heroic and praise poems of the Zulu *(izibongo)* and Basotho (Cope, 1968; Kunene, 1971), the court poetry of Rwanda recorded and presented by Coupez and Kamanzi (1970), and of course, the great epics: *Sundiata, Da Monzon, Mwindo,* and *Ozidi.* But perhaps the most distinctive body of oral texts that corresponds most closely to this notion of a canon is the Ifa corpus of the Yoruba (Bascom, 1969; Abimbola, 1977). If there is anything distinctive about this literature, it is what I'd like to call its organic mode of existence. In production, realization, and transmission, the text inheres in the physiology of the human frame and is *expressed* as voice, in gestures, and in immediate performance. The spoken word achieves here its plenitude as a total presence.

Albert Lord, following on the work of Milman Parry, has accustomed us to the formulaic structure of heroic poems. But orality is more than formulaic: it is the active and intensive deployment of parallelism, anaphora, parataxis, and other features, which give life to the structures of expression predetermined within the culture. Nor must we forget the special role played by sonic values in this literature, the onomatopoeia, ideophones, and especially tonal patterns that depend for their effect on the immediacy of realization peculiar to oral forms and thus proclaim the primacy of living speech in human language.

An important consequence of orality is the social significance of the literature in the face-to-face situations of traditional societies, which provide the context of its performance. We need to take account of the fact that the repositories of this body of texts are often specialized workers, "masters of the word" (Laye, 1978). Therefore, a significant part of this literature falls within the domain of the specialized activity of a category of producers of the particular cultural form represented by oral literature. Not infrequently, this specialization involves the use of deliberate hermeticism, as in the case of the Ifa corpus, which is exclusively in the care of priests of the divination cult *Babalawo*, literally, "fathers of the secret," in other words, guardians of the word. We may apply to this special category of individuals the well-known term *griot*.

We can conclude this cursory survey of oral literature in Africa by observing that it stands as the fundamental reference of discourse and of the imaginative mode in Africa. Despite the undoubted impact of print culture on African experience and its role in the determination of new cultural modes, the tradition of orality remains predominant and serves as a central paradigm for various kinds of expression on the continent. The literary component of this tradition, in both its expressive modes and with respect to its social significance, provides the formal and normative background for imaginative expression. In this primary sense, orality functions as the matrix of an African mode of discourse, and where literature is concerned, the griot is its embodiment in every sense of the word. In other words, *oral literature represents the basic intertext of the African imagination.*

The function that orality still fulfills in contemporary African society is most apparent as we consider the imaginative creations that derive immediately from the indigenous tradition, especially the new written literature in African languages to which Albert Gérard has devoted a comprehensive study (Gérard, 1981). The fact of a direct progression from the oral literature is important here, since it is a question not merely of drawing upon material from the oral tradition but essentially of re-presenting such material through the medium of print in order to give wider currency as well as new expression to forms that are already structured within the languages themselves. This practice does not preclude a modification of the traditional forms within the new modes; indeed, such modification is inevitable given the changed context of realization of the literature, which, with other contemporary forms that have developed from the oral tradition, are clearly marked by what we have noted as the assimilation of modes and conventions of the Western literate culture. However, the predominance of orality as a shaping medium is a determining factor of the process by means of which such material is recreated and endowed with a new mode of existence.

The adoption of the distinctive modality of writing in this literature has thus led to the development of a new literate tradition in African languages, one that remains bound by language and the distinctive quality of oral expression to the traditional literature. The literate tradition of works in the African languages has been brought into being primarily by writers who, though they may be literate in the European languages, have naturally gone directly to their native tongues for their writing. It is significant to observe that this tradition is being actively extended today by writers whose dual competence—in both an African and a European language—is an active one, demonstrated in works produced in the literary registers corresponding to each.

The best known instance of this phenomenon remains Okot p'Bitek, whose long poem *Song of Lawino* was first written in Acholi and later translated by the author into English. But even more interesting is the case of Mazisi Kunene, whose Zulu poems complement his work in English; in a similar way, Charles Mungoshi has created fiction in both Shona and English as expressions of the same creative impulse. In these and other cases, we observe African writers electing to express themselves in an African language and going back therefore to oral forms. This development has been thrown into special relief by the evolution of Ngugi wa Thiong'o's writing from English to Gikuyu. To judge from his own translation of the work into English, he has attempted in *Devil on the Cross* a direct representation of the oral mode in a written medium; the ideological intention of the novel has determined its allegorical and didactic character, in the manner of the traditional folktale or moral fable, hence his deliberate recourse to the narrative conventions associated with that genre.

The situation of dual competence in an African and a European language, which has led to writing in the literary registers of both by some African writers, is indicative of the situation of diglossia in which they are involved. For if at the moment, the direct and immediate recreation of the oral tradition in the mode of writing, either in an African language or a European one, is not yet widespread, the interaction of orality and literacy in the case of those writers who have established a visible traffic between the African languages with their distinctive forms of expression and the European linguistic medium is especially instructive. These writers provide clear evidence of the tense area of signification that lies between the native tradition of imaginative expression and the European literary tradition, a terrain through which every African writer has to find an expressive means to navigate for his or her own creative purposes.

The process involved in this movement between two traditions can be termed *reinterpretation* in the anthropological sense of the word. It is well illustrated by the so-called folk operas in Nigeria and the related forms of concert parties in Ghana and Togo. In these works we witness an effort to adapt the conventions of the oral narrative and traditional drama, both popular and ritual, to the exigencies of a new cultural environment dominated by Western influence: even where there is a written text, the voice as realizing agency remains absolutely primary.

If with oral literature we have an indigenous tradition, then with the writings in the African-language literatures that can be said to have proceeded directly from it, we are dealing with an endogenous development of a mode of expression for which the African imagination has found adaptive forms for its manifestation. In these two areas, orality functions as a maximal framework of expression.

In all other areas of literary production associated with Africa, this integral orality is either totally negated or profoundly modified by the written mode and the conventions associated with a literate culture, which intervenes to define a new framework of expression. It must be emphasized that this relationship is not a recent development arising out of the influence of the West but in fact reflects a long-standing situation. We need to recall in this connection that the oldest written tradition in Africa is associated with the Arabic language. This tradition goes back to the introduction of Islam in both East and West Africa in the period that corresponds to the European Middle Ages. Bound up with the central position of the Quran in the religion, it has determined a specific line of development in African literature to which the term *Afro-Arab* has been attached. The literatures in Swahili, Somali, and Hausa, in which Arabic script was until recently employed for writing the African language, provide the prime examples. In this Afro-Arab literature, there is already a radical break in relation to the indigenous matrix evoked above with regard to both the inspiration and the mode of expression. In the classic texts, the strong coloring by Islam can be said to establish a primary connection of this literature with Arabic literature and the literary tradition of the Middle East in general. However, in both Hausa and Swahili, there is often a harking back to an earlier tradition of orality, with poems composed in writing and then declaimed or sung in live performance. It is also worth noting that a new secular literature is beginning to emerge in these languages; the example of writers working in a realist mode in Swahili in socialist Tanzania indicates that the tradition of Islamic writing no longer determines either content or form in contemporary Swahili literature. The same observation can be made concerning North African literature in Arabic, including the recent development of Egyptian literature, notably in the work of Naguib Mahfouz and Nawal el Saadawi.

The other literary tradition that has made its impact on African literature is of course the European, its present dominance being, as we know, a factor of our historic encounter with the Western world. There is a sense indeed in which African literature in the European languages can be said to have begun with European writing on Africa, for the latter not only initiated modern discourse on Africa but also established the terms in which that discourse has been carried on until the present day. Generally, European works that take Africa as a setting comprise a corpus that has consisted largely of the literature of exoticism, a literature in which Africa provides a theme for what amounts to no more than fantasies. But even with the more serious novels in which the African scene is not employed as a mere backdrop, it features essentially as a symbol of moral states and existential issues—the classic examples here are Joseph Conrad's *Heart of Darkness* and Graham Greene's *The Heart of the Matter*. In these and other works that form what Michael Echeruo has called "the novel of Africa" (Echeruo, 1973), Africa itself is never an immediate reference, and the African is never envisaged as anything more than an element in a landscape to which the writer has ascribed a predetermined meaning. Thus, the continent itself is not only refracted through a European perspective, its peoples are also excluded as living figures (Coetzee, 1988).

The common feature of this category of literary works related to Africa is thus the absence of imaginative sympathy with the continent or its people as bearers of culture, a fact that the settler writer either denies or ignores. The dominant posture indicated by this literature is one of either indifference to the African continent or of outright antipathy. Indeed, the most salient aspect of European and settler literature with an African setting is the fact that it has served as the basis for a hegemonic discourse. Beyond the ideological significance of the content of this literature, it is easy to understand why it is unable, by its very nature, to strike a relationship with an African imagination defined by any kind of formal affiliations with indigenous modes of expression.

A possible exception to this observation concerns the work of that group of writers in southern Africa of European extraction for whom the African subject comes into direct imaginative focus. There is no doubt that South African writing has assumed a new direction as well as an unexpected dimension with the work of white writers like Alan Paton, Nadine Gordimer, Athol Fugard, Andre Brink, J. M. Coetzee, and Breyten Breytenbach and, before them, the work of Olive Schreiner and the early Doris Lessing. The heightened sense of involvement with the particular experience of the black community in relation to the political and social circumstances of the racial divide that for so long governed life within the South African context gives a distinct quality of reference to their work and marks it off from that of earlier writers like Roy Campbell and William Plomer. But besides the pattern of equivocations that, understandably, runs through the works of these writers, it is clear that they do not display the sense of a connection to an informing spirit of imaginative expression rooted in an African tradition. In a formal sense their works are bound just as much to the European literary tradition as are those of metropolitan writers. Nonetheless, they have a claim to be considered *African* writers, even if their expression has no connection to the African imagination in the sense in which this implies an immediate involvement with an informing African sensibility. Such a distinction is simply a recognition of the fact that while, from the thematic point of view, these writers can be identified with African interests, they stand apart in formal terms from "native" South African writers like Oswald Mtshali, Sipho Semphala, and especially Mazisi Kunene, for whom the compulsion to make just such a connection to indigenous tradition forms part of their expressive project. The distinction between the white and black South African writers becomes clearer when we consider the work of some Portuguese-born writers such as Castro Soromenho and Luandino Vieyra, who express an engagement with Africa not simply in terms of external allusion to forms of life but as a real, formal identification with local modes of expression, that is, not merely as thematic reference but also as touchstone of form (Bastide, 1960).

This observation leads to a consideration of modern literature written in European languages by indigenous Africans. The striking feature of this literature is a noticeable preoccupation not only with the African experience as the central subject of their works but also with the problem of a proper and adequate reflection of that experience, which involves, in formal terms, a reworking of their means of expression for that purpose. There are of course African writers who demonstrate no preoccupation with an indigenous mode, but the really significant writers are those who have addressed the question of an African manner of expression and of the establishment of an African imaginative mode derived from the oral tradition, along with the representation of an African universe.

Perhaps the most fruitful way of characterizing modern African literature in European languages in order to understand what appears to be its double formal relation—to the European conventions of literate expression and to the indigenous tradition of orality—is to see it as an effort to reintegrate a discontinuity of experience in a new consciousness and imagination. For the modern African writer, it has not been enough to attempt to come to terms with that experience; rather, in the new literature, what we encounter is a constant interrogation of both self and the original community to which that self is felt to relate in a fundamental way. Hence, we find in this literature an imaginative centering of the traditional society and culture in terms of both theme and formal procedures.

This double relation of modern African writers represents something of a dilemma, which stems from the apparent disjunction that separates their creative activity and effort from their material and language, between what is given as *signified* and the constraints of the *signifier*. This disjunction exists between Africa, considered as comprehensive reference for and image of experience, and European languages and the literary conventions associated with them. The result is that the tensions and ambiguities that mark the situation of African writers are reproduced within the very form of expression they are obliged to deploy. The question then becomes how to create a formal harmony between expression and the objective reference of that expression. Formulated differently, the problem of the African writer employing a European language is *how to write an oral culture.*

Various solutions to this problem have been attempted by various writers. The simplest approach has been direct transliteration of African speech into the European language. The case of Amos Tutuola is noteworthy in this respect, since his novels are really an extension of D. O. Fagunwa's work in Yoruba and therefore represent a continuous progression from the indigenous to the European. Tutuola can be considered an "unconscious artist" insofar as his language is the spontaneous recreation in English of the structures of the Yoruba language, which provides the linguistic and cultural framework of his imagination. In the case of writers such as Gabriel Okara (*The Voice*) and Ahmadou Kourouma (*Les soleils des indépendances*), the process is carried a stage further and becomes a conscious recasting of the European language in order to render both the speech patterns and thought processes of fictional characters. It is debatable whether, in Okara's case, the process really works; with Kourouma, any doubt about the possibilities it offers is dispelled by the remarkable coherence of his novel, by the way in which its language functions as the integrative medium of its structure. Despite variations in one's appreciation of their respective levels of achievement, the presupposition in both cases is the same: a reworking of the medium will result in an adequacy of representation and statement.

We witness a parallel process in modern African drama in the European languages, for it operates on the principle of what one might call *transfer*; the concrete enactment of real-life situations as demanded by drama compels a mode of representation that draws directly on the elements of cultural expression in the communal existence. These are projected directly on stage, and an approximation of the African speech within the European language is called for in such a representation in order to give a measure of verisimilitude to the work. Beyond this, the gestural features involved in drama afford a direct link to the ceremonial functions prevalent in indigenous expressive schemes, the ludic and didactic in the folktale as well as the symbolic in ritual forms, both sustained primarily by the oral mode. These two veins have been explored with particular success by Guillaume Oyono-Mbia, for the first, and by Femi Osofisan and Wole Soyinka for the second, in such a way as to suggest a renewal of dramatic aesthetics through the infusion of the African mode.

The more conventional approach to the question of writing an African content in a European language is what I call *transposition*, by which I designate the recuperation of African material and forms in the standard form of European language. It is of interest to note that the precedent for this approach was set by a Caribbean writer, René Maran, with his *Batouala* and even more in his little-known work, *Le livre de la brousse*, arguably his masterpiece. Besides these two novels, Maran wrote a series of animal tales, which may well have served as the direct inspiration for Birago Diop's *Les contes d'Amadou Koumba*. Published in the 1930s, Paul Hazoumé's *Doguicimi* may be considered an early attempt in this direction, although compared to more recent work, such as Amadou Hampaté Bâ's *L'Etrange destin de Wangrin*, its interest in this connection is reduced to a purely historical one.

The outstanding work in this genre, which inaugurates modern African literature as a mode of transposition in the sense I have given it here, remains Chinua Achebe's *Things Fall Apart*. The innovative significance of this work derives not only from Achebe's integration of the distinctive rhetoric of African speech into the conventional Western novel but also from the formal relation of the work to the two distinctive traditions, African and European, each representing an imaginative ethos corresponding to different structures of life and expression, which the novel holds together within its narrative movement and referential bounds. A primary indication of Achebe's approach to the problem is offered by his incorporation of folktales as allegories within the narrative development of at least two of his novels, which signals their directing function in the imagination at work.

The example of Achebe illustrates how the oral tradition has come to govern the processes of creation in the work of other African writers who have achieved significance in our modern literature. In the poetry of Léopold Sédar Senghor, the cadences of oral poetry underlie the flow of his processional lines in a verse form that is at the same time an elegiac and a heroic celebration of an entire continent and people. The affinity of Senghor with Christopher Okigbo on this point becomes clear as we progress from the latter's early work to his final sequence, "Path of Thunder." Similarly, Ayi Kwei Armah's *Fragments* and *Two Thousand Seasons* effect a deliberate return to the oral mode, in the former intermittently, in the latter as an organic foundation for his narrative, which presents in a collective plural the steadiness of the collective voice, which translates the persistence of communal being affirmed by the novel. It is this collective voice that Yambo Ouologuem subverts in his *Le devoir de violence.*

Perhaps the most significant integration so far has been managed by Soyinka in *Death and the King's Horseman*. The work is a play centered on a precise, crucial moment of rupture in the African consciousness. In formal terms, the play progresses from an immediate realization of orality as the expressive mode of a total way of life to what can only be described, within its specific context, as the tragic loss of the empowering function of the word in the universe of the African. The circumstantial interest of the play rests upon its theme of the encounter between the traditional ethos and Western values, between a metaphysical and a historical imperative. But it is the presentation of this encounter that gives force to the theme and significance to the work itself, for it enacts in language the form of the existential predicament it presents, the dilemma involved in the progressive decentering of the African psyche and imagination in a new dispensation that is imposing itself upon the African world. Part of the significance of *Death and the King's Horseman* is its demonstration that this process begins with language.

What this cursory examination has tried to establish is the fact that, beyond its function in the African tradition, orality also serves as a paradigm for the written literature in the European languages, a literature whose distinctive mark is the striving to attain the condition of oral expression even within the boundaries established by Western literary conventions.

It remains for us to consider one other area of African literature, the Black diaspora in the New World. The current interest in the folk origins of African-American literature and the possible resources offered by an oral tradition in Black America is related, as we have seen, to the need to define the distinctive character of this literature. At the same time, it prompts the question as to whether there exists a link between the literature of the Black Diaspora and African literature in its indigenous inspiration, whether the former can be seen as a manifestation of the African imagination in the sense in which I have been employing the term here. Certainly, a thematic connection exists, if only because of the reference to a common historical experience. Perhaps the best evidence for this link at the thematic level is to be found in the various autobiographies by Black writers. The value of such works as Camara Laye's *The African Child*, Ezekiel Mphahele's *Down Second Avenue*, Joseph Zobel's *La Rue Cases-Negres*, Richard Wright's *Black Boy*, and Goerge Lamming's *In the Castle of My Skin* is the testimony they provide of the black self emerging across the world as the product of a growing consciousness and of the black experience deriving from a common relation to the white world as a function of a common association with Africa.

In the literature of Blacks from the Diaspora, this association plays an important role both as focus of consciousness and, increasingly, as reference for self-expression. The controlling idea here is the awareness of a particularized experience—historical, social, and cultural—which gives rise to the sentiment of a distinctive identity. From this sentiment springs the affirmation of a specific feeling for the world, a feeling that demands to be reflected in a distinct expression. The postulate is of a Black literary tradition with roots in an oral tradition, one in which the slave narrative, considered today as the "master text" of African-American literary expression, has come to occupy a central and defining position.

Whatever one may think of this movement, it must be acknowledged that it was dictated by the actual development of the literature. The assimilationist position of Phillis Wheatley has receded so far that it hardly ever comes into view any more. In addition, the interrogation of racial roots, colored by the profound ambivalence we find in the work of the Harlem poets, has progressed beyond the hesitant recognition of a bond with Africa to a frank ancestralism, exemplified for instance in Paule Marshall's *Praisesong for a Widow*. An Afrocentric vision in Black literature in America thus appears as an essential element of a liberating consciousness.

The continuity of experience and expression that this ancestralism postulates is easier to trace and define in the cultural life of Black communities in the Caribbean and Latin America, and it accounts for the persistent African references in the literature from these areas. We know that in such developments as *negrismo* in Cuba, in which the poetry of Nicolás Guillén came to be central, and the Haitian Renaissance, practically called into being by the writings of Jean Price-Mars and nourished by the work of "indigenist" writers such as Jacques Roumain, Guy Tirolien, and Jean Brierre—writers whose spirit continues today in the varied production of René Depestre—the African vision is the determining factor in a renewal of idiom. The link between these movements and the Harlem Renaissance on one hand and the Negritude of Léon Damas, Aimé Césaire, and Léopold Sédar Senghor on the other is a matter of historical fact, one that suggests the emergence of a comprehensive Black idiom in the literature of the African diaspora, often as a matter of conscious reconnection to the mother continent through orality, as in the case of Edward Kamau Brathwaite. These developments suggest that Black writing in the New World has a certain claim as an avatar of the African imagination.

It is against that background that we need to appreciate the effort of theorization by black critics. Houston Baker's insistence in *The Journey Back* on the privileged status of the particular semantic field of African-American literature is predicated on the notion of an African-American vernacular, a point he develops further in his grounding of the black literary idiom in the cultural matrix of African-American musical expression in *Blues, Ideology and Afro-American Literature*. Baker indeed is not far from identifying in the literature what one might call a *black ethnolect*. Henry Louis Gates, Jr., has restated this position in structuralist and post-structuralist terms; for him, there exists an African-American literary tradition that manifests itself in the linguistic and tropological interactions between Black texts. Thus, "Black Language" provides the basis for the constitution of Black literary aesthetics. He goes further in this critical direction in *The Signifyin(g) Monkey*, in which he proposes an archetypal or eponymous figure for the African-American literary tradition drawn from the Yoruba pantheon: the trickster god, Esu, who he presents as the figure both of the language process in African and African-derived modes of expression and of the hermeneutic function of the critic. The indigenous African canon (Ifa, with the mediating role of Esu) opens up a perspective of Black intertextuality, with Black texts speaking to each other across time and space. The formal emphasis is evident with both Baker and Gates: the Black experience, for all its importance, is not enough as a basis for the definition or elaboration of a Black aesthetics, which must rely on language in its comprehensive sense for its proper validation.

In all of these efforts, and despite the formal bias that has been assumed in more recent work, we witness what is no doubt a form of essentialism. But the point is not whether this is founded in fact or not, but rather that we see at work among Blacks in the diaspora, writers and critics alike, a similar movement of mind and imagination as that taking place among the Africans, a conscious reference to a matrix of expression whose ultimate foundation is the oral mode. The essentialism is obviously a function of history in both cases, a matter of literary and affective affiliations consciously forged in many cases under the compulsion of social forces, but it determines a reflective adoption of a paradigm of imaginative expression that is African in origin and nature. In other words, the African imagination when viewed in the broad perspective I have tried to establish here and especially with regard to its written expression, is largely self-constitutive and therefore self-conscious. It manifests itself as a deliberate mode of discourse encompassed within a total strategy of differentiation. Nonetheless, it seems to me a notion that is just as operative as the notion on which it is based—the notion of Africa itself. For this reason, it seems to me to impose itself upon any form of critical apprehension that takes as its object any of the areas I have endeavored to outline here.

Orality, Literacy, and African Literature

Oho! Congo oho! Pour rythmer ton nom grand sur les eaux sur les
  fleuves sur toute mémoire
Que j'émeuve la voix des koras Koyaté! L'encre du scribe est sans
  mémoire.

Léopold Sédar Senghor, "Congo"

There seems little doubt that the attention devoted to the oral tradition in Africa in recent times has contributed in no small way to the renewed scholarly interest in the question of orality and its relation to literacy. It is of course true that the study of African oral forms has itself benefited from a preexisting climate of scholarly endeavor so that such research could be undertaken with seriousness. In this respect, it is worth mentioning two specific factors that were conducive to such a climate and thus facilitated the extensive consideration of African orality as a cultural phenomenon. First, the development of structural linguistics, in both its Saussurian formulation and its North American variant associated with Leonard Bloomfield, drew attention to the oral basis of language and all but made this fact into an orthodox precept of linguistic investigation. As is well known, the influence of structuralism extended beyond linguistics to stimulate in particular a renewal of literary theory, especially in the work of the Russian formalists, much of which, as is evident in the case of Vladimir Propp, was based on the examination of folk and oral material.

The second factor involves the work of Milman Parry, Albert Lord, and the Chadwicks and the way they encouraged a view of orality as a primary modality of literary expression. The direct impact of their work on traditional Western scholarship in its most venerated domain—the study of the European classical heritage—had the consequence of giving prominence to the question of orality in relation to literary expression and was ultimately helpful in promoting a revaluation of oral cultures and even, as in the case of Marshall McLuhan, prompting a reassessment of the literate tradition of Western civilization itself.

These developments favored a broadened awareness of literature and thus created the conditions for a scholarly investigation of African orality not merely in a purely linguistic framework, as in the early phase of Africanist studies, but also from a literary and artistic perspective. At the same time, the dominance of orality in the cultural environment of African expression seemed to offer possibilities for validating the endeavor to state the relevance of orality not only to a general understanding of the processes involved in human communication but also, and in particular, to formulate an all-encompassing idea of imaginative expression, one that would point toward a universal concept of literature.

But while this seems to be the prospect opened up by the close attention to oral forms that developments in scholarship in the earlier part of the twentieth century encouraged, the relation between orality and literacy has of late been perceived more often in terms of an opposition than a complementarity. There is now abroad, it seems, an effort to reverse the Saussurian order of precedence in which writing serves as a secondary medium lending material support to oral speech and to affirm rather the effective primacy of writing for communicative and cognitive functions. Thus, the values of orality are being more and more discounted, when they are not being actively deprecated, in favor of what is held to be the superiority of literacy, its greater adequacy in organizing human experience.

This bias in favor of literacy is perhaps most pronounced in the work of Jack Goody (1977, 1987), who virtually identifies literacy with the reflective consciousness. For him, orality represents an incapacity to handle logical processes and amounts to a less assured mode of manipulating the world; literacy thus provides the sole basis for any kind of sustained development of civilized life. A similar orientation emerges from the work of Walter Ong, whose position, though less categorical than that of Goody, proceeds from the same premise, for the term *noetics*, which he has proposed for the comparative study of differentiated mental dispositions as conditioned by orality and literacy, presupposes that the structure of the human mind is affected and even determined by the technology of linguistic expression and human communication available to the members of a society and of a culture at a particular point in their collective development. (Ong, 1982). In both cases, an inherent evolutionism pervades the treatment of the question. I have singled out these two scholars for mention, because the influence of their work has determined the prevailing trend in discussions of the question, which has led to the setting up of a sharp dichotomy between orality and literacy. These two notions are perceived as related to two modes of human communication through language, modes that are represented as indicators not only of two types of social and cultural organization but also, and more radically, of two modes of thought and even of existence. The following extract, which bears the stamp of Ong's ideas, sums up this point of view in an unequivocal way:

> To put it simply, orality is characterized by short memory, homeostasis in memory, speaker and listener sharing a site, hence shared tribalism, transience of texuality, poorer transmission, intimacy, direct social control, paratactic and non-cumulative narrativity, adjectival description, types as narrative personae. Literacy, on the other hand, is marked by physical textual permanence, longer memory, spatial freedom in textual transmission, isolation and alienation, individualist liberalism, syntactic and cumulative narrativity, introspective analysis. (Miyoshi, 1989, 33)

Insofar as the distinction being made here applies to the productions of the imagination, it is evident that the conventional Western novel is presented as a normative reference for all forms of literary creation and experience. More generally, the passage makes clear the value judgment implied in the dichotomy between orality and literacy, in which the former is associated with the communicative and expressive schemes of so-called simple societies, while the latter is deemed to provide the basis for the conceptual procedures and moral stances that have ensured the triumph of Western civilization. Thus, the notions of orality and literacy take their place as one more pair in the scheme of contrasted principles that serve, as Ruth Finnegan has remarked, to establish a kind of "great divide" between two spheres of human consciousness and achievement (Finnegan, 1973). This effort to create theoretical boundaries between peoples and cultures is a familiar feature of Western scholarship, which has bedeviled the discipline of anthropology in particular; as such, it raises issues that go well beyond the scope of my present subject. But I have felt compelled to show the way it operates and to suggest its direction in current discussions of the question of the relationship between orality and literacy in order to point up what I consider to be the simplifications that these discussions involve, especially the incomplete understanding of the true nature of orality that they display.

It seems to me therefore that a reappraisal of the question is required, and such an endeavor must start with a recognition of the differing contexts of the situations in which the two notions can be considered to be relevant. There is certainly no difficulty about conceding the obvious truth that, in certain important respects having to do especially with positive science, a literate culture has an overwhelming advantage over one that conducts its life through a purely oral mode of expression and that it enjoys its considerable advantages by reason of its prodigious capacity for the conservation and transmission of knowledge and the tremendous potential for the organization and transformation of experience that accrues to it as a result. It cannot be doubted that, until now,[1] writing has proved the most convenient means of processing information about the external world and has for this reason given a powerful impulse to the scientific and technological development we generally associate with Western civilization. Literacy has thus become a necessary condition for any conception of modern life. It can even be affirmed that books do not merely represent a convenient and serviceable format for the representation of discourse and the expression of ideas but comprise as well a comprehensive medium of human dialogue across time and space. Although this is manifestly an idealized conception of the function that books fulfill within a literate culture, it points to a sense in which literacy can be said to serve, at least in principle, the ideals of a humanistic liberalism.

The obverse of this relates to the real limitations, spatial and temporal, from which linguistic communication suffers in cultures that are either purely or predominantly oral. But it is possible to make too much of these limitations, for it cannot be said, as it is being constantly suggested, that oral cultures are so crippled by them as to be prevented from developing expressive schemes as complex as those of literate cultures. It is well to observe in this regard that many oral cultures have developed various strategies within the complex framework of their semiotic systems for overcoming the limitations of oral communication. In the African context one might mention the constant recourse to surrogates (the use of drum language is a notable example) and to other nonlinguistic symbolic schemes, which serve both to give spatial resonance to human speech as well as to extend the expressive potential of language. The temporal limitation involved in orality is also met by the mobilization of the entire culture—the incorporation of professionals of the word and intensive development of memory techniques are crucial elements—toward keeping alive in oral form those documents of the collective life to which a particular value has been assigned, a point to which we shall return presently.

Given these considerations, the theoretical assumptions that govern the prevailing distinction between orality and literacy need to be seriously modified and the value judgments that lurk within them directly challenged. What is involved in these judgments is an extreme valorization of writing, of its imagined autonomy as a spatial category of language. But this view can only be sustained by neglecting the fact that, whatever its capacity for the elaboration of language, writing remains a secondary form, a *representation,* at a remove from the vital immediacy of spoken language itself.

This point has a direct bearing on certain important aspects of the literary experience that I shall have occasion later to evoke; meanwhile, let me state that, when one considers the African situation, it is possible to affirm that, in the area of imaginative expression, the advantage may not be altogether on the side of literacy. It needs to be appreciated that orality has preeminent virtues as an expressive modality within the symbolic universe that all forms of social participation require for their full and proper mobilization. And as far as the African situation is concerned, if it illustrates anything, it is the impossibility of isolating language from the total field of social and cultural experience that orality conditions. Indeed, it is in this area that I am inclined to look for what may well constitute the distinctive contribution of African orality to the experience of literature: the reminder it provides that the use of language for imaginative purposes represents a fundamental component of the symbolic structures by which the individual relates to society and by which society itself relates to its universe of existence. My contention then is that it is truly rewarding to ponder the nature of orality for a more rounded view of literary expression as a dimension of experience.

This observation leads to a major issue at the heart of African expression, one that must count in any consideration of orality in relation to African literature: faith in the primacy of language as a vector of experience upon which all this expression rests. It happens to be the case that this is a faith that needs to be reaffirmed at this time in the face of a modern skepticism that animates certain currents of contemporary thought in the Western world. This new skepticism seeks to deny the capacity of language to disseminate values that are other than purely textual and formal, to generate meanings that reflect the dense texture of experience. This effort to dissociate language from the sense of a human world raises important issues in critical theory that I need not go into here, except to say that it proposes an impersonal conception of language that proceeds directly from habits of mind induced by writing, a conception therefore with which those of us with a background of an oral culture cannot possibly identify.

It is therefore in the firm and clear perspective of an intimate relationship between language and consciousness, between expression and experience, that I intend to consider the status of orality within the corpus of African literature. I start then with the presupposition that texts, whether written or oral (and we shall examine the question of what constitutes a text later), are embodiments of language, that they are products of human awareness and maintain a profound complicity with the consciousness through which such an awareness is mediated. Although it is recognized in many African societies that language has a reality all its own and even a certain potency intrinsic to it as a natural phenomenon (Zahan, 1963 Calame-Griaule, 1965), it is ultimately inconceivable without the expression that it enables and sustains. We may restate this view of language by observing that, however elusive and refractive words may be, they collaborate to vivify the abstract system of language and in so doing empower our efforts to create meanings, which are nothing other than the expression of our will to order experience.

These reflections should, I imagine, begin to make clear what I consider to be the possibilities of orality for the revaluation of literature in relation to experience and as a form of mediation between life and the imaginative consciousness. The African case seems to me especially instructive in this regard, and I shall now endeavor to develop this point with specific reference to the present literary situation in Africa, marked as it is by the complex relationship between orality and literacy, a situation reflective of the dichotomy that obtains in our dual experience of tradition and modernity.

Although it is only in recent times that African literature has been attended to by the rest of the world, literary expression is not by any means a recent development in Africa. This statement, for all its banality, is dictated here by the need to direct attention to the oral tradition, which has for ages served on the continent as an institutional channel for the intense involvement with language that we recognize as the foundation of literary form. More recently, with the introduction of writing, a new dimension has been given to imaginative expression on the continent; indeed, it can be said that, given the circumstances of this transition, literature has more recently come to acquire in its status as a social institution and as a form of cultural production a new prominence and urgency. From being a natural manifestation of the processes, structures, and dispositions of the various societies and cultures that made up our precolonial, traditional world, it has more recently developed into a mode for the articulation of a new, modern experience. Literature in Africa has thus become the area of an active and focused self-consciousness that extends in its implications into both a sustained interrogation of history and a determined engagement with language.

A significant part of this process of the revaluation of literature in Africa is the preoccupation with the nature, possibilities, and formal modes of literary expression itself. To put this another way, in trying to formulate the state of disjunction between an old order of being and a new mode of existence, literary artists in modern Africa have been forced to a reconsideration of their expressive medium, of their means of address. In the quest for a grounded authenticity of expression and vision, the best among our modern African writers have had to undertake a resourcing of their material and their modes of expression in the traditional culture. Because the traditional culture has been able to maintain itself as a contemporary reality and thus to offer itself as a living resource, the modern literature strives to establish and strengthen its connection with a legacy that, though associated with the past, remains available as a constant reference for the African imagination. The oral tradition has thus come to be implicated in the process of transformation of the function of literature and in the preoccupation with the formal means of giving voice to the African assertion.

These remarks, which apply primarily to the relationship between the oral tradition and the new literature in the European languages, can be further amplified by reference to the steady development of written literature in the indigenous languages, which represents, in many instances, a direct outgrowth from the oral tradition. The complexity of the literary situation in Africa can thus be appreciated when we present the full picture of imaginative production on the continent. We have a line of progression that can be said to have begun with the oral literature whose forms and functions still operate over a wide range of social and cultural activities in the traditional context and to a considerable extent in the modern world as well. This primary domain of literary expression is extended by a body of written literature in the African languages, which maintains a natural linguistic and formal relationship with the oral tradition but is already dissociated, as a result of writing, from the immediate insertion into collective life that orality entails. The emergence of a modern expression in the European languages has resulted in the creation of a third domain of African literature whose connection with the other two consists in the process in which it is engaged for the recuperation of the values—aesthetic, moral, and social—associated with orality.

I shall presently be considering the oral literature in its salient features and as a fundamental reference for the experience of literature in the African context. But as a preliminary, let me make a further observation in order to clarify the relationship that obtains between orality and literacy within the comprehensive field of African literature. The interest of the written literature in the African languages in this regard is obvious, since it demonstrates the direct connection between orality and literacy. In the specific case of the literature in Yoruba with which I am familiar, there is a sense indeed in which much of this literature relies for its effects on this connection and thus exists primarily as a form of "secondary orality."[2] We need to distinguish within the corpus of written literature in the African languages two distinct categories: the classical literature, represented principally by the extant works in Ki-Swahili in the so-called Afro-Arab tradition but including as well other works outside that tradition, such as those in Geez or Amharic in Ethiopia, and a second category, made up of the more recent productions in other African languages, which have resulted from the introduction of literacy from the West. To this latter category belongs the considerable body of established works in such languages as Yoruba, in which the development of a new written literature was pioneered by the novels of D. O. Fagunwa, and in Sotho, which has given us a modern classic, Thomas Mofolo's epic novel, *Chaka*. It is especially in this category that the process of direct transfer of the modes of oral expression into that of writing is clear. I should add that although the works I have cited are representative examples, they do not cover the entire range of present developments, for the spread of literacy is propelling the emergence of new African language literatures all over the continent. (Gérard, 1971, 1981).

The literature in the European languages is now generally recognized, in its formal significance, as an effort to approximate to the oral model, albeit within a literate tradition taken from the West; it is this feature that marks the most important African writing of contemporary times. The point that emerges here is that, through these two channels, the oral tradition continues to function as a fundamental reference of African expression, as the matrix of the African imagination.

This brings us to a direct consideration of the oral literature itself. There is an obvious sense in which it can be considered as the "true" literature of Africa. It is the literature that is still the most widespread and with which the vast majority of Africans, even today, are in constant touch, and it represents that form of expression to which African sensibilities are most readily attuned. The reason for this is not far to seek, for despite the impact of literacy, orality is still the dominant mode of communication on the continent, and it determines a particular disposition of the imagination of a different order from that conditioned by literacy.

We might consider at this juncture a question that arises immediately at the outset of any discussion of the phenomenon of orality in relation to imaginative expression: the levels of articulation that distinguish ordinary communication from what may be considered the literary uses of language. I have suggested elsewhere the three levels at which we might envisage the articulation of language in African orality and I will recall these and develop them further here in an effort to provide a clearer understanding of the distinctive features of oral literature, at least in the African context, as well as what I shall be proposing in due course as their comprehensive significance.

To begin with, there is, as in all cultures, an elementary level of ordinary, everyday communication, which is largely restricted to the denotative sphere of language; about this level, nothing more needs to be said. In African orality, we are plunged at once into the connotative sphere with the second level, signaled by the presence of those figurative and rhetorical forms of language that, as anyone who is familiar with African habits of speech is aware, occur as a frequent element of linguistic interaction on the continent. The culture itself offers prescribed forms of discourse, which define what one might call a "formulaic" framework for the activity of speech and even for the process of thought. To this rhetorical level of linguistic usage belong the proverbs and the aphorisms, which have a special value in practically every African community, a fact that accounts for their widespread development as fixed forms, culturally prescribed. What is more, the proverb can be considered as practically a genre in itself, and it enters as a device into almost all kinds of speech activity and is regularly made to serve a formal function in the extended forms of oral literature. When Achebe writes, adapting an Igbo proverb into English, that proverbs are "the palm oil with which words are eaten," he is drawing attention to the central position that the form occupies in African speech. He is also indicating the relish in words that has been cultivated in nearly every African society as a matter of cultural conditioning, a sensitivity to language that orality encourages, and the aesthetic function of the proverb which this cultural factor promotes.

But the consciousness of the role that the proverb fulfills in speech is not confined to the aesthetic appreciation indicated in the Igbo saying but involves as well a recognition of its possibilities for mental processes and even for cognitive orientation. For the proverb represents a compaction of reflected experience and functions as a kind of minimalism of thought. It is this awareness of the intellectual value of the proverb that is summed up in the Yoruba metaproverb: *Owe l'esin oro; ti oro ba sonu, owe l'a fi nwa* (Proverbs are the horses of thought; when thoughts get lost, we send proverbs to find them). As genre, the proverb provides a link between what I have called the rhetorical level of language and the third level, that at which, in African orality, the imagination finds its proper manifestation as *organized text* and even, in many societies, as a body of *consecrated texts*. I am aware that the notion of text as applied to oral expression can be ambiguous, but I believe it is just as relevant to orality as it is to literacy.

A variant of the opposition between orality and literacy is the distinction that has been proposed between text and utterance, a distinction that further affects the view of conditions under which instances of language are produced. In this view, an *utterance* connotes anonymity, a collective voice, whereas a *text* implies individual authorship, a singular consciousness. A little reflection should make clear however that this implication involves a restriction that is peculiar to literate cultures and that the distinction it rests upon is ultimately untenable. At best, it is merely a formal one that bears upon the modality of expression rather than on the substance. It is enough to consider the role of register in all forms of linguistic usage to understand that what is at issue here is the degree of elaboration in speech, which brings into view the character, level, and context of the speech act itself, whether it is oral or written. This seems to me to compel a more inclusive notion of text than is afforded by the sole reference to literacy.

From this perspective, we can define a text quite simply as an organized series of enunciations that combine to form a coherent discourse. In literary expression, the element of coherence is supplied by the imaginative path of the discourse and by the deployment of form in a stylized mode of language. Literary texts exist in this fundamental sense; indeed, what I have said of the proverb indicates that it is in fact a text in this sense but in a highly compacted form. It has now been established that in many African societies, extended texts based on the definition I have proposed can be identified quite frequently; they exist as autonomous and isolated works each of which is highly organized as a full and independent imaginative statement. What is more, in certain cases, these oral texts can be so rigidly fixed as to attain what can only be called canonical status; they represent "monuments," in Paul Zumthor's phrase, of the particular cultures in which they occur (Zumthor, 1983, 39).

The examples that come to mind in this latter respect are highly instructive of the relationship between literature and society in an oral culture, of the social applications of imaginative discourse in a situation in which language as embodiment of experience has become highly valorized. The case of the Ifa corpus in Yoruba culture comes immediately to mind. It is obvious that the sacred function of this corpus (linked as it is to the ritual of divination and associated with the hermetic character of the poems that comprise the corpus) has everything to do with the conservative textual requirement of the form (Bascom, 1969; Abimbola, 1977). In another case, the dynastic poems of the kingdom of Rwanda, the ideological factor is the predominant one, for the poems combine historical narration with eulogies of the ruling family in such as way as to identify the monarchy with the material and spiritual well-being of the state. It is of special interest to note that in this case, the textual integrity of the corpus is anchored in an elaborate metrical system; the social valorization of the genre exerts the pressure toward textual preservation in this form (Coupez and Kamanzi, 1970).

These two examples demonstrate that an oral culture is perfectly able to sustain literature in a strictly textual form. However, the reality of the African situation is that oral literature operates on a more flexible principle of textuality than is suggested by these examples. By its very nature, orality implies, if not absolute impermanence of text, at least a built-in principle of instability. But what may seem, from the point of view of literate culture, a disabling inconvenience has been transformed into a virtue in African orality, for although the textual elements, cannot be disregarded in the forms of our imaginative expression, they are more often experienced as the outline of a verbal structure and as reference points for the development of ideas and images, as suggestive signposts in the narrative or prosodic movement of a discourse that is still in the future. This outline is simply held in the mind and expanded by the performer into a fully worked-out discourse when the occasion arises for its actualization. The point is that an oral text is almost never fully determined beforehand, given once and for all, as in the case of written literature, which strives to endow the text with the permanence of a material object. An oral text is actualized in oral performance and is thus open and mobile; what can be abstracted as the verbal content of a given work is perpetually recreated, modified as the occasion demands, and given new accents from one instance of its realization to another.

This feature of oral literature is well illustrated by the folktale, possibly the most visible of all the genres of African oral literature. By its nature, the folktale is a genre that lends itself readily to improvisation, that allows ample scope for the free play of creative inventiveness around a cluster of motifs furnished by the culture and within a structure of formal functions, which may be considered to derive from the recesses of a universal imaginative faculty (Propp, 1968). But the same principle of improvisation is at work, in greater or lesser measure, in the major extended forms of African oral literature. The great praise poems that are performed in nearly every African community as repositories of social ideals provide a striking instance of this observation, for they are constructed on the basis of variations on a restricted number of themes and dominant images. These variations move through each poem as a succession of parallel enunciations whose progression is sustained much more by the inventive power of the performer than by the absolute prescriptions of a previously determined text.

Similarly, in the mythical narratives and epics that have often come down to us in several versions, we observe that the textual variations from one version to another are as much a factor of the memory and general disposition of the bards who recreate them as of the particular circumstances, the hazards so to speak, of their composition and transmission. Such is the case with the epic of *Sundiata*, to take a notable example, the national text of the Manding people spread across the Sahel area of West Africa, an epic in which the historical personality of their founding figure lives on in the collective memory of the people. But while the main outline of the narrative of Sundiata's life and career is clear in each version of the epic that has been collected or recorded, the details often vary from one version to another (Innes, 1974; Johnson, 1986). The same is true of the *Mwindo* epic in Central Africa (Biebuyck and Mateene, 1971) and probably too of the Ijo narrative saga of *Ozidi*, although J. P. Clark-Bekederemo, the Nigerian poet who recorded, transcribed, and published the work—with a magnificent English translation accompanying the original Ijo text—assures us that the version he recorded is standard throughout the Niger Delta (Clark-Bekederemo, 1977). In any event, many other examples of this feature of oral literature can be cited to confirm the point.

But as my remarks concerning the Ifa corpus and the Rwanda dynastic poems indicate, although we have at work this principle of flexibility and openness of the text in our oral literature, there is often a contrary movement that reins in the free play of invention involved in performance, for there is almost always a tension between the artistic liberty of the performer and the social and cultural control of texts that either have a sacred significance or are felt to have assumed the status of a communal asset. This tension is graphically illustrated in one outstanding case, the myth of the Bagre collected by Jack Goody, who notes the greater textual coherence of the myth in its ritual context as opposed to its more diffuse form in the less-constrained atmosphere of its secular recital (Goody, 1972). Similarly, in the case of the Zulu praise poems, *izibongo*, it has been observed that the formal features of these poems have gone through three distinct phases of evolution: the first is related to the period before the advent of Chaka, when the form was apparently relatively free; the second to the period of his ascendancy when, in line with the highly centralized political system he introduced, the form of the praise poem that served as the ideological expression of his rule became more rigorously organized; and finally the phase related to the post-Chaka period, when the praise poem lost much of its application and reverted in its internal features to a more relaxed form (Cope, 1968). It seems safe therefore to affirm, in the light of these observations, that oral literature in Africa displays an ascending order of textuality as we move from the minor to the major forms and as the constraints of social function dictate.

The point that emerges from all this relates to the status and situation of the oral text in what I have called elsewhere the "organic mode of existence" of oral literature. By this phrase I mean that the text in any of its manifestations is never an entity divorced from the conditions of its realization. Its existence is dependent on the human frame itself, first as an inert form in the memory and then in its dynamic form in performance, the point at which it becomes embodied in the full sense of the word. For it is at this point carried by the living voice that, through the modulations of various extratextual effects weaving through the text a network of resonances, gives it an immediate and effective presence. Beyond this, it is dramatized through the paralinguistic features of language itself and the extralinguistic devices of movement and gesture, often accented into dance (a reminder that meter in poetry was originally related to dance), devices by which language enters into active association with the expressive possibilities of the human body. Orality dictates then a total experience of literature, one in which the textual or verbal component is only one element, an important one it is true but nonetheless a partial dimension of a wider range of resources brought into play in the aesthetic and imaginative framework of that experience as a function of the whole sensibility. This amounts to saying that in the cultural and artistic context of African orality, *literature is nothing when it is not enactment.*

It is easy to understand that, under these circumstance, the faithful reproduction of the text on each occasion of its realization cannot be a norm. This faithful reproduction is neither a relevant nor a useful criterion of judgment, for it is obvious that we are dealing here with a non-Aristotelian conception of discourse; the principle of orality is essentially one of nonclosure. A concomitant of this principle is that of multiple creation, so that even where the text is fixed to an extent, it emerges as the end result of a continuous process of accretion of the textual elements going hand in hand with displacement and tending toward a synthesis that is almost always provisional. In other words, although there is always in oral literature a minimal text and often a *master text*, it functions basically as a defining context of imaginative projection initiated by the experience that gives it inspiration. The reference to the reality of the world of events and phenomena provides a pre-text, which is in turn given elaboration in language, constituted by the verbal resources that comprise the elements of the text and sustained by ancillary devices that can be termed paratextual but that enter into the total field of its meaning and contribute to its force of impression. Furthermore, the mobility of the text implies that the entire process of the generation and maintenance of oral texts—composition, performance, and transmission—obeys the principle of intertextuality, which impels every instance of oral literature toward a condition of collective appropriation.

This interplay of discursive forces within oral literature suggests that an attention to the modalities of oral expression, as exemplified notably by the African situation, stands to confirm a new consideration of literature in its immediate manifestation as constituted by the living forms of speech and thus illuminates those grounded aspects of literary experience that writing as a modality of human communication necessarily obscures. Whereas writing decontextualizes and disincarnates, orality demonstrates the contextual dimension of communication and restores the full scope of imaginative expression, which writing in its reductive tendency cannot fully capture or even adequately represent. Thus, orality proposes a dynamic conception of literature, one that envisages literature as *text in situation*.

It is no longer, then, a question of considering oral literature as verbal art but as a totality that conjoins communication and participation in the affective field of a communal event. And what may be designated as the "spectacular" aspect of orality becomes essential to what Bronislaw Malinowski, (1925, 1989, 315), has termed the "phatic" function of language, a function that underlies the communicative impulse of all literature and relies for its unhindered effect on the immediacy of the linguistic situation. It seems to me that it is only in an oral environment that this condition of immediacy is properly met, and where imaginative expression is concerned, only such an environment provides the live sense of situation in which literary values can take on their full human significance.

There is no reason therefore to suppose that the "metaphysics of presence," which this conception of orality arising from its imaginative functions dictates, is necessarily a negative thing. On the contrary, a complete experience of literature may well depend on what Robert Plant Armstrong has called the "affecting presence" in African art (Armstrong, 1971), which, for the experience of literature, orality so eminently promotes. This point has a relevance that is not limited to African forms, as is clear from the remarks of Walter Benjamin on the depreciation of the art of the storyteller in Western culture and on the loss of the "aura" of art in the age of mechanical reproduction (Benjamin, 1973). And it is significant that Walt Whitman should have sought to give epic voice to young America in the cadences of the Old Testament, in the form of an orality that, through the habit of reading the Bible aloud, which was still prevalent in his day, provided a reference for shared literary and spiritual values and favored the sense of an organic community in which the bardic role he assumed could take on meaning.

It is this intrinsic quality of presence to which all forms of discourse aspire—none more than literature—and which is so fully exemplified in the African oral tradition, that our modern writers are striving to reinterpret on a large scale. For what gives interest to the literary situation today in Africa is the way our written literature, in both the indigenous languages and the European languages, enacts a dialectic between orality and literacy. I would like to suggest that this relationship of expression and function among the three domains of imaginative expression in Africa represents a renewal of the literary phenomenon with what may well be universal import. It promises not only a revitalization of the internal process of literary creation but also a reaffirmation of the significance of literature as something more than a cultural ornament that a society may provide itself but rather as an essential human value.

This seems to me then a direction in which Africa stands to make its greatest contribution to the world literature that the great German poet Johann von Goethe envisioned long ago as the most enduring heritage of the human community. Africa stands to offer, as its proper accomplishment of that heritage, a conception of literature as not merely an intense medium of human communication, but also, and more important, as the privileged mode of a ceremonial whose vital necessity springs from the deepest impulses of the human disposition itself.

3

African Letters

The Making of a Tradition

In the introduction to the first edition of his collection of tales (published in 1947), the late Birago Diop explains the circumstance in which he came to produce the work that has secured for him an enduring place in the corpus of modern African literature. Ascribing the tales to the family *griot*, Amadou Koumba, Diop downplays his own participation in their composition; he makes the modest claim that his role was limited to transcribing the tales as he heard them from the *griot* in their original versions in Wolof and translating them into French so as to make them accessible to a wider audience of readers. It is this condition of their generation as written texts that is reflected in the titles of the first two collections, *Les contes d'Amadou Koumba* and *Les nouveaux contes d'Amadou Koumba*. The *griot*'s name is conjoined to the material that Diop presents as a way of insisting upon its true provenance.[1]

Nonetheless, in publishing these tales, Birago Diop put his signature to them. It is not clear whether this is to be taken simply as an indication of his role as transmitter or whether it represents more than a gesture in deference to the Western convention that requires that a written text be assigned to an individual—who thereby assumes responsibility for its existence both as a material object and, more important, as a mental product. However, as we read these tales, we become aware of the complexity of the situation that has called them into existence in the particular form in which Diop has offered them to us; if he did, indeed, take them over from Amadou Koumba, he did not simply write them out, but he *rewrote* them. In other words, he sought to achieve much more than a simple act of carrying over into the sphere of experience designated by his acquired French/Western culture the material he had received from the expressive universe of his Wolof/African environment.

At least two processes are at work in the unfolding of these tales in their written/French version, in the composition of which Diop appears simultaneously as both scribe and author. He may be considered (by his own account) to function as a scribe in the sense that he is an ancillary agent to the tales' perpetuation in writing, a human medium for their consignment in a fixed, durable state. On the other hand, he emerges as an author in the sense that he constitutes an individual, imaginative consciousness engaged in an act of its own pure creation. In this respect, it is obvious that the renarration of these tales in French entailed for Diop an active effort to recreate the oral genre in writing in such a way as to capture the original tone within the diacritical framework in which it had come to be enclosed and whose expressive function it was now required to fulfill. The primary consideration for Diop was thus to ensure a continuity of spirit between the traditional tale in its natural sphere of integral orality and its new form, a secondary orality sustained by writing, to create the feeling that the written form itself had been generated directly from the oral within a common field of expressivity. Indeed, in his handling of the form, Diop does convey, for anyone familiar with the procedures of the African folktale, the distinct impression of a direct progression from the tales of Amadou Koumba to his own, despite the change of linguistic vehicle and, to some extent, the change of rhetorical registers that the material had to undergo.

Moreover, Diop's retelling of these tales conforms to the conventions that originally governed the transmission of the form: each performer in the culture was free to reinterpret the tales and to give new shape, new direction, and even new meaning to what was considered a communal holding, an intertextual resource. However, Diop's recreation of the tales in French involves the intervention of two critical factors: writing as the modality of expression and a second language introduced as the expressive medium. Not only is the determining structure of that language brought into play but so are the literary conventions that are associated with it. In this respect, the palpable influence of La Fontaine, apparent in Diop's adoption of a neoclassical style and urbane manner, suggests the way in which the whole tradition of French literature, as it has been transmitted to the colonized, "assimilated" African, exerts a direct pressure on Diop's transposition of the tales into a French key of expression.

This amounts to saying that the oral form has been reinscribed by Diop into a new mode of existence so that his signature registers, in effect, a valid claim to an individual act of authorship in the full sense of the term; he can be regarded as a responsible and autonomous creator of his own discourse. Furthermore (and this is part of the second factor) Diop was not simply moving from one modality and from one paradigm of language—from one system of *langue*—to another but also from one plane of discourse to another. By making manifest the vernacular form in the second language, a language imposed by the exigencies of history, he was also bringing to light and into a new prominence a suppressed reality of his indigenous environment, thus affirming it as an autonomous area of values. Presenting the tales in French rather than in Wolof thus involved both displacing them from their original setting as well as reactualizing and revaluing their significance within the "logosphere," the total universe of discourse represented by the colonial situation. By rewriting these tales in French, Diop was making a statement with a specific resonance in the particular circumstances of his writing, for in the historical context of his work, the act of writing proceeded largely from an ideological impulse: the necessity of challenging the colonizer's claim to the exclusive privilege of voice.

In this same perspective, writing became for Diop a willful act of recuperating an original voice, for which Amadou Koumba served as a reference, as the comprehensive figure and embodiment of a tradition that Diop felt compelled to reclaim—less perhaps as a prodigal son than as one who had ventured forth from the cultural and spiritual home and brought back in triumph a new and precious acquisition, the colonizer's language. What seems, then, in Birago Diop's introduction, like an extraordinary gesture of modesty and even of self-deprecation turns out to be an assertive posture, a way for him to state his affective relationship to that vast territory of imaginative and symbolic values that tradition offered him as a primary endowment but which he stood to complement and even to intensify in the movement toward a new expression dictated by his circumstances.

I have chosen to dwell on the work of Diop at the outset of this chapter for two reasons. I am paying homage to the memory of a master of the word (*un maître de la parole*) who has now left us to join the company of the ancestors. The homage seems to me appropriate given the importance of Diop's achievement; his genius manifests itself in the incomparable felicity of his rendering in the French language of the oral tradition, and in his assured handling of a central form of the African imagination. Second, his imaginative engagement with tradition, felt as the anchor of consciousness, of a presence in the world, impels him toward an expressive form through which tradition finds its most visible exemplification. Yet, the necessity of employing the language of the colonizer relates his expression to a non-indigenous, Western frame of reference whose pressure on objective life and inner mind accounts for the pronounced state of transition that has marked the modern phase of African experience. Diop's work thus provides a striking illustration of the complexities and paradoxes with which the African writer has had to contend in elaborating a new expression in the modern age. His example suggests the way in which writing places the modern African in a field of tension generated by this double perspective established for the African in the dialectic of tradition and transition. African letters in their historical and thematic development provide testimony to the fact that this dialectic is not simply a view of the mind but a situation lived in its full immediacy.

In his magisterial study of the modern African novel, Senegalese critic Mohammadou Kane places tradition at the center of its thematic and formal organization as the fundamental concept that makes for its intelligibility (Kane, 1982). Although he privileges the African novel of European expression, there is no doubt that all forms of modern African expression display the same intense engagement with the question of tradition. The coexistence of two sharply differentiated modes of life on the African continent and the dualisms observed at practically every level of life, consciousness, and expression that this situation implies have imposed tradition as a primary reference not only for the literary imagination but also for African discourse in general. It is, of course, the textual manifestation of the various modes of response to this situation and the different directions of thought it proposes to African self-reflection that constitutes the corpus we refer to as *African letters*.

I would like to offer an appraisal of the significance of the question of tradition in African letters within the historical perspective that seems to give the question meaning. But before doing so, let me make two clarifications that I consider essential for a proper comprehension of the subject. The first concerns the term *tradition* itself in its relation to modern African expression. There are two distinct though connected senses in which the concept of tradition can be applied to African literature in the European languages. In the first place, tradition features as a theme in both imaginative works and ideological writings, as a focus of preoccupations that govern the production of a reflective discourse, itself centered upon the experience of an existential predicament: the sense of a profound cleavage of consciousness in the Westernized, acculturated African. In this sense, what is important is not so much the objective situation of the modern African in relation to the customs, institutions, cultural practices, and so on that comprise the living reality of an indigenous African tradition as it continues to have an existence and to establish norms of conduct and sensibility. What matters is the affective stance that tradition determines and the imaginative projections and intellectual reconstructions that it conditions in the specific historical context of its thematization within African discourse (Balandier, 1984). In the second place, tradition itself derives from the process of discourse to which it gives rise. This is a pattern traced by tradition's successive stages, and it gives a certain coherence, both historical and conceptual, to the discrete segments of the discourse, despite the internal contradictions it displays or, to change the metaphor, despite the transitions and modulations that mark its general orchestration.

The other clarification concerns the notion of *letters* as it applies to the African situation. The term calls attention to the phenomenon of literacy, and it may suggest that the dichotomy evoked in citing the work of Birago Diop can be reduced simply to an opposition between an oral tradition associated with Africa and a literate tradition associated with the West. In reality, the term African letters cannot be identified solely with ideological and literary productions in the European languages. For an antecedent literate tradition associated with the Arabic languages and with Islam has been available to vast areas of the African continent south of the Sahara for centuries, long before the incursion of Europeans. That tradition, which established a literary connection, among others, between black and white Africa, continues to this day in its various transformations and might even be said to constitute a classical tradition of African writing.

To appreciate the continued vitality of this tradition, it is enough to consider the way in which the legacy of the *tarikhs*, historical writings, and devotional literature introduced by the Arabs is reflected in the so-called Afro-Arab literature in Swahili and Hausa. We might note in passing that it is within this tradition that the formal inspiration of Yambo Ouologuem's *Le devoir de violence* is more correctly located, rather than in relation to André Schwarz-Bart's *Le dernier des justes*, which has been assumed to be its unique model. It needs to be stressed that the literary tradition in Africa that derives from the Arabs has not only had direct historical consequences for millions of Africans, even in the non-Islamic areas. It has also continued to function as a reference and even as an immediate force in the lives of countless contemporary Africans in the predominantly Moslem areas, who situate themselves in the world less with reference to Western civilization and its organizing ethos, founded upon the Christian religion, than with reference to the civilization of Islam and the redemptive value attached to this religion by its adherents.[2]

To mention these areas of literate culture is immediately to draw attention to the complexity of the literary situation in Africa. The varied character it presents is further complicated by the more recent development of a body of written literature in the indigenous African languages—Sotho, Zulu, Yoruba, Ewe, and so on—which owe their existence directly to the introduction of a literacy based on the Latin script introduced in the wake of European political and cultural incursions into Africa. The interaction of these traditional literatures with both the oral tradition and the European legacy of letters constitutes another major area of African expression, one that cannot be ignored in any comprehensive discussions of the literacy phenomenon in Africa (Gérard, 1981).

These references that adumbrate for us the notion of letters in Africa provide the comprehensive context for both the theme of tradition in African letters and the debates that have surrounded the language question in African literature, a question to which the theme stands in obvious and close relation. As we shall see, it is clear that the preoccupation with identity indicated by this theme also predominates in the passionate involvement with the issues concerning the nature and function of literature in the African context, which have been raised in these debates since the 1960s on the subject of African literature as both a cultural phenomenon and as an object of academic study.

It is essential to bear in mind, then, that the two channels of African letters I have just mentioned, along with the oral tradition itself, which provides a comprehensive background for all modes of African imaginative expression, have their importance. Each exists as a reflection of a substantial dimension of the African experience and possesses authority as a constellation of texts (oral and written) with both literary and cultural significance. It remains true, nonetheless, that the main focus of interest suggested by the term African letters is the body of works produced by Africans in the European languages. The reason for the present prominence of this area of African letters has to do, of course, with the circumstances of our historic encounter with Europe, marked by the violations that we have had to endure in the long and painful drama of slavery, colonialism, and the devaluation of the Black race by the ideology of racism. These are factors that have been central in our recent experience, have determined our perception of our contemporary circumstance, and have therefore influenced the dominant themes and orientations of our modern expression.

Moreover, and as an immediate implication of these factors, it is here that the notion of transition in African letters can be said to receive its sharpest outlines; it is precisely as a result of the dislocations occasioned within our societies and cultures by the impact of Western civilization that we have been compelled to the readjustments to which our modern literature bears witness and provides the clearest insight. What is reflected above all in this literature is the movement of the African mind, considered as a complex of thought and sensibility, in response to history. What is more, a major stimulus to this movement of mind has been the problematic relation of the African subject to the European language, which functions as a conditioning medium of our modern expression. These are the factors that have been singularly foregrounded in the process by which tradition has been thematized in African letters. To an examination, perforce schematic, of these factors and an exploration of their determination of the course of African letters, I shall now turn.

In *Criticism and Ideology* (1976), Terry Eagleton remarked upon the circumstances in which a new public discourse took shape in eighteenth-century England, typified by the work of Joseph Addison and Richard Steele, upon "the conditions of possibility" of the emergence of both this discourse of the public realm and of the person of letters as its embodiment. Eagleton's description of these conditions applies as well to continental Europe, especially to France, which witnessed in the same period the rise of a new class of writers, whose interest and style of discourse are exemplified in the person and the work of Voltaire, the quintessential man of letters.[3]

It is of some interest to note that African letters emerged precisely in the same period, as a small but significant form of participation by the first group of enfranchised and acculturated Africans in one of the great controversies of the day, the question of African slavery. Voltaire's intervention in this question—in the celebrated description in *Candide* of the Surinam slave and his unhappy lot—-is, of course, well known, as is the moral dilemma the institution of slavery posed to liberal thought in Europe in the Age of Enlightenment and beyond. The particular significance of the Africans' participation resided in their determination to bring their personal experience to bear upon the discussion of this question. The specific lines of development in the reflective discourse enacted by African letters thus began to be disseminated in this early literature of the eighteenth century, at a period when the historical encounter between Africa and Europe began to reveal itself in its full tragic dimensions. The point, then, is that African letters in European languages were called into being in the first place primarily by a sense of historical grievance, and they have been sustained for some two hundred years now by our continuing need to situate our collective existence—our very being as Africans—in the new perspective mapped out for our historical experience by the encounter with Europe.

It is no accident that what is now recognized as the most significant African work to emerge from this early period is an autobiography, *The Interesting Narrative of the Life of Olaudah Equiano, or Gustavus Vassa, the African*, published in 1789.[4] The autobiographical genre affords scope for precisely the kind of introspection inspired by the actualities of experience that the circumstances of these early Africans in Europe required. Equiano's work inaugurates African letters in this perspective and lays out in recognizable outline the province of their essential concerns; it serves to identify the point of departure of both the written self-representation they offer and the process of self-reflection they delineate (Ogude, 1982; Costanzo, 1987).

In an early chapter of his *Narrative*, Equiano employs what Henry Louis Gates, Jr., has termed "the figure of the talking book," which, as he observes, recurs as a frequent trope in other slave narratives of the period (Davis and Gates, 1985). What the passage reveals is first of all the ironic stance Equiano adopts towards his earlier naiveté as a young African making his acquaintance with the Western world, a stance now made feasible for the adult narrator by the fact that he has in the meantime not only acquired a familiarity with books but has also developed into a man of the world. With this passage, Equiano broaches a major theme of his works: his understanding of literacy as an empowering medium. Reading is a liberating force in the new dispensation, and writing—as self-expression—is a means of coping with an unprecedented historical experience. It thus becomes clear that Equiano's account of his desperate effort to acquire the ability to read and write determines a fundamental level of his narrative; it develops as an account of the progressive integration of the black/African self into the white/European world, and in this development, it proclaims an adventure of assimilation.

As an extension of this significance, writing also served Equiano as a means of establishing his credentials to consideration as a legitimate participant in Western civilization. The picaresque style is a prominent feature of the *Narrative*, but it is a feature that is given a purposeful direction related to Equiano's situation. In narrating his adventures, he does not merely offer the story of his progression through life but an image of himself with which he expects his European audience to identify. It needs to be stressed, in this regard, that Equiano's work is oriented specifically to his English readers as a reminder to them of his service, in war and otherwise, on behalf of the national community to which he seeks full admission. The account of his years as a slave serves further to provide evidence of his loyal devotion to various masters and of his trade, which enables him eventually to buy his freedom in a fair transaction; it is an indication of his aptitude for participation in the new mercantile civilization, which placed a premium on economic exchange, including the slave trade. His repeated invocation of providence as a factor in his life is intended as proof of his adherence to Christian tenets, which, as he is careful to point out, he embraced as a matter of rational choice. But most of all, it is upon his ability to assimilate and manipulate the new "technology of the intellect" (to borrow an expression from Jack Goody), painfully acquired in the most improbable of circumstances, that he most fully stakes his claim to consideration. In a real sense, therefore, Equiano's *Narrative* is his *apologia pro vita sua*; running through the work is a strongly articulated plea addressed to his white, European audience for recognition despite his race, his exotic origins, and his earlier servile condition—in a word, his *eccentricity*. Yet he is deliberate in drawing attention to this defining eccentricity, signaled by his racial and cultural difference. For the fact that his autobiography begins with an evocation of his African childhood registers at the outset a sense of loss, a sense that he insists upon throughout his *Narrative*, both directly and in other ways that are less obtrusive. Indeed, the whole book can be read at the fundamental level of its intention as a rhetorical gesture against the state of dispossession implied by his enslavement and his alienation. That writing was also a means of salvaging his deprived selfhood is made evident in the use he makes of his African name to advertise himself in the title of his book, alongside the imposed one, which is presented as its shadowy alternative. All this attests to an abiding sense of origins and marks a gesture of self-affirmation as African subject.

It is thus significant that, throughout the *Narrative*, Equiano is constantly at pains to mark his distance from the European world, as much in the open rebukes he addresses to its tolerance of slavery as an institution as in the more subtle suggestions of his feelings of disaffection toward its representative humanity—the exceptions he makes in this respect are strategic to the polemical purpose of his book. It is especially in the reflections upon the language in which he writes, which are scattered throughout the *Narrative*, that we most discern Equiano's sense of his marginality to the civilization into which he has been thrust. The necessity of employing the language in which he encounters the negative representation of himself and of his race—which he has undertaken to reverse—forces his mind upon the meanings of the terms by which this representation is elaborated. This leads him to a recognition of the interested, *aberrant* character of these terms, in the original essence of the word: their wandering off course insofar as they seek to apply to his own reality, which he is able to grasp as a function both of his essential human condition and of his African antecedents. Equiano's reflections on language thus amount to a challenge to constituted meaning in European discourse about the African; incidental to that challenge is the insight he attains into the relative and unstable status of meanings, the contingent nature of language itself.

Thus, the play of irony in his book becomes bidirectional: aimed in a mild way at his earlier, "uncultivated" self—in terms of European modes of life—but also and more insistently directed at the European world itself in the moral stances he adopts toward this world. Here, it is the irony of Jonathan Swift that is replicated, albeit in a less ferocious vein but from the vantage point of an objectively distanced angle of vision, that of the embattled consciousness of the African. With Equiano, the "anguish of affiliation"[5] that finds expression at one level of his *Narrative* is poised at another level against an anxiety of self-recovery implicit in the continuous appraisal of Europe that his work offers. It cannot yet be argued that writing served him as a mode of disalienation, but it provided a means of advance toward such a project by enabling him to take his bearings in the world, to make a determined gesture toward a sense of his real location within the scheme of experience. In this sense, Equiano's *Narrative* looks forward to the existential themes of Camara Laye, Cheik Hamidou Kane, and most of all, Chinua Achebe, who has recognized in Equiano a primary literary ancestor.

Equiano belonged to the first group of African practitioners of the written word to appropriate the European languages in a discursive project whose aim was a critical confrontation with a Western representation of Africa (Miller, 1985). That this representation had a practical import, which was amply demonstrated by the dismal existence of the black slave, only gave a special urgency to the writing. These early black authors took up the pen to narrate their own lives in order to enlighten the white world as to the pathos of black experience. Their works were marked by an explicit conflation of the individual with the collective, for they needed to testify on behalf of their entire race in its state of historic dereliction.

The invocation of Western values was essential to the purpose of these early writers. It served not merely to appeal to the moral conscience of Europe but also, and more important, to refute the European thesis of their nonparticipation in a human essence. For, as Gates has observed, it was for them a question of writing themselves into the human community, an entry that could only be secured by their observance of the rules of rationality entrenched in the conventions of Western literate discourse (Gates, 1987).[6] But their appeal to these values and these rules came to have implications that they could not be conscious of, or even if they were, they could not avoid. The polemical thrust of their work had to be subsumed within an apologetic rhetoric that advertised its conformity with Western norms, in terms of its mode of discourse and also in relation to the rhetorical obligations that this mode laid upon the African writer. Thus, their works came to be produced in each case as a mode of self-validation. They contain, from this point of view, an implicit recognition of the ascendant status of the Western frame of reference, perhaps even of the validity of the scale of values that it enjoins, compelling therefore, at the very least, a minimal adherence of the African subject who seeks to have a voice with which to express the African experience or present an African perspective on the world. This observation further suggests that, in their minds, there coexisted a minimal awareness of an alternative, African frame of reference, embodied certainly in a historical community, one provisionally marked by suffering but one that might also signify a source of authentic human values.

The effect of these contradictory pulls on the African imagination has endured over the two hundred years or so that Africans have been writing in the European languages. From the beginning, a dual consciousness has been its fundamental component and underlying principle. As a concomitant of this situation, the African writer has had to shoulder the burden of working out a form of mediation between the two frames of reference of this dual consciousness at both the thematic and formal levels of expression. In other words, the tradition of African letters in the European languages has been founded upon a situation marked by a profound and radical ambivalence about both theme and mode of expression.

In his *Souls of Black Folk*, W. E. B. Du Bois has given memorable expression to the sentiment of ambivalence in the African-American context, but its general relevance for all Black, Westernized individuals was demonstrated well before his formulation—in the tenor of the ideological writings that constituted the predominant form that African letters took in the nineteenth century. There is a point to evoking Du Bois here, since the formation of African intellectual life in this second period was in large part fostered by the activity of Black diaspora figures as an extension of their preoccupation with the problems of the Black experience in the New World. This preoccupation had African ramifications, which arose from the association in Western ideology of blackness as a category of being with Africa as an area of values or, more precisely, nonvalues. The exiles followed up this association in their minds and, in the case of such figures as Alexander Crummel and Edward Wilmot Blyden, through their personal initiatives in Africa itself.

The sociological conditions and the intense intellectual atmosphere in which the African question was debated by the Black intellectual elite in the nineteenth century has been well documented by several scholars (Lynch, 1967; July, 1968; Fyfe, 1972; Moses, 1989). I will only add a few observations. First, we need to bear in mind that the major preoccupation of all these intellectuals, without exception, was what they saw as the historical necessity of upgrading African societies and cultures—with reference to the norms of Western civilization. This is evident as much in the assimilationist position of Crummel, whose work evinces an obsession with what he saw as the inadequacy of Africa, as in the "relativist" views of Blyden, whose lifelong promotion of the "African idea" gave him the preeminence in African intellectual history that he now enjoys. For both men, who were contemporaries and represent for us today the opposite poles of the African response to the solicitations of European culture, the ultimate objective of African development consisted in approximating European conditions of life, which stood unquestionably as the ideal of "civilization." In their view this process was to flow from a strenuous cultivation of the intellectual and moral values of European civilization. The special regard they both had for Western scholarship attests to the conviction they shared that it was the underlying and enabling factor of European achievement. They believed, consequently, that Western scholarship would be of instrumental value to African progress toward the recognized ideal. In other words, they both conceptualized African destiny as the necessary alienation of the African from his traditional background.[7] My second observation concerns the way that they each diverged from this common position. For where Crummel's assent to this alienation was wholehearted, Blyden's came to be qualified by his adherence to the nineteenth-century organic conception of national communities inherited from such Western intellectual figures as Johann von Herder and Giuseppe Garibaldi. The application of this conception to Africa and the black race became evident to Blyden from a consideration of the distinctive patterns of cultural expression on the African continent, more so as his New World antecedents predisposed him to a global vision of Africa as a "nation" in the nineteenth-century understanding of the word. Thus, he came to posit an "African personality" with an objective correlative (to use T. S. Eliot's term) in the configuration of social arrangements and communal values that, as he maintained, gave coherence to African life and established its validity on its own terms.

The coherence of Blyden's thoughts is ensured by his vision of the harmonious integration of the elements that structure what he already understood as "the triple heritage" to which Africans had henceforth to relate, elements clearly indicated in the title he chose for the collection of his essays published in 1882 in London, *Christianity, Islam and the Negro Race*. But it was obvious to him that the self-negation to which the pressures of European ideology impelled the assimilated African could only vitiate this process of integration, and he understood the need to place a special emphasis on the human quality of the indigenous element in his conception of the emergent culture of Africa. This task he undertook in his little book *African Life and Customs*. The work is less an exercise in ethnography than a form of exegesis, which takes the African universe as a text to be unraveled and interrogated for its inner significance. The significance was predetermined by Blyden's need to justify African traditions and to demonstrate the existence of an informing spirit of African culture in its profound connection to a vibrant order of life. And it is this logic of Blyden's project of rehabilitating Africa that led him to propose a view of African tradition as the cultural and spiritual ground of the African personality—a common denominator of the black self rooted in the interaction of race and culture, a universal Black racial identity that, as Robert July has remarked, was in effect a forceful anticipation of Léopold Sédar Senghor's Negritude in all of its essential tenets (July, 1964).

Blyden's influence on the intellectual community in British-controlled West Africa in the early years of the twentieth century was, as we know, considerable, and his ideological position became consolidated in that community's work. Although he was not a native-born African, he had endowed the notion of tradition in Africa with an intellectual and moral sanction that derived from the recognition of his formidable mental powers and from the persuasive force of his uncommon gift of communication. But with these African intellectuals, tradition was no mere theoretical construct, less still an object of conjecture; it presented itself as an overwhelming phenomenal presence, the concrete and visible form of their antecedents prior to their enforced submission, in body and soul, to the impositions of Europe.

The main interest of the intellectual and ideological activity of the Westernized African elite in the succeeding period was the way in which their discourse, firmly centered on a reconsideration of tradition, issued into an intense cultural nationalism that became linked, in turn, to political agitation in the pursuit of social and political objectives within the colonial framework. Writing became for this elite not just a means of mapping the world and taking one's bearings in it but of making one's way in it. A functional relation was thus established in their work between discourse and *praxis*; one might say that, for them, the rhetorical and discursive became, to use Carl von Clausewitz's famous expression, politics by other means. This active orientation of their discourse is well illustrated by the publications and activities of the Gold Coast intellectuals—Joseph Caseley-Hayford, John Mensah Sarbah, and J. B. Danquah, in particular—who were not content to be just spokespersons but were activists in a cause that, for all its class basis, they were able to assimilate to the collective interest of the entire African population. Within the political and social context in which the works of this social and intellectual elite were produced, the literary effort became identified with an ideological project, which often turned out to be coextensive with an aggressive militancy. The parallel between the cultural nationalism of the Gold Coast intellectuals and that of the Nigerian elite, who gave character to what Michael Echeruo has described as "Victorian Lagos," reinforces the general application of this observation (Echeruo, 1977).[8]

There, is however, a pathetic underside to all of this ideological activity, a drama of consciousness that the tone of African nationalist discourse is unable to conceal despite its vigorous orientation toward political objectives. For the appeal to tradition in cultural nationalism is not a mere rhetorical mode of self-justification; it rests on a firmly entrenched subjective disposition, the sense of a constituted identity disrupted by the cultural impositions of Europe. There was, thus, a felt need to make a reconnection to this identity in order to restore the African to an integrity of being and consciousness. In the imaginative writings that led to the literary renaissance in the years after the Second World War, the pathos entailed by this drama of consciousness, implicit in African cultural nationalism, comes into full view.

No area of African letters demonstrates the preoccupation with the problem of identity as much as that represented by the work of French-speaking African writers associated with the Negritude movement. There is something schematic about explaining their anguished concern with this question in terms of the special circumstances of their relation to French culture. As should by now be obvious, theirs was a preoccupation that was general, commanded by the cultural and ideological imperatives of the colonial situation (this term to be understood as designating the comprehensive historical situation of the Black race in its relation to the Western world). As we have seen, although there is no direct circumstantial connection between Blyden's African idea and Senghor's concept of Negritude, there is a thematic and, I daresay, structural connection that explains the practically identical terms in which the theory of Africanism promoted by the two men came to be conceptualized.[9] There is no doubt, however, that it is in the literature of Negritude that the question of tradition and of divided awareness has been thematized in the most forceful way in all of our letters. And it is pertinent to observe that ambivalence is the hallmark of Negritude. It accounts as much for the surging passion of David Diop's poetry as for the austere grandeur of Cheik Hamidou Kane's novel *L'aventure ambigüe* (*Ambiguous Adventure*), whose hero serves as the emblematic figure for the very condition that has generated the novel in the first place; the novel presents itself, indeed, as a barely mediated form of factual reporting. This is of course the same condition that dictates the composition of Birago Diop's tales. I might add that, even beyond the circle of professed adherents of Negritude, the same condition operates as a potent factor of Francophone African expression, for example, in the mordant irony of Ferdinand Oyono's portrayals in *Le vieux nègre et la médaille* (*The Old Man and the Medal*) and *Une vie de boy* (*Houseboy*) or in the vehemence of Mongo Beti's satires of the colonial situation in his first four novels. We might add that this quality of vehemence in the first phase of Beti's work is in itself revealing of the deep mechanisms from which it springs. And the late Tchikaya u Tamsi's poetry is nothing other than a sustained introspection whose violent imagery enacts the dissonances of consciousness rung on the same key of ambivalence.

This character of Negritude and of French-speaking African literature in general is, of course, most prominent in the open declamations of Senghor's poetry. It ought to be emphasized that Senghor's poetic expression, in its lyrical aspects, does give prominence to the themes of renewal through a pastoral and telluric evocation of the African environment. But it is a theme developed upon the ground of a heroic and elegiac paean to the past. Senghor's work has the special significance of giving amplitude to the contemplation of the past, which the dual consciousness dictates almost as a matter of course, and his merit, which is rarely conceded, is his determined exploration of the ambivalence by which his imagination is wholly conditioned. His frank recognition of its implications as a factor of his personal experience clears an imaginative path toward his quest for a reconciliation of the conflicting demands of his divided consciousness, an integration in which the contradictions of a double relation to the world have been superseded by a third term of being. His poetry takes its complexion and is given direction by this fundamental aspiration to a new wholeness, an aspiration to which he gives voice in the explicit tone of these lines, which conclude the poem "Le Kaya Magan" in the volume *Ethiopiques*:

Car je suis les deux battants de la porte, rythme binarie de l'espace, et
  le troisime temps
Car je juis la mouvement du tamtam, force de l'Afrique future. (105)

[For I am both sides of a double door, the binary rhythm of space
And the third beat, I am the movement of drums
The strength of future Africa.] (79)

Senghor's conceptual formulation of Negritude follows a corresponding
trajectory punctuated by his encounter with Western texts. His revaluation of Africa exploits the propositions of Henri Bergson's intuitionist and
vitalist philosophy and the idealizations of Africa's cultural history offered by Leo Frobenius. Thus, he is able to undertake a reversal of the
negative connotations of Lucien Lévy-Bruhl's ethnographic characterization of the mind of non-Western people, and especially of Africans, in
such a way as to accommodate the French scholar's categories within the
affirmative scheme of his own anthropological vision and so endow them
with a positive significance.[10]

It is fair to observe that despite Senghor's effort to establish Negritude
as an effective reference for thought and action in contemporary Africa,
its literary expression in the work of the Francophone African writers,
with the possible exception of Birago Diop, hardly progresses beyond a
psychological fixation upon the issue of ambivalence itself and a rhetorical celebration of tradition, invoked as a sanction for metaphors of the
self, which African texts of racial and cultural retrieval deploy. With the
English-speaking writers, and especially the Nigerians, on the other hand,
the engagement with tradition becomes more substantive; it goes with a
real feeling for the continuities of life, which the impositions of Europe
have impinged upon radically but not quite arrested. The contextual relation between the literature of Negritude and the work of the Nigerians
is demonstrated by the continuity between the poems of the pioneers in
English-speaking Africa—represented in the Nigerian context by Denis
Osadebay and Mabel Segun in particular—and the early phases of the
poetry of J. P. Clark-Bekederemo, typified by the long poem "Ivbie"; the
work of Gabriel Okara, typified by his "Piano and Drums"; and all of the
work of Christopher Okigbo before the sequence "Path of Thunder." The
point is that, in its emergence, Nigerian poetry in English displays unmistakable affinities with Francophone expression that are impossible to
ignore. But the Nigerian writers' appeal to tradition is more firmly set
within a framework of concrete evocations that derive from a much more

assured grasp of observed, specified modes of life. There is, therefore, a closer relation between the poetic consciousness and the structures of apprehension suggested by the traditional background, as these structures come through in cultural practices that continue to animate the indigenous sensibility.

It is in this light that one must understand the dominant presence in Okigbo's poetry of the emblems of Igbo traditional life, which serve as symbolic supports for the ceremonial scheme by which the collective consciousness in that society is mobilized. Okigbo's evocations are pervaded by a sense of ritual proceeding from the imagistic immersion in tradition, which thus comes to underwrite his conception of poetry as a hieratic mode, as a system of epiphanies (Anozie, 1972). In the case of Wole Soyinka, there is a conscious movement toward the recuperation of a primal vision proposed by Yoruba myth and toward a coincidence with an ethos fashioned by the binding structures of life it animates. This movement represents not only a means of reconnection with a grounded authenticity of experience but, more important, a revitalization of consciousness.[11] With these writers, the concern is with arriving at an understanding of the processes of the communal existence as it is situated between the appeal of tradition and the imperative of history.

No African writer has explored this situation as extensively as Chinua Achebe. In his work, ambivalence becomes submerged by the calculated objectivity of his theme of culture conflict. Yet it is a theme that is ultimately defined by a crisis of identity as profound as that fictionalized by Cheikh Hamidou Kane. It seems to me that an attentive reading of Achebe's novels quickly uncovers the traces imprinted upon his expression by this crisis of identity at levels of significance deeper than what appears on the surface of his prose. There is a sense indeed in which these levels provide the true point of entry into the meaning of his work; the turning outward of the writer's self-questioning provokes his global interrogation of history. The concern with the vicissitudes of history dictates, in turn, the reconstruction of the past in *Things Fall Apart* and *Arrow of God*, projected forward along a line of vision that encompasses the dilemmas of the present depicted in Achebe's other novels. In *Anthills of the Savannah*, these dilemmas are dramatized through the explicit political theme, but it is in the figuration of the discordances that this theme exploits that Achebe conveys its particular meaning. There is no better indication of Achebe's acute insight into the state of fragmentation that his novel dramatizes than his constant shift of registers as the action moves from one sector of Nigerian society to another. His use, once again, of a parable of art in the novel—of the folktale as a kind of metafiction that mirrors and refocuses the text in order to insist upon the moral function of art— becomes a personal statement of an envisioned coherence, which (as he is fully aware) the lived referent of his own work does not begin to approximate. In this instance, the notion of art as parable of life reflects a desperate imaginative effort to subdue a refractory present. Taken together, Achebe's novels comprise not only a narrative of the perverse course of history in our lives as Africans but also a meditation on the imponderable nature of the historical process itself. They represent, in other words, a metanarrative whose somber significance has to be measured in the light of the objective tension in our contemporary situation between a sense of tradition, which cannot be implemented as a viable dimension of the collective experience or even of the self, and modernity, which for a variety of reasons remains problematic.[12]

But if tradition cannot be wholly assumed in immediate experience by the modern African writer, it remains a stronghold of the African imagination within which it is given formal organization and new modes of significance; in other words, it affords a means of fulfillment at the level of art itself. A significant aspect of the thematic engagement with tradition has thus been its implications for the formal procedures of African expression in the European languages. This point arises in the first place from the writers' compulsion to recast their linguistic medium as well as the conventions taken from the Western literate tradition in order to reflect more adequately the African inspiration and reference of their works; this process manifests itself in what we might call an aesthetic traditionalism.

The effort to achieve a formal correspondence between the writer's African references and the European language he or she employs has, as one of its objectives, the achievement of a distinctiveness of idiom within the borrowed tongue by an infusion of the European language with the tonality of African speech patterns. But this objective is clearly secondary to the larger design, which consists of projecting through a second language and into the modern framework of life and expression the structures of apprehension and of the imagination that endow the communal existence with meaning in the traditional context. Tradition as theme, both as the figure of a disrupted African essence and as a focus of self-reflection, thus comes to function as well as a condition of form.

The pressure of the oral tradition on African writing that this condition dictates has been commented upon by several writers. I have attempted to formulate a view of orality as a matrix of the African imagination and to identify the four main procedures—transliteration, transfer, reinterpretation, and transposition—that African writers have employed in their efforts to integrate oral structures of expression into Western literate conventions.[13] I would like here to propose a comprehensive perspective in which these efforts can be seen and to suggest that the interaction between the oral tradition and our modern expression, so vividly illustrated by the example of Birago Diop's reinscription of the African folktale in French, marks the point of convergence between two orders of life, a process that becomes signified in a new language.

The literature abounds with examples of this integrative function of aesthetic traditionalism in modern African literature. I have already indicated how Okigbo's poetry refigures in English the ritualistic tenor of Igbo traditional life in a mimetic transposition of its ceremonial emblems. The same procedure can be discerned in the work of Kofi Awoonor, whose *Songs of Sorrow* expands the formulaic scope of the Ewe dirge in a lament related to contemporary experience. Similarly, Mazisi Kunene's rememoration of the exploits of Chaka in his epic poem is remarkable for the way in which he accommodates the movement of English blank verse to the heroic accents of the Zulu *izibongo*, or praise poem. And the late Okot p'Bitek's reworking into English of his long poem *Song of Lawino*, originally conceived in Acholi, demonstrates perhaps more than any other work the generative power of tradition in modern African literature, which conditions the convergence between orders of experience and their representation in language. Soyinka's dramatic practice and whole conception of tragedy provide, perhaps, the most arresting illustration of this process of convergence; the unresolved tension between Western norms of individual responsibility and the Yoruba sense of collective destiny around which so much of his drama revolves contributes to the charged quality of his language, which finds supreme exemplification in *Death and the King's Horseman*.[14]

We have to refer once again to the outstanding case of Chinua Achebe. So convincing is his work in this respect that it has induced Lyn Innes to base her discussion of his novels on the theoretical postulate that Achebe's fiction represents nothing less than a dialogic transformation of the Western novel into a new form of the narrative genre (Innes, 1990). Her reference to Mikhail Bakhtin can be amplified in this case by observing that Achebe's achievement consists precisely in the poise he maintains between the two poles of the narrative mode elucidated by the Russian critic: on one hand, the analytical sensibility that the conventional novel as a genre offers Achebe, its close circumscription of individual character and its temporal grounding in the present and ideological orientation toward the future; on the other hand, the formal indications in his work of the epochal significance of his theme, the intimations of an imaginative awareness closer to the epic, which is considered a "high genre" associated with a determined universe of life and reflective of a mental disposition related to a complete order of history (Bakhtin, 1981; see also Priebe, 1988). Indeed, it is specifically through the formal tension between these two poles in the overall economy of Achebe's work that its significance as a brooding upon the asperities of history is given its proper effect and wider resonance.

We might point to a similar tension in the much-neglected work of Elechi Amadi, especially his powerfully realized novel *The Great Ponds*, whose theme is enclosed within the world of the past and opens to the world of the present in the final pages to suggest the violent shift of the temporal register of African experience. We might note, too, that, on the Francophone side, the example of Birago Diop has been enlarged upon in his ironic way by Yambo Ouologuem in *Le devoir de violence* and more pointedly by Amadou Hampaté Bâ, with *L'Etrange destin de Wangrin*. Both works suggest a redirection of the French-speaking African novel toward new perspectives of expression to which Ahmadou Kourouma has given a dramatic dimension in his two novels, *Les soleils des indépendances* and *Monnè, outrages et défis*.

These examples suggest that what I have called aesthetic traditionalism has more than a formal value, that it fulfills a reflective function as well and therefore goes deeper into the recesses of the imaginative consciousness of modern Africa. We can speak, then, of a new mediation of the African imagination, which consists of a reworking of tradition at the formal level and a creative interaction between the two modes of imaginative discourse made available to the African writer. Yet, by its nature and in the present circumstances of the production of an African discourse, it remains a compromise. It raises the question of how far European languages can, as Achebe puts it, properly bear the weight of the African experience, whether the very use of these languages does not ultimately undermine the quality of the experience that the African writer is at pains to convey; in other words, the problem here concerns the ontological status, as it were, of an African work in a European language.

From the point of view of the sociology of literature, the most important issue raised by this ambiguous situation concerns the fractured relations between the African writer who employs the European language and the varied audiences for the work produced in that language. We have, first, the European audience to which the African writer is bound by language and established conventions of literary reception but which cannot be expected to coincide fully with it. Second, we have the African audience educated in the European languages, often at best a tiny minority, but which shares with the writer the system of references that inform his work, a common background that enables its members to "naturalize" the content and procedures of the work (which thus designates them as its ideal readers). Finally, we have the larger African population upon whose experience the writer's expression is presumably centered but who have no linguistic means of access to this expression. This issue takes us into the terrain where aesthetic questions make a direct connection with social considerations and, in the postcolonial situation, with ideology and politics. It is in this context that Ngugi's interventions on the question of the language of African literature and the development of his work have assumed a referential value. That value cannot be isolated from the pronounced state of crisis into which African existence and consciousness have been plunged in recent years nor from the drastic reorientation of African discourse in relation to the question of tradition through which the impact of the postcolonial situation has been registered in African letters.

I suggested earlier that the theme of tradition, despite its inspirational role for the writer's celebration of an original community in a state of historical and cultural siege, presents the African writer with a predicament of an existential and affective order. In effect, what is primarily involved in this predicament is what, in another context, T. S. Eliot has called "the problem of belief." For example, is Ogun, the Yoruba deity who features as the organizing symbol of Soyinka's mythology, merely a master trope, a formal category of his system of images, or an authentic agency of the writer's imaginative grasp of the world, constituting, therefore, a principle of conduct in that world? For Soyinka, as for other African writers concerned with the problem of "racial retrieval," the appeal to myth and other forms of the archaic imagination—identified as a collective resource from which to derive a new relation to the world—leads inevitably to insoluble problems of self-definition in the here and now, to serious dilemmas in the formulation of a consciousness adapted to the exigencies of the modern world.

A second consideration arises immediately from this observation. The appeal to tradition has grave ideological implications insofar as it makes for a conservative attitude; it predisposes the writer toward a romantic apprehension of the past and, in its promotion of reverence for tradition as an absolute value, necessarily impedes a radically critical appraisal of that past. Against this, the possibility offers itself of a stance that places the whole question of tradition in a relative and progressive perspective, a more forward-looking position that accepts the discomforts of transition as a necessary condition for the creative transformation of African society. This question prompts a third one: what is the relation of the text to history, to the real world that is represented in it? The question concerns the effective value of writing, whether the imagination can be anything more than a resting place for the troubled awareness of the contemporary African in what, to echo W. H. Auden, we have come to sense as our "age of anxiety." In short, the point at issue is whether literature can represent an effective summons to action in the contemporary context, a fount for the forging of a new will and vision.

These and other questions define the intellectual context in which the African situation commands reflection at the present time. I cannot hope to provide here anything like an adequate account of recent developments in African letters. The best I can do is to draw attention to two features that seem to mark these developments in such a way as to have given African letters a markedly new direction. The first concerns the decisive shift of African discourse from the vertical perspective, in relation to the European frame of reference in which it had been situated, to a horizontal one, outlined by the coming together of issues internal to the African situation in its specific configurations. The specific polemical relationship of African discourse to the Europoean discourse on Africa has lost a good deal of its urgency, if not its point. Thus, where before African responses proceeded more or less on a common front, so that, to use Mao Tse-tung's expression, the secondary contradictions internal to the African situation itself were subordinated to the primary contradiction of the colonial situation, these secondary contradictions now have been forced into prominence and have resulted in a new field of expression occupied by a multiplicity of equal and contending discourses.

This is not to say that the question of tradition is no longer an issue; on the contrary, it remains central to African preoccupations but in a context and with a pertinence transformed by the developments I have mentioned. Tradition is no longer accepted as a given of African consciousness, girding us with the force of evidence and essentialism so that we can oppose the cooptation of our minds and sensibilities by the discourse of Europe. Tradition has become problematic in a strictly philosophical sense; it has come to be deprived of its axiomatic and normative significance and has been made answerable, therefore, to a new effort of redefinition. It has thus become the subject of a lively and even intense controversy, calling forth various and contradictory responses.

The range of these responses can be measured by the nuances that obtain between the various positions that have emerged on the question. Senegalese scholar Cheikh Anta Diop represents something of a transitional figure in these debates. Against the massive postulate of an African essence implied by Senghor's formulations, Cheikh Anta Diop has propounded a more dynamic theory of Africanism, a distinctive disposition of the African personality whose determinations go back to the civilization of ancient Egypt. Yet his thesis involves no more, ultimately, than a projection of this abstract personality from a metaphysical onto a historical plane. Soyinka's response is even less differentiated than that of Cheikh Anta Diop. For despite his well-publicized stand against Senghor's Negritude, it becomes clear from a consideration of his work that he only burrows deeper into the essentialism that underlies the concept as he endeavors to give a more vivid realization to the "magnitude of unfelt abstractions" that Negritude represents for him. Soyinka thus opposes Senghor's concept with an organicism that amounts in reality to a more thoroughgoing traditionalism. It is in this light that we must consider as curious the failure of Chinweizu and his cohorts to recognize in Soyinka's work a fundamental element that is in profound agreement with their indigenist and nativistic precepts beyond the gratuitous modernism, which is all they seem able to apprehend in his work (Chinweizu et al., 1980). It is, of course, true that their prescriptions for the "decolonization" of African literature address the issue of tradition as a guiding principle of African creativity at an essentially superficial level of awareness and, in terms of literary expression, of execution.

What is clear in all of these responses is that the prior acknowledgment of tradition as a determining factor of African identity provides the point of departure for reflection. With Marcien Towa and Paulin Hountondji, who stand at the other end of the spectrum, no such a priori obtains; what appears to be their theoreticism is allied to a pragmatism that firmly repudiates the metaphysical preoccupations that these other responses indicate. The positions represented by other authors, such as Odera Oruka, Kwasi Wiredu, and Kwame Gyekye on the Anglophone side and on the Francophone, the late Alexis Kagame and Stanislas Adotevi (to name just a few), can be placed at various points along this highly variable spectrum. There are, to be sure, difficulties and even contradictions in individual positions. The case of Soyinka, analyzed in a penetrating essay by Biodun Jeyifo—who graces his hesitations with the erudite description of "aporias"—is perhaps the most interesting in this regard (Jeyifo, 1988).[15]

The more varied mix of voices heard within African discourse today attests to the infusion of the body of African letters with new intellectual energies, and these have resulted in vigor of articulation that reflects a new concentration of consciousness focused specifically on the postcolonial situation. The leavening role of Frantz Fanon's work, which raises this new consciousness and thereby opens up new perspectives for African reflection, cannot be overemphasized. This brings me to another feature to which I would like to draw attention: the agonistic character that African discourse has taken on in our present context. Fanon's work, apart from the immediate impact of his prescient analyses of the postcolonial situation, signals a clear demarcation of functions between the intellectual as nationalist and the intellectual as critic of the social order. (Nda, 1987).

In the area of imaginative expression, in particular in fiction, we encounter the new critical tone of African letters at its most incisive, inherent in what I have called elsewhere the new realism, which has emerged as the presiding spirit of recent African literature. The new realism in this understanding goes beyond the theme of disillusionment, and is indicative, rather, of an expansion of the horizons of African discourse, inseparable from a newly developed critical stance on the part of the African writer but native to the writer wherever the literary imagination is confronted with the vagaries and moral ambiguities of human experience.

The emphasis on the moral significance of the new literature is intended to reflect its relatively scant attention to the objective factors involved in the social and economic dynamics of the contemporary African situation. This judgment needs to be qualified only in the exceptional cases of Sembene Ousmane and Nugui wa Thiong'o, both writers with explicit ideological concerns. On the other hand, in the novels of Ayi Kwei Armah, Nurrudin Farah, Mongo Beti (in the second phase of his writing career), and several younger writers who have come into prominence in recent years, such as Sony Labou Tansi, with his exuberantly baroque imagination, and Ben Okri, with his relentless disruption of our normalized perceptions—in all of this fictional production, what we have is a literature of dissidence rather than a literature of revolution, a symbolic mode of dissent rather than a programmatic expression of the possibility of future social adjustments.

This explains why the mood reflected in the novels of the new realism is so closely linked to an unprecedented exploration of fictional language. There is an implied critical stance in the deliberate projection of African realities in the new light of formal procedures, which depart from the regularities of the standard realistic novel, a stance that proceeds from an uncompromising commitment to the truth of the writer's vision. The project of the new realism is to lay bare the stresses that weave through the fabric of the contemporary African situation and to explore this situation in its full range of moral significance and in its most profound human implications, those inner tensions that the conventional novel seems inadequate to fully encompass. The specific moral objective of the new African fiction is thus bound up with a general and resolute experimentation with form, based largely upon the application of the procedures of European modernism in the creation of what are manifestly parables of the African condition.

It is of considerable interest to note that the new realism incorporates within its deployment of European modernism what I have referred to as aesthetic traditionalism, in a recombination that is often employed to dwell upon the tense relation between tradition and the contemporary situation, as in Kourouma's *Les soleils des indépendances*, Armah's *Fragments*, and Chenjerai Hove's *Bones*. This approach becomes ironic and even self-conscious in Femi Osofisan's play *Eshu and the Vagabond Minstrels*, in which Brechtian dramatic techniques provide the frame for a transposition of the Yoruba festival mode; the dramatist exploits Brecht's notion of *Lehrstuck* in the guise of a Yoruba moral fable precisely in order to subvert the idea of tradition itself.

In Ngugi's work, the thematic preoccupation with social and moral comment on the postcolonial situation and the formal implications of aesthetic traditionalism come together to force a return to the use of an

African language as a medium of expression. Ngugi has recounted the circumstances that led him to break with the English language and to reeducate himself in the use of Kikuyu for his writing (Ngugi, 1986), but the transition simply makes apparent the logic of a development that has been inherent in his work from the beginning. The sense of tradition is pervasive in all of Ngugi's work, reflected as much in his themes and overt references as in his imagery. His heavy reliance on a rhetoric derived from the Bible in his first four novels written in English provides, perhaps ironically, the strongest indication of the shaping influence of this sense of tradition upon his imagination; it is clear that this derived idiom offers him an equivalent in English to an oral mode and also provides him with a demotic language appropriate for representing the universe of life and values with which he identifies his own Kikuyu society. But in his recent work, it is not so much his concern for authentic expression as the compulsion he feels to give effective potential to his writing—in the new context of African realities—that has dictated his return to his linguistic origins. The moral and social significance he attaches to this return is made clear by the quest for sustaining values embarked upon by the hero of his novel *Matigari*, a work that can be considered the supreme parable of the "African condition." For Ngugi, it seems to me, it is less a question of reinstating the self in its integrity as of recovering a purity of vision and a force of will adequate to confront the urgencies of the present moment.

Ngugi's adventure with language is indicative of the tension between tradition and transition in the modern African imagination and, indeed, in all of our contemporary apprehension. With his work in Kikuyu, coming after his achievement in English, Ngugi has opted to resolve in a radical manner the state of ambivalence that this tension has instilled at the heart of African letters. His effort to disengage his writing from the constraining framework of references determined by the linguistic bonding of Africa to Europe marks a gesture of refusal toward the cultural subjugation that this bonding entails, the implication it carries that Africa is an obscure province of "the empire of signs" instituted by Western civilization in its worldwide expansion. But although his endeavor to bring African expression full circle back to its foundation in language goes a step beyond Birago Diop's enterprise, it is as a reality newly inscribed in letters that he is obliged to carry this expression forward to new ground. Like Diop, he has had to give the African forms of fable and myth a new mode of existence in written texts. His solution still entails a recourse to the modality of writing, an acceptance of it as an imposition along with all the other aspects of our historical experience that have been imprinted on the pattern of our contemporary existence and can no longer be erased from either our lives or our consciousness.

But Ngugi's adventure is also instructive in another direction. It illustrates the way in which, as Africans, we have had to employ writing for the full exploration of what Soyinka has called "the movement of transition" in our collective existence. The process of elaborating a new and distinctive expression represents, in itself, the making of a tradition of letters, one that retraces the course of our modern adventure and may well take novel and unexpected directions in the future. Significantly, the idea of tradition has featured prominently in the process, both as theme and as determining factor of the very form of our modern expression. Above all, the idea of tradition has served us essentially as a focus of consciousness and imagination and thus enabled us to formulate a vision of our place in the world. In that sense, and despite the ambiguities its central place in African letters has involved, it has fulfilled a most important function: helping us to negotiate a path for our awareness toward a new mode of integration in the modern world.

4

Dimensions of African Discourse

It is now more than two hundred years since, as Africans, we have been using the European languages for self-expression. The circumstances in which these languages (English, French, and Portuguese, in particular) became available to us are too well known to require elaboration. What needs to be recalled for my theme is the fact that they bear the stamp of a tragic irony that, with remarkable prescience, William Shakespeare dramatized in the antagonistic relationship between Prospero and Caliban in *The Tempest*. An important component of this relationship, as the play stresses, is the question of language, that is, of the modes of perception and of representation that govern the master/slave dialectic.[1]

These circumstances, in their real historical manifestations, have determined the contours of modern African expression in the European languages. The themes and preoccupations that are central to the development of this expression and the uses to which the acquired literacy upon which it is grounded has been consciously put point to an imperative of the African consciousness: the intensive exploration by our writers, both at the imaginative and conceptual levels, of a peculiar and singular historicity. Whether in the form of imaginative literature or in directly ideological terms, writing has served us as a means of appropriating the European languages in an endeavor to transcend the vicissitudes of a problematic experience, in an effort toward an expressive grasp of the world in which that experience unfolds.

The close correspondence between the two channels of African discourse I have indicated becomes evident when it is observed that the themes and textual modes of the imaginative literature regularly present themselves as imagistic transpositions of explicit preoccupations at the level of the ideological; they give the indirection of form and of metaphor (in the large sense of the term) to sentiments, attitudes, and ideas—to activities of consciousness—that stem from an immediate engagement with experience. Both can thus be regarded as alternative and even alternating modes of the same textual response to a collective experience, exemplifying in a particularly striking way what Edward Said has called "the situation of writing in history" (Said, 1980, x).

The imaginative and ideological forms of African expression in the European languages thus constitute a specific configuration of discourse, which though not by any means uniform, univocal, or homogeneous, is nonetheless coherent, centered as it is upon a dominant issue: our historic encounter with and continuing relationship to the West and the varied implications of our modern experience as it has been determined by this historic encounter.

My intention in this chapter is not to propose one more exposition of the themes of African writing (which has already been well surveyed) but to highlight those aspects of African response to the incursion of Europe and the West that may help to clarify the processes and issues involved in the development of African discourse in the broad sense. I will situate African writing within the three contexts that seem to me to bring out its proper dimensions: as racial reference, its central place within Black expression and hence its specific affiliation to the movement of Black affirmation in the Americas; its relation to the emerging discourses of the Third World, as part of a general contestation of the hegemony of the West; and finally, its relevance to certain currents of thought in the West itself, with which it can be placed in a certain relation of congruence. In this last respect, we witness a transformation of African discourse in the postcolonial period into an internal debate that inaugurates a distinctive form of public discourse in Africa, focused on the question of modernity. My overall aim is to present African discourse as an affective and cognitive process whose textual expression continuously interacts with the concrete reality of history and significantly bears upon the urgent concerns of the contemporary world.

The most striking aspect of African discourse is of course its character as a movement of contestation. Starting with the work of the eighteenth-century Black writers, this discourse has determinedly confronted European representations of Africa and of the Black race and dedicated special attention to the objective historical conditions of the race, first during slavery and later under colonialism. A conditioning factor of African response has thus been, quite simply, an acute racial consciousness in direct reaction to the negativizing premises of Western racist ideology. Thus African discourse has been historically projected in an essentially adversarial posture and has thus assumed a polemical significance. In whatever accents African response has been given expression, whether in an openly combative form or a discreetly pathetic one—with gradations in between—the discursive project has taken the form of an ongoing, principled dispute with the West over the terms of African/Black existence and, ultimately, of being. The example of Aimé Césaire, whose poetry embraces the African experience in its full ramifications—historical, moral, and even metaphysical—becomes especially instructive in this regard. All of his expression is predicated upon what he calls "the true operative power of negation" (*le vrai pouvoir opératoire de la négation*), upon the subversive impulse of a poetic language resolutely pitted against Western prescriptive terms ("Barbare," in *Collected Poems*, 212). His work sets in train, as it were, a poetics of aggression that elaborates a system of "counter-interpellations" (to use Louis Althusser's term) opposed to the cooptive force of Western imperialism and cultural impositions.

Writing has also served us as the means of a pointed indictment of the European oppressor in the relentless documentation our literature provides of the stark realities of the Black experience as a historical consequence of conquest and domination. The resort to the autobiographical form by the early black slave writers (Equiano and others) attests to the function of witnessing, which the African writer has been compelled to assume from the beginning. There is perhaps no better instance of this immediate documentary and testamental significance of African writing than that offered by the ironic fictions of Ferdinand Oyono, whose depiction of colonial violence is built upon the image of the prison as the fundamental institution from which colonialism is generated and by which it is maintained. And it is the concrete grasp of the actualities of the colonial experience laid bare in works such as these that Frantz Fanon has enlarged upon in his analyses of the colonial situation to present a graphic image of what, with Michel Foucault, we now recognize as the "carceral society."

The point that emerges from this aspect of African discourse is its strongly articulated sense of historical grievance. The fact itself has further implications, beyond its immediate reference to our relationship with the West, for it has determined in African (and Black) thinking and attitudes a conflation of the categories of race and culture, which still exerts an axiomatic force even in the postcolonial period. The positing in this discourse of a sharp dichotomy between an aggressive Western civilization and a humane African sensibility has implications for the African debate on modernity, which we shall have occasion to consider. For the moment, we might note that the moral perceptions that inform the African sense of racial and historical grievance issue into a comprehensive critique of the West, a questioning of its assumptions about itself and of its vision of the world. Under the pressure of experience, our writers have had to undertake a critical reassessment of the colonizer, of the philosophy of life that is assumed to underlie his disposition toward the world, and anticipate in the course of this reassessment some of the key strategies of contemporary Western thought.

The complementary aspect of this stance of negation is the mobilization of the collective will and consciousness, which African writing has sought to enact at the discursive level. Our expression in the European languages has not only functioned as a mode of contestation of the colonial ideology but also has served an emancipatory project. It is of course in this respect that the various theories of Africanism that have sprung up in the Black world have had their strategic importance. Of some of the relevant figures, let me simply refer here in passing to Edward Wilmot Blyden and his concept of the "African personality," Martin Delany and Marcus Garvey, with their various exemplifications of the Back to Africa movement, W. E. B. Du Bois with his militant Pan-Africanism, and of course, Léopold Sédar Senghor and his theory of Negritude.

The ideology of race promoted by the theories of Africanism associated with these figures, which go hand in hand with movements of racial solidarity, sustains in the literature a form of Romanticism that seeks to legitimize and underwrite a myth of universal Black identity. In the African context, this has had the largely salutary effect (thought not without its problems and contradictions) of a revaluation and celebration of indigenous cultures, a process exemplified in the *gravitas* that writers as different as Senghor and Achebe ascribe to the universe of life that they posit as their true antecedents (what Senghor calls *le royaume d'enfance*, the realm of childhood) and on which they stake their sense of origins. That the process of revaluation also embraces the modes of expression associated with the traditional world gives rise to what I have called an aesthetic traditionalism, a poetics of indigenism that shapes the formal structure of much of the imaginative literature. For, in the discursive context of the colonial situation, language, as an essential medium of human articulations and cultural processes, becomes a strategic site of African revendications, a significant modality of cultural nationalism. The tremendous effort of historical scholarship that supports this movement of cultural nationalism gives further density to the African assertion by seeking to project African being-in-time along an autonomous axis of historicity (Gordon, 1971).

The immediate import of these imaginative projections and intellectual efforts is perfectly clear: as counterdiscourses, they represent not only a repudiation of the negative representations of the "native" in the imperialist ideology, they also articulate the claim to an alternative cultural history to the Western. It is especially in this connection that theories of Africanism assume an incisive relevance for Black intellectuals in the New World, in what has come to be known, by analogy with the Jewish condition, as the Black Diaspora. They imply a reinvestiture of the Black self, a reincorporation, in the strong sense of the word, that establishes a new compact of the racial and historical community through congruence with its origins. For the Black intellectual in Africa and the African Diaspora, severed from a sense of immediate connection with the original community, an appeal to the background of African traditional life and history represents a form of spiritual homecoming, a *nostos*.

The preoccupation with the racial question thus provides a primary dimension of African discourse. This dimension, which incorporates all of the significant aspects of cultural nationalism that the discourse promotes, links it in an immediate way with Black consciousness movements in the New World. Indeed, the historical and thematic links between modern African expression in the European languages and African-American and Caribbean literatures proceed in formal terms from their common origin in the work of the early Black slave writers of the eighteenth century. These links have determined a cycle of reciprocities that finds a pointed illustration in the derivation of the Negritude movement itself from the Harlem Renaissance as a direct outgrowth of the thematic and ideological expression of African Americans (Kesteloot, 1991). And the idea of Black identity to which the Harlem poets and artists strove to give expressive form finds with the French-speaking black intellectuals its ultimate formulation in a concept of black racial essence.

The essentialism implied by this concept, which informs the various theories of Africanism of which Negritude is a summation, still holds sway in some crucial respects. For instance, what I have called the cycle of reciprocities between Black discourse in the New World and in Africa is being sustained in the work of a prominent segment of the black intelligentsia in North America (Asante, 1987, 1988). Such developments as the Black Aesthetics movement initiated by Addison Gayle, Stephen Henderson, and others and the Afrocentrism of Molefi Asante constitute restatements in African-American terms of the essential tenets of Negritude; they proceed from the same vision of a common backdrop of origin, culture, expression, and sensibility. In the critical work of scholars such as Houston Baker, Jr., and Henry Louis Gates, Jr., who are promoting a theory of "vernacular" literary and cultural expressions of the Black community in the United States with direct reference to African-derived paradigms, we observe an effort to conceptualize the Black self as a continuous process of self-realization with organic roots in the ancestral soil. Whatever value one is inclined to attach to the propositions that these various scholars offer of the Black estate in the Americas, they attest to the fact that there remains a wide area of overlap between African discourse and African-American imaginative self-awareness and intellectual self-reflection.

These manifestations of Black racial consciousness denote a form of collective self-projection through what one might call a strategy of differentiation. We need not inquire here into the validity or truth claims in strict anthropological or philosophical terms of the formulations proposed by African discourse and its extension in the New World. Because they present themselves essentially as a refutation of the category of the radical "other" imposed on the colonized Black, they function, *ipso facto*, as a repositioning of the collective self in a willed act of renewed self-apprehension.

In its polemical stance, then, African discourse presents itself as a thorough-going deconstruction of the Western image of the Native, the Black, the African. Because we were represented as the absolute "other," we were well placed to develop a minority discourse that marks the extreme position of dissent from the systematizing, totalizing thrust of the Western imperialist system. This dissent has force not only in its bearing upon the application of the Western conceptual system in its concrete effects to our historical situation but upon the structure and the universalist ambitions of the system itself.[2] In this sense, the discourse of Africanism as elaborated by Black intellectuals on both sides of the Atlantic must be seen as a reinscription of an antecedent Western monologue on

Africa and the non-Western world, its displacement and transformation by a new, assertive self-expression on the part of a subjugated and previously voiceless humanity.

The general pattern of this challenge to Western discourse has been indicated for the colonized writers of English expression by Ashcroft, Griffiths, and Tiffin in their comprehensive survey, *The Empire Writes Back,* and the mechanisms they have described as typifying this expression can be identified in anticolonial and postcolonial literatures in other languages. The pattern involves notably the refusal of privilege to the language, literature, and thought systems of the colonizer and to the framework of references stipulated for the colonized writer by a metropolitan paradigm. This refusal is complemented by an assiduous cultivation of a sense of place, which finds expression in a localized idiom made coterminous with a radical sense of identity. What is implied here is a determined inversion of the order of precedence decreed by the colonizer from an entrenched center of power. The conceptual formulation of this new disposition discernible in Third World discourse is carried through by an intellectual effort that runs parallel to the imaginative expression. Edward Said's *Orientalism* represents perhaps the most powerful instance of this effort in the elaboration of a postcolonial discourse whose theoretical implications are being explored today in the work of other Third World intellectuals, including Abdelkebir Khatibi, Gayatri Spivak, and Homi Bhabha.[3]

The historical reference for this dimension of African discourse in its transactions with Third World literary and intellectual responses to Western imperialism is the Bandung Conference of 1955, considered the primal event of decolonization in our time.[4] The specific impulses at work in the postcolonial literatures that may be placed in relation to this event thus operate as potent factors to decenter and relativize the conceptual and moral order of the Western world and to promote a pluralism of voices with a legitimate claim to universal hearing. The pressures they exert move toward what one might call a global deregulation of the Western paradigm, as much in feeling and expression as in thought.

The allusion to Bandung and to decolonization underscores the constitutive role of African and Third World discourse in the formation and consolidation of anticolonial nationalism in contemporary times. These discourses assume a political significance as an integral component of ideologies of national independence, which gave orientation to anti-Western sentiments in the non-Western world and culminated in the emergence of new nation-states in Africa and Asia after the Second World War. The rhetoric of cultural and racial affirmation involved in these ideologies thus served as the mental levers in the struggle against the objective structures of imperial domination and colonial dependency. The implication of African discourse in these developments extends its affiliation to the literature of race and black identity, giving it a relevance with more than a circumscribed significance. But despite this extension of its primary affiliation, it is probably correct to state that the African/Black response to the West remains very particularized, as much in the specific terms of its expression as in its general thrust.[5] The nationalist project in the imaginative literature and ideological writings in the African context was centered primarily on considerations of the historical fortunes of the Black race, of which the African continent was taken to represent the ancestral core and spiritual homeland. African nationalism thus developed as a continuous progression from Pan-Africanism as the continent assumed the attributes of a "nation" in the comprehensive and unified vision that Pan-Africanism fostered among Black peoples. As I have pointed out elsewhere, nationalism in Africa only assumed distinctive territorial expressions in its final phase, in relation to the spheres of domination determined by the partition of the continent among the imperial powers (Irele, 1981, 1990, 117–24).

It is thus in a large and diffuse sense that imaginative literature and other forms of discourse came to serve nationalism in Africa. And as in all forms of literary expression dedicated to the promotion of nationalist consciousness, the dominant symbols tend toward a celebration of community projected through imaginative form. The master text in the case of Africa remains Chinua Achebe's *Things Fall Apart*, by reason of both its innovative significance for the emergence of modern African literature and its ideological project as a vindication of a unique mode of life and apprehension, despite the inevitable ambivalence that runs as an undercurrent to its portrayal of an indigenous African society and culture. Here, as elsewhere, literature provides an aesthetic and moral sanction for an idealized vision of the community defined, on the one hand, in terms of inclusion—of the indigenous group's singularity and its commonality of history, culture, and sentiment (although in Africa and Third World nationalisms, this commonality does not always extend to language)—and on the other hand, in terms of an exclusion of the colonial master himself from the human category to which the group feels and indeed knows itself to belong. The claim to self-determination thus becomes founded upon a cult of difference all the more plausible in that it seems ratified by the visible imprint of racial and ethnic characteristics.

This insistence on difference involves an apparent irony of the nationalist posture as it emerges from African and Third World discourses, for it seems to imply an assent to the terms of the colonial ideology, predicated as this is on the idea of the incommensurability of the human essence of the colonizer and that of the native. It thus appears as if what I have called "the strategies of differentiation," which animate much of African discourse, produce the paradoxical result of an entrenchment of the categories of the colonizers.[6] The essential point, however, is that this affirmation of difference not only authorizes the claims implied in the nationalist project to an autonomy that is political, it also in its fullest sense enacts a movement toward an absolute form of self-recovery, toward repossession in cultural and existential terms.

This observation points to what is perhaps the most salient aspect of the idealism (in all of the senses of the word) inherent in the myths of the nation constructed by African and Third World discourses: the utopianism and even millenarianism with which they are pervaded. These myths articulate the aspirations of colonized, non-Western peoples to a new mode of insertion into the flow of history as well as to a modernity in which their sense of initiative can receive unhindered play. This second aspect of African and Third World utopianism has implications for the further development of the intellectual adventure of the non-Western world, for it happens to be the case that, in the particular circumstances of decolonization in the twentieth century, the accession to modernity could only take place under the rubric of the nation-state, both as a notion inherited from the West and as a functional unit for modes of social organization and economic production compatible with the exigencies of the modern world, a point to which we shall soon return.

Thus, if nationalism in Africa and the Third World aspires in each domain of its expression toward a reintegration of the communal past within the collective awareness, it has perforce to acknowledge an epochal break with the past provoked by the colonial, Western incursion. The historical consciousness implicit in nationalism thus involves in this case an acute sense of discontinuities in the history that the colonized themselves have undertaken to refashion. In the African context, the career and work of Kwame Nkrumah strikingly exemplify the nexus intro-

duced by this logic of decolonization between a celebratory traditionalism mandated by his nationalist convictions and a utopian vision of
African reconstruction in the contemporary world.[7]

As an idea, then, colonial emancipation is predicated on the hopes
of new beginnings for historical communities striving for a new mode of
existence; it is thus enmeshed in an unusually complex relation among
past, present, and future. In African discourse, especially, this relation is
inscribed within the tense dialectic of tradition and modernity. The high
valuation of racial and cultural antecedents, of what is imagined and
projected as their coherence, has had to be balanced against the recognition of the new imperatives of modernization dictated by the impact
of a triumphant West. What this implies is nothing less than a drama of
conflicting normatives,[8] and it is this drama that defines for Africans
today the specific form of what has come to be termed "the dilemma of
modernity" (Cahoone, 1988).

It is especially in this respect that the contemporary climate of
thought in the West interests us, an interest that is the most recent indication of the deep and long-standing overlaying of African thought
onto the movement of ideas in the West. In significant ways, African
discourse, along with other "minority" discourses, has urgently antici-
pated some of the current concerns in Western thought. These anticipa-
tions were not necessarily theorized, or if they were, as in the case of
Fanon mentioned earlier, they were not formulated in exactly the same
terms as the currents of thought now commonly grouped under post-
structuralism and postmodernism. But the ideas that are coming out of
the Western world today strike us with a certain familiarity, for they address issues of authority, pluralism, and especially the relationship between discourse and power to which we have had perforce to pay special
attention by reason of our historical experience. These ideas are also concerned with the question of discursivity and its crucial function in the
claims to legitimacy and normativity in the social sphere, a question that
goes to the heart of our modern experience as a result of our encounter
with Europe.[9]

This parallel provides confirmation of the fact that there have been
significant points of intersection between the unfolding of African discourse along its polemical trajectory and intellectual and social developments in Europe, at least since the eighteenth century. African discourse, by the force of circumstances, has had to integrate important

elements of the Western structure of mind to which African intellectuals have had to relate. This is obvious enough in the case of what we may term the "liberal" tradition of Western thought, within which powerful voices have been raised on our behalf since the beginning of our encounter with Europe, voices with which we have found good cause to identify.[10] The critical interrogation going on today within Western thought concerning its own systems of knowledge and values corresponds in certain important respects to the exigencies of this liberal tradition. Moreover—and this is the point I wish to stress—it accords with the perceptions of African intellectuals of the contradiction between the humanist claims of Western civilization and its practical effects on subject races, in other words, its profound dissimulations.

But the real significance of the convergence that can be claimed between African discourse and the critical activity now taking place in the West emerges from the wider perspective of a global debate on the question of modernity. It is at this level that one discerns a third dimension of African discourse. The dynamics inherent in contemporary discourse in Africa, as indeed in the Third World as a whole, takes us well beyond the immediate ideological and nationalist project the discourse patently serves. It involves not only a reappraisal of the terms of the relationship between the West and indigenous cultures and societies but also an interrogation, often anxiety-ridden, of the societies themselves. This interrogation is inherent in the nature of the nationalist project itself, in the peculiar conjunction between the archaisms that modulate its deeply affective function and the prospective significance of the utopianism by which it seeks to mobilize the collective will.

It is important to place this process of self-interrogation as it has manifested itself in Africa in the historical and philosophical framework of modern experience worldwide in order to grasp this dimension of African discourse. Modern nationalism, in Europe and elsewhere, has derived much of its impulse from the pressures brought about by the vast social transformations set in motion by the industrial revolution, which profoundly altered the modes of transactions between individuals and between communities and redefined their relation to the world. Much of modern thought and scholarship has been conditioned by the need to confront the existential implications of these changes. Thus the Enlightenment has come to represent the point of cleavage between what Karl Mannheim has called "conservative thought" and the various ideologies of progress that have derived from the unprecedented development of science and its technological applications since the eighteenth century (Mannheim, 1953).[11]

The massive reorganization of life in political, economic, social, and cultural terms brought about by the industrial revolution has provoked varying responses from writers and thinkers in the West, some of which might be said to offer parallels to nativistic movements in the non-Western world and to provide a common ground for the debates on culture and the whole question of modernity both in the West and in the Third World, most especially Africa. In the more significant of these responses, the quest is for a mode of experience that retains the immediacy of the "simple life" of traditional societies conjoined with an inwardness of experience as opposed to the complex organization of industrial society and the spiritual disarray and alienation that it is presumed to entail. This quest is obvious in literary Romanticism in Europe, and a Romantic strain can be said in this sense to pervade the conservative ideology of Burke and the nationalism of Herder, and it can even be discerned behind Hegel's idea of the "organic society."[12] The case of Russia, which remained more or less on the fringe of Western civilization for much of its history up to the Bolshevik Revolution, is particularly illuminating in this regard. Movements such as that of the Russian Slavophiles, with their affinities for the mysticism of the Tolstoyans and even for the philosophical anarchism of Kropotkin, offer perhaps the most revealing instance of the way in which the advance of modern civilization has produced malcontents even in Europe (Walicki, 1975; Avrich, 1978).

The tension that all of these responses address is summed up in the distinction made by Ferdinand Tonnies between *Gemeinschaft* (community), with its connotation of close bonding between the members of a determinate and specified group, and *Gesellschaft*, with its implication of an impersonal order of social organization. This distinction reflects a concern for a warmly human rather than a purely rational scale of values, which Max Weber has singled out as the organizing principle of modern society.[13] And it is in the general light of a profound dissatisfaction with this principle that a reappraisal is taking place today in contemporary Western thought of "instrumental reason" as a factor of modernity. The interplay between thought and change—evoked in these very terms in the title of Ernest Gellner's book—that underlies the responses mentioned above becomes directly relevant to a consideration of African discourse, for it sketches out the background to the felt pressures of modernization in all societies and cultures that have experienced the impact of industrialization either directly, as in Europe and North America, or indirectly through foreign influence or imperialism, as in non-Western societies. The Russian case, despite its peculiarity, offers close parallels to the African situation.

The point, then, is that a general preoccupation with the dilemmas of modernity runs as a *leitmotif* in Western thought at least since the Enlightenment; it is hardly surprising therefore that it should also constitute the unifying theme of the reflective activity embodied in African discourse, which has developed in the context both of Western cultural impositions and of the far-reaching dislocations that these have engendered in African cultures and societies. The combined effects of the humiliated feeling of colonial dependency and of the cultural malaise flowing from these dislocations have determined something of a standard trope of the African imagination in which Africa, associated with the security of origins, is represented as being violated by an aggressive and unfeeling Europe. This is, of course, the basis of the Romanticism that informs what I have alluded to as the myth of identity in African discourse, conditioning the disaffection toward Western rationality, which is associated both with colonial domination and an unsettling modernity that is its immediate consequence. African literature in its genesis and development has revolved so much around the theme of culture conflict carried by this master trope that it has become a commonplace of its reception and analysis.

Yet, it is important to note that what appears to be a fixation on the dialectic of tradition and modernity also reflects a quest for a new direction for collective initiative, for the intellectual foundations of a movement of African renewal. The theories of African socialism propounded by figures such as Senghor and Julius Nyerere in the immediate aftermath of African independence have no other significance; indeed, they issue largely out of the utopianism that, as we have seen, underlies the nationalist consciousness in Africa. And, as is evident in the case of Nkrumah's "consciencism," they represent a focused endeavor to negotiate a mode of accommodation between Africa and the West (Senghor, 1964; Nkrumah, 1970; Nyerere, 1973).

This aspect of contemporary African thought has been thrown into special relief by the current debate on the question of African philosophy. An extension of the Negritude debate, the present discussion centers upon an argument about the philosophical status of traditional African systems of thought and their capacity both for providing a satisfactory explanation of the world comparable to Western systems of knowledge and for enabling effective action in the modern world. The epistemological issues involved in the debate have thus been subordinated to a consideration of the options open for the process of renovation in Africa, options that condition strategies for ensuring the destiny of its peoples in a world governed by the institutional imperatives of the nation-state and dominated by a universal technicality, in short, for the instauration of an acceptable order of life in Africa in contemporary times.

The intellectuals associated with this debate—such as Marcien Towa, Paulin Hountondji, and Achille Mbembe—have initiated what one might call a "contradictory discourse," which breaches the consensus around a uniform vision of Africa and is more in tune with the dynamics of the social and cultural processes at work in cultural and intellectual production in contemporary Africa. By fostering a new orientation toward a critical appraisal and revision of earlier formulations of African discourse, they have given a new focus to intellectual activity in Africa in the postcolonial period.

The Zairean writer Valentin Mudimbe has argued that the development of African discourse has been essentially a function of what he calls, in Foucaultian terms, the depositions of the Western archive (Mudimbe, 1988). What he means by this amounts to saying that this discourse is merely derivative. However, it is possible to propose a more positive estimation. From a consideration of what I have called its dimensions, it is indeed perfectly legitimate to postulate a close connection between African intellectual efforts and Western discourse and, specifically today, critical activity in the West. The immediate conclusion one can draw from this connection is that African discourse is not by any means marginal but, on the contrary, is central to contemporary concerns.

While there exists a congruence between the temper of contemporary thought in the West and African concerns, it does not seem to me that this quite indicates a coincidence of interests. Western thought at the moment, in its distinctive anti-foundationalist current, is engaged in the process of unraveling its tradition, specifically, the tradition that came into sharp focus in the eighteenth century; it is marked, in other words, by a comprehensive skepticism with regard to its defining legacy of rationalism and by a disengagement from its predicates arising from a profound distrust of what has come to be seen as its reifications. On the other hand, the direction of African discourse has been toward the privileging of thought as an active modality of existence. It seems to me, therefore, that the terms of late twentieth-century Western thought do not correspond to the imperatives of intellectual enterprise in the present African context.

We cannot then, as Africans, have much use for what can be described as the uncharted nihilism of this aspect of contemporary thought in the West—for the morose antihumanism of Foucault or the corrosive intelligence of Derrida.[14] An active intellectual vigilance is therefore in order on our part. The plain fact is that history has not been for us a phantom play of mirrors but rather a harrowing experience, vividly rendered in our imaginative expression and reflected in the general tenor of our discourse. This fact imposes on the African intellectual a certain moral responsibility, for at this stage of our historical and intellectual adventure, we cannot do with anything less than a forward movement of thought and, above all, will.

Study in Ambiguity

Amadou Hampaté Bâ's
The Fortunes of Wangrin

The name of Amadou Hampaté Bâ, the veteran Malian scholar of African folklore and traditional culture, is now firmly associated with a famous remark he once made at a UNESCO conference in Paris concerning the oral tradition in Africa: "En Afrique, chaque fois qu'un vieillard meurt, c'est une bibliothèque qui est brûlée" (In Africa, each time an old person dies, it's a library that burns down). The remark has acquired the status of an aphorism, expressing as it does, in graphic terms, the urgent necessity of collecting the oral tradition in Africa before its final disappearance with the last of its guardians, in whose memory its textual values are preserved. The import of the remark derives in the first place from what it demonstrates of the mode of existence of the oral text in Africa. No better formulation than that offered by Hampaté Bâ could be given to the idea of the "organic" nature of the oral tradition, of its material basis in the living presence and manifested being of its creators and of those individuals charged with its perpetuation as an essential component of the communal awareness (Bâ, 1981). These individuals function not as mere inert repositories of texts but as their recreators in the immediate context of performance.

Hampaté Bâ's words carry an unmistakably positive valuation of the oral tradition, for although they cannot be construed as a naive expression of cultural nationalism, they certainly stress the urgency of the task that lies ahead in the effort to save what he considers to be an inestimable and endangered cultural and spiritual legacy. The terms of his statement are proof of his state of mind, for the phrase is shot through with a tragedy that indicates a sense of calamity at the prospect of the disappearance of the values of this legacy in our present situation of intense social and cultural change. At the same time, his statement draws attention to the essential fragility of the oral tradition once it is deprived of the institutional framework within which it functioned. It points to the evanescent nature of the spoken word, which is that of life itself; as the living carriers of the oral tradition disappear, and its formal texts can no longer be relayed through a new succession of active agents, its mode of existence is undermined, and the textual values that comprise it can find no other means of embodiment than those offered by the alternative tradition of a literate culture, symbolized in concrete terms by the Western institution of the library. The terms employed by Hampaté Bâ thus dramatize the process of displacement of the oral tradition in Africa as a contemporary culture is being elaborated on the continent. It is a recognition of this truth that Hampaté Bâ's remark registers, and we cannot doubt that it is his purpose to draw attention to the necessity of ordering this process of displacement in such a way as to effect a transposition of the oral tradition in Africa into a literate one as harmoniously as possible. This involves not merely fixing the texts in writing—doing this ensures that they are indeed preserved but only as mummies presented to our curious gaze—but also adjusting their forms to the new medium so as to revitalize their meanings in the new context of situation created by the emergence and development in Africa of the structures of a modern civilization.

Hampaté Bâ's individual contribution to this process has been by all accounts an outstanding and even exemplary one. As the catalogue of his publications prepared by Alfa Sow indicates (Sow, 1970), his interests and activities as a lifelong scholar of African folklore and traditions have been both extensive and eminently productive. Indeed, his contribution to knowledge in this area has been nothing less than distinguished. It is enough to cite his monumental reconstruction of the oral tradition of the Pular empire of Macina (Bâ, 1984) to indicate the honored place that his work now occupies in African historiography.

But what is significant about his efforts on behalf of the oral tradition is not so much their scholarly orientation as their creative intent and value. The remarkable aspect of Hampaté Bâ's work is that he has not been content merely to collect oral texts and to reproduce them either in the original language or in French translations. His approach has been based rather on an understanding of the disparity between the oral and the written media, which makes the latter inadequate for a proper presentation of the oral texts without adaptation. His method has thus consisted in recreating these texts anew in written form. In his French translations of oral literature, in particular, this method has had the admirable effect of producing works in which the original texts assume once again their literary status in their new language and new medium of expression. Thus, a work like *Kaidara*, for example, presents not simply an academic or ethnological interest related to initiation rites among the Pular but a properly literary one. It represents a transposition into a distinctive idiom of the original poem, which comes to bear the stamp of an individual sensibility manifested in a personal relationship to the universe of ideas and values of which the text is an expression in the original context and language of its composition. One might indeed observe that Hampaté Bâ negotiates a new path to this relation by means of a reconstitution in French of the meaning of this text in Pular.

Hampaté Bâ's career thus illustrates the dialectic of the oral and the written in contemporary Africa and its insertion within the sociological and cultural context of the production of meanings and the creation of values that now prevail on the continent. As Alain Ricard has observed, his work not only straddles two traditions, it amounts to a personal appropriation of the intrinsic values of oral literature for an imaginative purpose (Ricard, 1985). What gives point and effect to this appropriation is the realization that in employing the written medium, in particular the European language, to render the oral literature of Africa accessible to a wider audience, one can only hope to transmit the imaginative values it proposes by remaking the texts that constitute it as literature, so as to reactivate their essential human significance. With Hampaté Bâ, as with Birago Diop and John Pepper Clark-Bekederemo, the transposition of the oral tradition into a new key of expression and into a new mode of existence passes through a veritable process of *poiesis*.

This process is exemplified in a peculiar way in the work before us in the singular character of its conception and execution. More than any other work in the whole corpus of contemporary African writing, *The Fortunes of Wangrin* represents a mediation between the African tradition of orality and Western narrative conventions as formalized in written texts. Such indeed is the nature of this mediation that the work seems to propose a new category, if not a new form, of imaginative discourse in Africa. The most striking aspect of this work is the original way in which it both accommodates cultural references from its hinterland of denotations—its two areas of reference are represented by the social and cultural forms of life in traditional Africa and the modern forms as they begin to unfold under colonialism—and also integrates the formal properties of imaginative expression in both the African and Western registers. No less significant is the fact that this integration in terms of content and form produces a certain tension within the work, which paradoxically contributes to its cohesion.

When we consider the overall scheme of the work and the complications Hampaté Bâ introduces into its structure, it becomes at once apparent where its originality resides. *The Fortunes of Wangrin* purports to be the story of Wangrin's life as recounted in the Bambara language by the man himself to the author, who proceeded to reproduce it in French as the biography of an exceptional individual with whom he has had acquaintance. It is clear that we have here two series of mediations: first, between the oral text as received and recorded by the author in its original language of delivery and its reformulation in French as the written text of the published version he subsequently offered the world; and second, between the presentation of a real life experience for whose veracity the author vouches (thus, a *biography*) and a narrative progression, enforced by the use of the third person in its development, whose elements have had to be constructed in conformity with the demands of aesthetic form. Wangrin's experience comes to be presented to us in essentially imaginative terms, in other words, as a work of fiction or, more specifically still, as a novel.

These two series of mediations are further intensified in their effect by subsidiary devices, which contribute to the formal pattern and the scheme of reference of the work. For it is not only the voice of Wangrin but also that of his griot, Dieli Madi, and of his archrival, Romo Sibedi, which are mediated by the authorial voice. What is more, none of these voices is ever made to speak for itself, but they speak instead for the common background of experience and values from which they all issue, as we are made aware from the outset when Hampaté Bâ brings in the figure of Fodan Seni to present the setting of his narrative in a symbolic and mythic overture to its development. The meanings that these various voices propose comprise a vision of life whose articulations the author has had to make intelligible to his audience and which by that fact is distanced from him in the act of reconstruction that is implied by writing. Because the development of the narrative is carried through in the framework of a realistic mode, these voices continually challenge the conventions of the form in which they are given expression. They set up a contrary and dissonant mode rung upon the realistic key of the work, while at the same time they are harmonized within its total movement to bring out its significance. It is this tension that animates the work: the tension between a register of experience and its expression.

We thus have a curious relationship established in the work between the two imaginative traditions enclosed by its system of references, which translates as a reciprocity between the two narrative traditions associated with them. Within the space of a written text in a European language, not specifically adapted but given a purposeful inflection, Hampaté Bâ incorporates the essential features of the oral narrative at significant points in his work in order to reflect their appropriateness to situations and for special effects. Their conjunction with the narrative procedures sanctioned by the Western model thus enlarges their scope and gives them an unusual resonance. At the same time, although he writes with conscious reference to this Western model, he does not feel so constrained by the framework of its conventions that he is unable to go beyond its limitations. His departures from the established code of the Western narrative rely on the resources of the oral tradition, which in turn provide a new dimension of expression to the adopted model. The formal complexity that results from this reciprocity, this circular movement in Hampaté Bâ's treatment of the text, will be examined later; it is sufficient to note at this stage that it produces what by normal canons of literary judgment would be considered a mixed and even indeterminate genre of the narrative. It is obvious, however, that this formal aspect of the work is inherent in the disparate character of the material that provides its content, a disparity that Hampaté Bâ exploits to the fullest in its organization and in the orientation of its meaning, so that the work evinces an ambiguity of an essential order. We can sum this up by observing that the pervasive ambiguity of reference in the work determines a corresponding ambiguity of form.

No more appropriate reference could be imagined for the kind of ambiguity that informs this work than the context provided by the colonial situation. It is a truism, one that needs to be restated here, that the Western colonial imposition has been the single most disruptive factor in the African experience. To say this is not to open an ideological issue but to situate the African condition in its proper historical perspective and its objective manifestations today. The colonial impact had the effect of a comprehensive reordering of African societies and consequently of a massive reorientation of their historical evolution. Although the traditional institutions have generally opposed the erosion of the social structures that sustained them and the forms of cultural expression that validated them, they appear in retrospect to have been moving against the current of a historical process that was from the beginning irreversible. The state of disarray produced by this dialectic of history is still far from resolved, so the psychological and moral disorientation that has ensued remains with us a major preoccupation. In this sense, the colonial experience has a continuing importance as a cardinal reference for the modern African consciousness and imagination. It has specifically provided the dominant theme of our modern expression, and the pathetic development that this theme has systematically received in the works of our major writers represents perhaps the most significant feature of our literature in the European languages. A title like Chinua Achebe's *Things Fall Apart* is sufficiently indicative of our thematic preoccupation with the pathos of our historical experience that the point need not be stressed further.

The classic statement of this theme is contained in Cheikh Hamidou Kane's *L'aventure ambigüe*, a work that reflects in its very title the angle of reference to the colonial experience with which we are here concerned. The fact that it offers a parallel of historical context and geographical setting to *The Fortunes of Wangrin* is of considerable interest; in both works, we are taken back to the early years of French occupation in Sahelian West Africa to the period of transition between the final dissolution of the precolonial Islamic states in the region and the full establishment of the French colonial administration as the point of departure of the narrative. Moreover, Kane designates his novel a *récit* (rather than *roman*) presumably in order to emphasize its basis in historical fact, while Hampaté Bâ presents his work as a true account of events experienced by an authentic individual. The interest of the parallel between the two works resides in the fact that while they both refer to the same moment of historical transition, their perspectives differ markedly. Kane's work presents us with a meditation upon the state of ambiguity; Hampaté Bâ dramatizes it. With Kane, the conflict in the real world of the historical situation from which the spiritual adventure of his hero, Samba Diallo, proceeds is never portrayed; the concrete framework of life in which his drama of consciousness takes place is never fully realized. With Hampaté Bâ, the adventures of Wangrin arise out of the interplay, sometimes brutal and at other times subtle, between the contending forces in the social universe of the narrative; his fortunes are constantly and intimately involved in the drama that unfolds between these forces, a drama not only of events but also of wills. At the moment of historical divide between two dispensations, Wangrin moves to the center of the intense confusions that constitute the drama of ambiguity in the colonial situation.

It is significant to note the way in which Wangrin functions at various levels in the work as regards both the situations depicted in it and the narrative procedures by which they are conveyed, what may be considered the work's determining structures. As the subject of the book, he represents of course its focus, but the spotlight trained on him illuminates as well the web of human relations and the clash of various forces that stand in objective opposition to one another in the social universe through which he jostles his way. It is indeed something of a paradox that the half-illiterate interpreter, placed between the world of the French colonial administration and that of the indigenous political system, placed also between the world of the common African and that of the local notables, should stand at the vantage point from which to view the colonial universe in the round and to understand the tensions with which it is wracked as it comes into being.

Wangrin's scope is thus far more comprehensive than Kane's aristocratic hero can possibly take on, and his career offers a fuller and more representative testimony of the historical moment of the development of colonial rule. As we follow his adventures, we are led through the network of the French colonial administration as its machinery is being elaborated and put in place and thus into the day-to-day realities of the system of colonial imposition. A whole subterranean sphere of history is opened up to our intelligence. History itself comes alive in its immediate impact upon the individuals caught up in its movement. As we read Hampaté Bâ's work, we are persuaded that this was indeed the lived experience of Africans at that time and in that place.

It is this concrete quality of representation that distinguishes Hampaté Bâ's engagement with history. From this point of view, *The Fortunes of Wangrin* is a chronicle that presents an extraordinary documentary interest. The details it provides of the early period of colonial rule in French-speaking West Africa are so vivid that the picture of the times that emerges from the book goes well beyond anything that an academic history, however meticulous, can ever hope to offer. It is evident that we owe this richness of representation to Hampaté Bâ's own experience as well as to his narrative skill; there is a real sense in which the memorialist is at work in these pages. Moreover, in its expansiveness, his chronicle often assumes the quality of a pageant, of a tapestry of life as it was still regulated in the early years of the twentieth century in the savanna states before their institutions were finally dismantled by the French. There are evocations of the splendor that attended the ruling class, carried through a range of references that have both a documentary and a poetic value. The constant mention of gold in particular begins to seem a discreet metonymic device to characterize the civilization that the ruling class personified, apart from being a measure of the economic system on which it was based and an index of the opulence of a privileged minority. Our sense of the pageant quality of Hampaté Bâ's evocations is heightened by the processional character of his descriptions and the symbolism of open spaces that pervades the narrative, a feature it shares, incidentally, with Kane's novel.

It is important to draw attention to this conjunction of the documentary and the symbolic in Hampaté Bâ's reconstruction of this civilization, for it has more than a picturesque interest. It makes a historical point that is at once poignant and significant. We come to realize that the whole panoply of life, the whole ceremony of manners and values reproduced here, is that of a civilization that is on its last legs, doomed to yield to a new order the open spaces it had for ages inhabited. The economic system that provided its material basis is beginning to crumble and the relations of power that functioned within it are being subordinated to a new and different political arrangement. In specific terms, we become aware that what Hampaté Bâ recounts is the process by which the transition from a feudal system to a new economic order determined by the interests of French capitalist imperialism got under way in West Africa. A new impulse is seen at work upon this civilization, a quickening of historical time that rends apart the illusion of a "life for values," which it had engendered in the consciousness of the populations embraced within its objective fold.

Viewed from this perspective, the figure of Wangrin assumes a progressive significance. The new situation opens up the prospect of action for men like him, who are quick to see the signs scattered on the sun-baked walls of the palaces of the ruling class and to read into them the promise of the new dispensation inaugurated by French colonialism. Wangrin is thus the exemplar of the new class that European imperialism created all over Africa: petty bureaucrats evolving into a moneyed bourgeoisie. Hampaté Bâ's account is all the more valuable in that, though in a fictional mode, it avoids the melodrama with which Yambo Ouologuem presents the same historical process in *Le devoir de violence (Bound to Violence)*.

The dialectic of history, of permanence and change in the African experience, finds then in Hampaté Bâ's chronicle a dramatic expression. His work not only captures the objective process of this dialectic, it illuminates as well its subjective aspect, the tremendous pressures of adjustment entailed by the colonial experience. And it is here that *The Fortunes of Wangrin* sets out in the most graphic way the moral issues thrown up by the process and thus assumes a spiritual significance, in my view as worthy of attention as that proposed by Kane's novel.

It is interesting in this regard to consider the ironic stance that, as narrator, Hampaté Bâ maintains throughout the work toward the outstanding trait with which he endows his creation—the profound amoral nature of Wangrin. The impression of irony derives principally from the fact that the gap between our moral sense, based on the code of judgment we normally apply to instances of human behavior, and our tolerance for Wangrin's deviation from this code, is never fully bridged; our tolerance cannot go far enough to enable us to grant assent to Wangrin's ways.

Yet, for all that, we do identify with the man, as we identify with Molière's Scapin but not with Tartuffe; the fascination Wangrin exerts on us forces us to suspend our code of judgment even if we do not lose sight of it completely. The constant undermining of our identification with the character does not, it seems to me, diminish the effect of *catharsis* produced by his tragic end. It is not only that we admire the intelligence and energy that Wangrin brings to his immoral behavior as that we come to understand his profound motivation, inherent in the situation that he so fully embodies. Wangrin has grasped with remarkable intuition the truth of his situation: in a world of changing values, there can be no established code of conduct until the dust of history has settled. As the old institutions lose their relevance and the new ones, freshly introduced by the French, are yet to acquire the moral sanctions of a proven legitimacy, the movement of transition creates a situation of intense moral ambiguity. At the precise moment in history in which Wangrin has his existence, no one need have any allegiance except to himself, for in the moral penumbra that settles in the space between the two systems of references, to identify with one, to conform to its codes, is to make a choice that is in the circumstances problematic. The solution that offers itself to Wangrin is to move on to a third ground in which he makes his own rules as a means of self-fulfillment.

It is important to grasp this determining factor of Wangrin's psychology as it comes through in his actions. It would be superficial to see him as a simple rogue, as an opportunist ready to turn every situation to his advantage, for the course he chooses is not without its perils, and he himself is fully aware of the fact. The picture of intrigue on all sides, of generalized corruption and moral confusion that emerges from Hampaté Bâ's account of the early years of the French colonial administration produces the impression of a dangerous environment in which the only strategy of living appropriate to the situation and for survival is to get the better of others before they are aware of the fact. Wangrin's peculiar position is such that he can never take things for granted, so that the tension of anticipation becomes the motivating force of his personality, the basis of his *hubris* both as a historical individual and as the imaginative hero of Hampaté Bâ's narrative.

The heroic dimension of Wangrin is thus not in doubt, and we accord him the recognition that is due to the great project he wished to make of his existence in the improbable circumstances of his particular situation. It does not matter that this project turns on the idea of material success for, paradoxical as it may seem, it has for him the same spiritual significance as for the Calvinist in the primitive phase of capitalist accumulation: it is his guarantee of salvation in a world of uncertainty. Nor does it matter that his amorality is undiscriminating, so that at one moment it appears as a challenge of the colonial system, as in his confrontation of Villermoz, and at another as a cynical disregard of the elementary values of human solidarity, as in his dealings with Romo Sibedi. The reversal of values is consistent with his need for self-affirmation. In this, he is not only at one with the fundamental ambiguity of his situation, but he also actively enters into its tensions and moral contradictions and confronts its exigencies in a purposeful quest to master his situation. The pursuit of material success thus becomes for him a means of sublimation, and his amorality defines the modalities of an existential posture toward a hostile universe upon which he seeks to impose his individual will. The essence of his adventure is thus a desperate effort toward self-realization: by seeking to give effect to an autonomous intention, he gives direction and meaning to his own existence.

The significance that we are led to attach to Wangrin's adventure is thus in certain respects the same as that of Kane's Samba Diallo; he too is a prototype of the alienated African in the colonial situation, in need of a spiritual compass to chart his course in the world. It is true that Wangrin's intelligence is not applied to lofty reflections upon the nature of his alienation nor is his disposition toward a stoic withdrawal from the turbulence of his world. He is not, however, unreflecting nor is he without a spiritual conception of the universe, if we are to take his profound animism overlaid by a superficial adherence to Islam as an expression of spirituality. His disposition is rather toward action, which in the circumstances is the only means available to him to surmount his alienation in the particular form in which it manifests itself. In his own obscure way, he too seeks a fixed point of awareness around which to organize a consciousness of himself that is whole.

But if that much we can understand of the man, the excess of his project and his inordinate pursuit of it caution us against an endorsement of his pact with destiny. The murky details of this pact and our own moral instincts awaken in us a premonition of disaster long before it takes place. This is of course the normal pattern of tragedy, which not only takes an unusual turn here but assumes a special and intense character. Wangrin's fall takes place as much in the social sphere of the action contained by the narrative of his life as it is ordained in the realm of the supernatural, which casts a constant shadow over his life. His enigmatic career is thus inscribed within the enfolding enigma of the natural order itself. This is registered by the fact that the motif of his characterization is that of the trickster figure in the African folktale tradition enlarged here to the dimension of an archetype. And it is as such that he passes into the domain of tragedy. His ambiguity persists even in the manner of his characterization, for he is a comic figure who progressively takes on the attributes of a tragic hero. Wangrin is never as great in his days of glory as he becomes in adversity. Thus, the final note on which Hampaté Bâ rests his narrative is not that of just retribution meted out for a metaphysical indiscretion of the Faustian type but of a tragic irony: Wangrin's display of a rugged resignation to fate, which mocks his worldly project, and his ultimate triumph of spirit.

It is a remarkable tale that Hampate Ba offers us in *The Fortunes of Wangrin*, and no less remarkable is the manner of its telling. As I have already observed, the work involves a mediation between the Western conventions of written literature and those of the oral tradition in Africa, between two idioms of the narrative, which reciprocate their effects to reinforce its meaning. To appreciate the peculiar originality of Hampaté Bâ's approach, we need to examine the way in which this mediation operates in the formal organization of the work. The basis of this organization is the free interplay of the three modes of narrative that Hampaté Bâ employs: historical discourse, realistic fiction, and fable. Although each mode moves at a distinctive level in the narrative progression, they run into each other in such a way as to produce in the whole a special tonality of imaginative expression. It should furthermore be observed that each mode encompasses an area of Hampaté Bâ's interests as a scholar and writer, so that the work represents in its texture a summation of his productive and creative career. The atmosphere of *The Fortunes of Wangrin* recaptures to a certain extent that of his earlier biography of the Islamic mystic Tierno Bokar (Bâ, 1980); its factual quality derives from his experience of the French colonial administration and of scientific work as a historian; while the sociological framework is his own background, an environment with which he is not only familiar but which he has explored in the course of ethnological investigations. Above all, the literary foundation of the work lies in his assimilation of the forms of the oral tradition of his region to which he has devoted a lifetime of study and with which he has a double relation—as their interpreter to the world, collecting, translating, and presenting them, and as a poet in his own right, who has assumed their heritage. All of these aspects of Hampaté Bâ's interests are able to contribute to this work so effectively because they are held together by a powerful creative impulse that establishes its own laws in such a way as to impose on the heterogeneous character of the work a general order of form and significance.

This heterogeneous character is what first strikes us as we approach the work. The matter-of-fact air of the foreword, in which Hampaté Bâ recounts the circumstances in which the book came to be written and provides a general portrait of its subject, does not quite prepare us for the flourishes of the overture that immediately follows; our sense of fact in the one is at once undermined as we pass on to the other. It is this principle of narration that governs the development of the details of

Wangrin's life in the rest of the book. As we have seen, these details are situated in a concrete framework of time and place and give to the work a solid documentary foundation and character, to such an extent that we are prepared to accept them as fact. In formal terms, they lie at the biographical surface of the work, which is made up of what appears to be a random collection of events. The episodic character of the book at this level relates simply to the vicissitudes of a life in its uncertain course toward its term. The events that comprise this life have an interest only insofar as they can be seen to form a pattern, to have a unity not only in their reference to an exceptional personality but also in their progression toward the making of a destiny.

It is from this perspective that a biography approaches literary significance, and many works exist that have crossed the border between fact and fiction in the narration of a life. One thinks in particular of the fictionalized biographies of Robert Graves, and African literature itself offers the example of Camara Laye's account of his own childhood in *L'enfant noir* (*The African Child*), complemented by those parts that relate to his adult life in *Dramouss* (*A Dream of Africa*). It may be remarked in passing that the parallel between Laye and Hampaté Bâ is made more pertinent by the fact that the latter has given considerable development to the precedent established by the former.

It is fair to observe, however, that despite these particulars it is the fictional level of *The Fortunes of Wangrin* that predominates, established as it is both by the structure of the work and by the deployment of expressive means through which this structure is elaborated. Indeed, the biographical and documentary references of the work can be considered a literary device, foregrounding its fictional stance and serving to establish the major key of its narrative mode: that of the realistic novel. Again, we have a precedent for this in African literature, in the case of Ferdinand Oyono's *Une vie de boy* (*Houseboy*), which also purports to be the story of an African life in the colonial situation and progresses toward a tragic conclusion. There is a similar logic of development, which marks Hampaté Bâ's work as fiction in the technical sense of the term. The events it narrates, the actions it presents, the motivations it probes all organize themselves into a plot structure as definite as that of any conventional novel. The episodes from Wangrin's life at this level lose their random character and enter into a formal scheme of functions within a thematic development. This implies that analysis of the work from the formal point of view would need to start by reversing the documentary perspective in order to see the way in which Wangrin himself functions as a character in a novel whose picaresque nature at once becomes evident. He is indeed the classic *homo viator,* whose experience extends in space and whose adventures become facets of a quest motif. His birth and early life, his pact with his tutelary deity, his struggles and trials, his rise and final degradation can thus be defined as focal elements in the progression of a single theme that may be qualified in any number of ways but whose imaginative and symbolic import is not in doubt.

It should be observed that as the narrative develops, there is a constant crossing of the documentary and the fictional perspectives, so that Wangrin often reemerges in his status as a real life reference for the story; he is both real and imagined, with a simultaneous existence within the text and outside it. This interaction between fact and fiction is reinforced by the notes, which serve as detailed ethnological commentary to the text in its documentary aspects and specify at the same time its referential code for its intelligibility as a work of fiction. Unlike Achebe, who works this code into his novels, Hampaté Bâ makes it an explicit adjunct to his text.

The most important marker of the fictional status of the work remains of course the language. Even at its most factual, denotative, and referential, the language constantly points to a significance beyond the historical. The self-consciousness of the language is evident in the overture with its dramatic statement, like an extended opening chord, of the enigma of Wangrin. But even as we pass on to the story of Wangrin's life in the first chapter, the descriptive style conforms to a convention that we recognize as that of the nineteenth-century Western novel. We are made aware at once of the character of the language as a form of *écriture,* to use the term proposed by Barthes, that is, as the idiom of a certain kind of institutionalized fictional writing. It is here especially that Hampaté Bâ's departures from the Western conventions are most telling. The proverbs, songs, and praise poems with which the text is interspersed serve not merely as verbal equivalents of the cultural context of the narrative but also—and essentially—as devices whose purpose is to add luster to the drab tone of its realistic development. They thus fulfill a function that is properly poetic. We may add that a characteristic aspect of this function in the present context is the incidence of hyperbole, which forms an essential aspect of African imaginative expression as exemplified by the novels of Amos Tutuola. These devices derived from the oral tradition introduce a distinctive element into Hampaté Bâ's narrative, which has to do with its character as a fable. They evoke an atmosphere out of keeping with the standard notion of a novel and hint at the symbolic connotation of the work, which the intervention of the supernatural in the narrative serves to intensify.

In a penetrating structuralist analysis devoted solely to the overture, Nouréini Tidjani-Serpos has demonstrated how it provides a paradigm for the work's narrative structure as a whole (Tidjani-Serpos, 1984). His analysis reveals that the germ for the development of the work in all of its aspects is indeed contained in this short piece. But its dominant note is symbolic and mythical, and it runs through the narrative as a base over which its realistic tones are orchestrated. To a rationalist mind, perfectly attuned to the well-tempered key of the Western novel—exemplified even now by its nineteenth-century manifestations—this cohabitation of the realistic and the mythical in the same work administers something of a shock. It is easy enough to understand and to accept the supernatural in the folktale or the presence of myth in a poem. No doubt too, the fantastic tale exists and is practiced as a form of written narrative, but it announces itself as a genre, even as a subcategory, whose relation to the novel is a special one. It is a different matter with a work like Hampaté Bâ's whose realistic thrust is overwhelming but is finally undermined, as it were, by a mythical element moving under its ground.

An obvious explanation for its acceptance in this case is the fact that it is an African work, written by an African with deep roots in the traditional culture, who is giving expression to a mode of vision distinctive to his background. He therefore shares certain assumptions about reality with his largely African audience, in whom an active sense of the supernatural informs an apprehension of the world. This has a consequence for the way in which the work must be read and experienced, for the mode of what Jonathan Culler calls "naturalization" in literary competence has to conform with the mode of vision that determines the structure of the work itself, the general referential code of its constitution as imaginative expression.

The choice of the conventional form of the Western novel by Hampaté Bâ requires a further explanation. It is obvious that he is not working against the structures of the genre as a modernist writer would, conscious all the time of the conventions he is subverting. Neither is he the kind of naive artist that Tutuola has been made out to be. In this, as in other works, he is in full control of his medium, deploying its effects with a sureness of touch that the present translation happily captures for the

English-speaking reader. It seems to me rather that Hampaté Bâ has sought in this work to give a new dimension to an established form so that its meaning can have a proper resonance in the environment of its creation. For Hampaté Bâ, the novel is not so much the African tale writ large as an expressive medium offering new possibilities for presenting the total canvas of experience as apprehended in the African conception of the world. The common notion of life as a passage through a dark world is central to this conception, and the narrative of a singular experience must take on an elemental character to reflect this notion adequately. *The Fortunes of Wangrin* provides an illustration of this relationship between life and imagination, which prevails in the African consciousness.

To see Hampaté Bâ's work in this light is to recognize that it testifies to the ambiguity of Africa itself, caught between tradition and modernity, a continent in which, in the midst of transformations brought about by the technological revolution, minds are still haunted by the symbols of a culture intensely engaged with the mysteries of life and of the universe. Art in a modern form that explores these symbols to give them a new meaning has a continuing relevance not only for the African but for the rest of the world. In this sense, Hampaté Bâ's work can be said to transcend the situation of ambiguity that governed its inspiration and elaboration.

Narrative, History, and the African Imagination

Ahmadou Kourouma's
Monnè, outrages et défis

Fiction is history, human history, or it is nothing. But it is also more than that; it stands on firmer ground, being based on the reality of forms and the observation of social phenomena, whereas history is based on documents, and the reading of print and handwriting—on second-hand impression. Thus fiction is nearer truth. But let that pass. A historian may be an artist too, and a novelist is a historian, the preserver, the keeper, and the expounder, of human experience.

Joseph Conrad, "Henry James:
An Appreciation"

Let me begin with a reminiscence, one whose relevance to my subject will, I hope, soon become apparent. I remember that, when I was a little boy in primary school in the late 1940s in Lagos, we used a textbook entitled *Itan Eko* for our history class. This was a book written in the Yoruba language on the history of Lagos, which is today capital of the independent African nation of Nigeria. Looking back over the years, in the light of my subsequent education and the conditioning factors of a later awareness, two things now strike me as peculiar not only about the book but also about the history class for which it served as textual support.

The first aspect of this peculiarity has to do with the content of the book itself, the nature of the history it presented. While it recounted in a reasonably clear chronology the facts relating to the history of Lagos—from its beginnings as a fishing village to its days as a colony of the Benin empire to its subsequent independence, which it lost in the nineteenth century, this time to become a crown colony within the British empire—facts that are indeed verifiable, the whole mode of its narration was firmly situated within what we would call a mythic framework. The early rulers of Lagos emerged from this narrative as proper figures of legend, endowed with supernatural powers on which they relied constantly for their dealings with both their subjects and their adversaries; they performed such feats as turning into boa constrictors in certain situations of tension (notably in battle) and recovering their human form when such situations had been resolved. Moreover, they invariably lived to a very advanced age; a detail I can still recall concerns one of these rulers who was so old that he had to be carried daily into the sun to be revived (a trope, incidentally, that is used to poignant effect in Wilfrid Owen's well-known poem "Futility"). This easy conjunction of fact and fable ran through the entire book, which appears in this light as quite simply a transfer from the realm of oral tradition of elements of indigenous lore concerning the historical origins of Lagos into the mode of print, of literate discourse.

The second aspect concerns the form assumed by our history class itself, its strikingly different character as compared with other classes—say, geography or arithmetic—conducted in English. For despite the presence of the book and the institutional setting of a Western-type classroom, our history class, based as it was on the material contained in the book, was inevitably transformed into a narrative session in the oral tradition. Our history teacher was fully disposed to enter into the role of the traditional storyteller: at each lesson, he took on a presence before us as successive embodiments of the characters in the historical drama he was recounting; he enacted this drama with expressive gestures and in vivid images of his own creation and used the book merely as a prompt for what was in effect a narrative performance. Thus, the history class was in its essential character like the storytelling sessions with which each of us was familiar from our experience at home, as a given of our cultural background. What is more, the continuity between the history class in school and the storytelling sessions at home was emphasized by the fact that, as pupils, we were an active audience for our teacher, who brought us into direct participation in his narrative by making us take up refrains or even whole sections of the various songs with which the narrative was regularly punctuated, a device that, as in the folktale sessions, functioned as an integral element of its construction.

This distinctive character of my early introduction to the study of history provides me with two lines of reflection on the association between narrative and the African imagination: the centrality of the oral tradition as a continuing reference for African imaginative discourse and the significance of this reference in the elaboration of expressive forms by which the intimate relation between narrative and history is established.

As Louis Mink and Hayden White, among others, have reminded us, all history begins as story; the narrative element is the point of departure for the interpretive endeavor involved in the discipline of history. If we take once again the example of Yoruba historiography as it has evolved in this century, we are struck by what might be considered a progression from the kind of historical narrative I began with at school to histories of a more "textual" character, written in English, which aspired to a more "scientific" conception of historical narrative.[1] Yet, both types are expressions, though sharply differentiated in the modes of their phenomenal realizations, of the same fundamental impulse: to recollect the past as a function of one's existence in the present. In other words, they represent narrative projections of a fundamental historical consciousness. The difference is that in the latter kind of historical writing, the "logical" element has come to predominate over the poetic and the rhetorical; where one remains bound to a celebratory mode of discourse, the other tends toward the analytical, a distinction analogous to that between diegesis and exegesis.

A further clarification I think it important to make, one that is perhaps elementary but fundamental to my argument, concerns the distinction between the two senses of the word *history*. The first sense denotes a configuration of events in themselves, as it were—the *res gestae*—as lived and experienced in the remote or recent past; these constitute what may be considered the real, concrete facts of historical experience in its full immediacy. The second sense relates to the story of these events, the facts connected with them, and their recollection in narrative form.[2] In this latter sense, a certain reality of the past is mediated by consciousness in the effort to grasp its significance. The effort of recollection serves to order the experience of the past in the mind and may well lead to the discernment of a pattern in the events upon which the mind's activity is engaged. This produces the effect of an unfolding through time of an intelligible process; it becomes integrated, in other words, into a philosophy of history. The point here is that all history, as narrative, inhabits the space between apprehension and comprehension.

What emerges from this restatement of fundamentals is the fact that the imagination plays a crucial role in any narrative recollection of the past, if only because that past is no longer part of the immediate experience of the traditional storyteller or the modern historian; for both of them, the task or vocation consists precisely of a discursive or textual reconstitution of the completed past. The process of reconstitution, as Hayden White has stressed, not only obeys a principle of selection and rearrangement of the material to be presented in narrative form, it also involves the calling into play of distinct rhetorical strategies. The formal properties of historical narration establish a real equivalence, therefore, between history, which aspires to a full correspondence with reality, and fiction, which, as pure act of imagination, has no such pretension. The maximal distance between them presupposed by this remark is purely theoretical; both are in fact governed by the same protocols of narrative art.[3] Furthermore, the narrative strategies deployed within both have this in common: they serve to organize consciousness and thus to fulfill a "synthetic function," not only at the level of constituents of form operating within the aesthetic bounds of narrative itself—as James Phelan, to whom I am beholden for this term, has observed (Phelan, 1989, 132–46)—but also, and more fundamentally, they establish a significant relation to experience in the world beyond the text. Since there has been some contention on the question of the relationship between the text and the world it represents (the *hors texte*), let me quote Roland Barthes on this point: "Narration can indeed receive its meaning only from the world which makes use of it: beyond the narrational level begins the external world, that is to say other systems (social, economic, ideological) which no longer include narratives only but elements of another substance (historical facts, determinations, behaviors, etc.)" (Barthes, 1975, 264–65).

In this extract, Barthes situates history, in the primary sense of real events that constitute the realm of the *hors texte*, in a continuous relationship to narrative precisely in order to point up the fact that the impulse to narration derives from what one can only call an existential dimension of experience and that we respond to narratives from a grounded interest in the conditions of life. From this point of view, history, in the secondary sense of story, as much as fiction, can be considered a necessary function of the imagination in its organizing relation to the actualities of existence.

It is this formal equivalence between history and fiction, determined by the intrinsic properties of the narrative genre, which accounts for the incessant traffic that takes place between them, highlighted in the particular case of the historical novel, of which Tolstoy's *War and Peace* provides the supreme instance. This factor, which conditions the possible assimilation of history and fiction to a single mode of discourse, also points to to a certain principle of reciprocity between them, a kind of reversibility in their nature and status. It is this principle that is so well demonstrated in the oral tradition of Africa and of other preliterate and preindustrial societies, in which the boundary between history and fiction is, for all intents and purposes, nonexistent or, indeed, inconceivable, a boundary that, when all is said and done, is ultimately a view of the analyzing, positivist mind intent on ascribing truth value to one and withholding it from the other. What these remarks amount to is this: the purpose of all forms of narrative, whether fictional by design or factual in intent, is moral and ultimately metaphysical—the reformulation of experience in such a way as to endow it with a large significance.

I want to suggest that something of the same principle of reciprocity that obtains between history and fiction operates not only in African oral tradition but also in modern African literature; it has a significance for contemporary African life and expression on a much broader front than is suggested by the thematic association of this literature with the colonial experience. The postulate here is that of a continuity of form and function between the oral tradition and modern African imaginative expression, a continuity that rests primarily on the African writer's conception of literature as testimony.[4]

It has become a commonplace of critical discourse bearing upon the status and "conditions of possibility" of modern African literature to assert that the novel, considered as a literary genre conditioned by the modality of writing and associated with the Western concept of individualism, is foreign to Africa. We need to bear in mind, however, that the art of the narrative, elaborated within the framework of orality, has always been and remains an essential component of cultural production on the continent.[5] While the minor forms of oral expression represented by folktales and moral fables provided a comprehensive normative reference for the moral life in precolonial African societies, the more extended forms, such as the praise poems, epics, and myths, functioned as the principal channels of historical awareness, as the imaginative commemoration of a common past serving to celebrate the collective compact in the present. The narrative forms in particular, woven as they often are around the figure of a cultural hero, partake necessarily of the nature of myth. The historical element in these narratives is thus endowed with a powerful symbolic charge; history is felt to be part of a primordial order of experience. Mircea Eliade's elucidation of the conception of time and its function in myth is apposite here: time presents itself in these oral narratives as a basic category of consciousness, as an invariant of the natural process and, indeed, of being. It is thus invested with a sacred character that substantially informs every new undertaking and refers it back to an original model *in illo tempore* (Eliade, 1954; also McNeil, 1992, 3–81). It becomes possible in this perspective to understand the way in which the major forms of the African oral tradition were also employed to project structures of the collective mind, which served as explicative narratives of the world. In this respect, they present themselves as "grand narratives," in the sense that Jean-François Lyotard has given to the term (Lyotard, 1979, 35–43). They correspond to his conception of narratives as expressive formulations of systems of knowledge (what he calls *le savoir narratif*) when he refers to them in order to insist upon their supersession by and in postmodern society, a point to which I shall return.

That the rhetorical and poetic properties of myth constitute the essence of myth in what Georges Balandier has called "societies of tradition" (*les sociétés de tradition*) has come increasingly to be recognized by the discipline of anthropology.[6] We cannot, however, ignore the fact that these narratives fulfilled as well a comprehensive ideological function; they often served quite simply as legitimations of systems of power and domination within traditional societies with a manifest hegemonic significance. The prominence that the question of the social uses of discourse has acquired in contemporary Western theory obliges us to take account of the problematic nature of narrative in the light of its ideological function, even outside the context of Western debates. It is possible, however, to take a more comprehensive view of the matter and to recognize that these narratives, which form part of the total semiotic universe of the culture, offered points of orientation and provided a global system of reference, which enabled members of these societies to relate in a lively way to one another, *even in the mode of contradiction*, on the basis of a common set of assumptions about the world. This is especially true of precolonial Africa in which narrative forms of various registers were integrated into the fabric of social life at every point and level of its articulation; the oral mode of performance in any of these forms facilitated an immediacy of response that went beyond the purely aesthetic to embrace the symbolic and cognitive spheres of awareness. Orality involved a direct "somatic" representation of and participation in narrative; stories were obviously not *read* but experienced in a total manner, whether we are dealing with the simple folktale or the more elaborate forms of myth.

Narrative was thus an institutional factor of social life in traditional Africa, as elsewhere; cultural production was bound up intimately with social processes. It can therefore be said that, as in all preindustrial societies and cultures, a fundamental connection was established through narrative art between imaginative form and the dynamics of social life underlying the collective consciousness.[7] If, then, the ideological cannot altogether be dissociated from the cognitive, ethical, and symbolic functions that various forms of narrative assumed in traditional society, it remains true that it is through their connectedness to the superstructural sphere that collective life, in its most vivid aspect, was animated in those societies. When we consider, then, that narrative provided not merely the formal basis but the essence of myth and went into its construction as a comprehensive system of the world, we are led to modify the celebrated formula by Claude Lévi-Strauss and to declare that myths in those societies were fictions not so much to think with as to live by.[8]

Thus, while it would be disingenuous to subscribe to the notion of unanimity in precolonial or traditional societies, especially in Africa—for we know that powerful internal tensions frequently shook them—the impression of unity and the image of coherence that they conveyed were perhaps not altogether factitious. The important point, however, is not whether this impression corresponds to reality, but the compelling significance that the image of traditional life and culture has retrospectively assumed for modern African experience, the way in which its global configuration in African minds has come to serve as a reference for an antecedent order of life and to represent for the modern African writer an original paradigm of being and consciousness.

It is in this light that we must appraise what has been for so long the fundamental theme of modern African literature in the European languages: the cleavage of consciousness provoked by the encounter with Europe. In this literature, the existential predicament presented by this interaction, in all its moral and affective import, is directly associated with history; the problematic present is experienced as the unresolved sequel of a devastating history. It is not only a secure sense of being-in-history that is no longer available to the African but also a proper sense of belonging in the world; both have, therefore, to be constructed, striven for, in other words, *imagined*. Narrative, in the form of the novel, has afforded a privileged mode for this process of reconstruction.

In order to illustrate this phenomenon in our letters, I would like to focus here on one of the most significant African works to be published in recent times, Ahmadou Kourouma's second novel, *Monnè, outrages et défis*.[9] Although not exactly a historical novel in the conventional sense, the fact that the work draws directly upon the actual facts of the history of French colonialism in West Africa for its theme and for its system of allusions makes it particularly interesting for considering the function of narrative in its projection of the historical consciousness in modern African literature.

Kourouma's novel takes us from the moment of French conquest in the late nineteenth century (the defeat of Samory by the army of Faidherbe) through the period of consolidation of French rule, the turmoil of the two wars, right up to the political developments in the former Afrique Occidentale Française (AOF) on the eve of independence in the late 1950s. These facts provide the historical points of reference for Kourouma's narrative, which details the African experience as henceforth dependent on an external will and purpose, which emanates from the colonial *métropole*; the new history of the region is not so much obliterated as subsumed within the history of France, with all its vagaries and in all its vicissitudes. Kourouma's novel thus offers an extended chronicle of the colonial imposition in this region in what may be considered its full historical span.

It is in the nature of the events with which it deals that Kourouma's novel develops primarily as a narrative of dispossession, traced in the reversals suffered by his fictional kingdom of Soba. The kingdom is evoked by the narrator as a society in full disarray, a process that is figured in the steady decline of its ruler, Djigui—the focal character around whom the narrative revolves—from a state of primal vigor into physical and moral decrepitude. This process of degeneration becomes central to the narrative and symbolic scheme of Kourouma's novel, for it is a negative transformation of the African world that provides the keynote of its development. We get a sense of the drastic nature of this transformation from the changes rung in the novel upon the imagery with which it is pervaded. Djigui is presented in the early part of the novel as the traditional figure of legend:

> Nous fûmes fiers de le voir se former, s'épanouir, s'endurcir; il grandit et se répandit. Tout le Mandingue parla de lui, et à force de le dire, il devint ineffable et multiple; il acquit la force de réaliser tant de choses prodigieuses.

> [We were proud to see him develop, flourish, harden; he grew and spread out. All the Malinke nation talked about him, and the sheer force of words made him ineffable, multifarious; he acquired the power to achieve so many prodigious feats.] (17; all translations are mine)

The underlying metaphor in this extract is, of course, that of the tree, emblematic of the rootedness and solidity of Djigui and the society, which is both his realm of authority and the locus of his being. Moreover, the actualizing force of language is emphasized in this passage (*à force de le dire*), as constitutive of the essence of the king's mythical stature. But just as language locates him in this initial realm of political and mythical power, so his objective devaluation after the conquest of Soba by the French comes to be denoted as well in language, summed up in a proverb that alludes to the fact that, when the crocodile has been domesticated, it is no more threatening than an ordinary lizard (*un lézarde vulgaire*). The dark irony that informs Kourouma's narrative throughout appears in its full dramatic import when the same mythic register in which Djigui's initial attributes are characterized is recalled in this apocalyptic evocation of the season of drought that later devastates his kingdom:

> Les nuits de lune se remplissaient de brouillards fauves et crus qui emmuraient. Au premier chant du coq, la terre crépitait sous nos pieds, le soleil bondissait du levant comme une sauterelle pour réaliser midi qui, de sa plénitude, dominait; le firmament s'élevait, s'éloignait, bleuissait et s'étrangeait même pour les hirondelles. Les jours étaient sans vent, sans voix, sauf, de lointain en lointain, ces éphémères et riens de tourbillons de poussières coniques qui tentaient de caresser la terre avant de

se fondre dans les mirages. Nous en avons vu d'incroyalbes: des arbres
pris de convulsions pousser des soupirs et sécher.

[The moonlit nights filled with wild and raw mists. At the first cockcrow,
the earth crackled under our feet, the sun bounded from the east like a
grasshopper to attain the height of midday which reigned over all in its
full intensity; the firmament rose bluish above us, withdrew itself, becoming a stranger even to the swallows. The days were windless, without
a sound, save for the slight, timid gusts of conical shaped sandstorms
which, as they moved farther and farther into the distance, tried to caress
the earth before losing themselves in mirages. We witnessed unbelievable
sights: trees taken with convulsions, giving out sighs, and withering.]
(202)

Beyond Kourouma's creative manipulation of French here, we note the
connection between the desolate aspect of the kingdom of Soba, as a
result of its violent invasion by the colonizer, and the disorientation of
the native population. This aspect of the impact of conquest is brought
into focus as essentially an effect of language. Consider the narrator's
presentation of the original model of the African universe as structured
by the relation between the customary words and the grasp of reality
they enable:

Certes, ce n'était pas le bonheur pour tout le monde, mais cela semblait
transparent pour chacun, donc logique; chacun croyait compredre, avait
attribuer un mot à chaque chose, donc croyait posséder le monde, le
maîtriser.

[It was most certainly not the reign of happiness for everybody. But
everything seemed clear to everyone, therefore logical; all thought themselves to understand, had given a word to every thing, and thus believed
themselves to grasp the world, to master it.] (20)

We move from this state of achieved coherence established through
an ordering of language to one of an unsettling contingency in which
the process of apprehension of the world has been rendered highly problematic. The trauma provoked by the dislocation of the system of symbolic references that sustained and gave meaning to collective life is
summed up in this reflection by the king's principal griot, Djeliba:

Apprendre les nouvelles verités. L'infini qui est au ciel a changé de pa-
roles; le Mandingue ne sera plus la terre des preux. Je suis un griot, donc

homme de parole. Chaque fois que les mots changent de sens et les choses de symboles, je retourne à la terre qui m'a vu naître pour tout recommencer: réapprendre l'histoire et les nouveaux noms des hommes, des animaux et des choses.

[To learn new truths. The Infinite in heaven has changed words. The land of the Malinke will no longer be the abode of heroes. I am a griot, hence a man of words. Each time words change meanings and things their symbols, I return to the land which gave me birth to begin anew, to learn history afresh and the new names of men, of animals and of things.] (41)

This statement by Djeliba registers not merely the profound demoralization of the people but also, and more fundamentally, a veritable epistemological crisis, which strikes at the foundations of their mental universe. In a real sense, the impact of the colonial imposition manifests itself in its furthest reaches as a pathology of language, and to overcome it requires an effort of reconfiguration of the world, an effort to establish a new congruence between the structure of words and the universe of experience. It initiates, in other words, a new process of symbolic reappropriation of the world, through language. It is the difficulty of being, entailed by the working out of this process, that constitutes the essential theme of Kourouma's novel. *Monnè* affords from this point of view a large and penetrating insight into the rigorous nature of the colonial imposition; apart from the exactions it involves, conquest implies a radical reordering of life and values, and with that a new dispensation to which Africans have had painfully to negotiate a mode of accommodation in both body and mind.

The significance of language as a factor in the colonial relationship is highlighted in Kourouma's work not only as theme but also as an internal dimension of the novel at the level of both expression and structure. In his earlier novel, *Les soleils des indépéndances,* Kourouma had undertaken a wholesale recasting of French on the lines of his native Malinke, as a means of providing his readers with an expressive mode of entry into the universe of his fiction. His procedure in the new novel is less radical, but it is still a modified form of French that he employs, one that reflects the ambiguous character of the transactions between the colonizers' linguistic code and the indigenous forms of signifying the world. Kourouma's idiom, as it is deployed in his second novel, is singularly adapted to the narrative of the transformations that take place both in the objective world of his characters and in their subjective dispositions. It has, besides, a determining effect on his conception of narrative structure, for although the novel adheres to the chronological progression of events as dictated by its reference to the facts of history, the narrative unfolds less as a linear plotting of these events than as a cluster of marking episodes, each of which is related, as in the folktale tradition, to a proverb or aphorism, which serves as its motif and whose meaning it illustrates. The progression formed by these proverbs and aphorisms, which are employed textually as headings for the novel's chapters, lays out the ground plan of its narrative development.

The consonance between theme and structure in Kourouma's novel, in which the forms of orality serve as the vehicle of historical consciousness, is brought out by the prominence accorded in it to the figure of the *griot* as a social and cultural agent. At the thematic level, we witness the transformation of the traditional role of this figure as mediator between sectors of the indigenous community into that of interpreter between the African king and the French invader. Much of the novel is made up of the reflections of the two principal griots, who occupy a decisive position in the discursive space of the novel. Indeed, the fate of the kingdom of Soba, at one crucial moment of its confrontation with the French forces, is made to hinge on the intervention of a griot, who deliberately mistranslates the discourteous words addressed by Djigui to a French officer in order to save the king from himself, and, thus, to preserve the kingdom from total destruction.

But it is primarily at the structural level that Kourouma's novel illustrates the preeminence of the *griot* as the organic bearer of the collective memory. The collective first person plural dominates the narrative, representing the voice of the *griot* whose function it is to bear witness to the movement of history. The novel thus provides a verification of the identity between the function of the *griot* in tradition and the African writer in the modern context; it presents itself as a reformulation in textual terms of this function, which Kourouma himself seems to have assumed in the writing of his novel. Set against the collective voice, however, is that of the omniscient narrator, who distances himself somewhat from the events he is narrating, and the occasional eruption into the narrative stream of the first person singular, which is the voice of the king himself in his moments of self-awareness. The interactions among these voices, in a constant interplay between the diegetic and the homodiegetic, makes for the shifting perspectives and modalities of Kourouma's narrative, a process that sets up a peculiar tension in its mode of representation.

It is instructive in this respect to note the way that the framing device of the novel emerges as a function of this interaction of narrative voices. At the end of the novel, in what appears to be an epilogue, the collective voice informs us that the chronicle just concluded looks forward to a new and strenuous chapter in history:

> La Nigritie et la vie continuèrent après ce monde, ces hommes. Nous attendaient le long de notre dur chemin: les indépendances politiques, le parti unique, l'homme charismatique, le père de la nation, les *pronunciamentos* dérisoires, la révolution; puis les autres mythes.

> [Nigritia, life, continued after this world, these men. Awaited us, along our hard road: political independence, the single party, the charismatic leader, the Father of the Nation, the laughable *pronunciamentos*, The Revolution, and all the other myths besides.] (287)

The testamental import of Kourouma's novel rests on this final note of desolation. But it is prefigured in the prologue, which undertakes to explicate the meaning of the novel's title in terms both of the affront to consciousness that the narrative is about to document and of the disparities in race, religion, and world view (as codified in language) between the parties involved in the colonial relationship within which this affront is proffered and on which it is predicated.:

> Un jour, le Centennaire demanda au blanc comment s'entendait en français le mot *monnè* . . . Parceque leur langue ne possédait pas le mot, le Centennaire en conclut que les Français ne connaissaient pas les *monnew*. Et l'existence d'un peuple, nazaréen de surcroît, qui n'avait pas vécu et ne connaissait pas tous les outrages, défis et mépris dont lui et son peuple pâtissaient tant, resta pour lui, toute la vie, un émerveillement, les sources et les motifs de graves méditations.

> [One day, the Patriarch asked the white man how the word *monnew* was known in French. . . . Because their language had no word for it, the Patriarch concluded that the French had no experience of *monnew*. And the existence of a people, who were moreover Christians, and had never lived through, never known all the affronts, exasperations and acts of contempt from which he and his people suffered so much, remained for him, all his life, a source and reason for deep meditations.] (9)

We might observe, that, within the novel itself, the concept of *monnew* is elucidated more succinctly in the expression *les saisons d'amertume* (seasons of bitterness), which recurs several times as a kind of leitmotif through which the theme is constantly restated throughout its narrative development. The framing device brings home to us the fact that the entire movement of the novel serves to chart the long course of the agony and frustration of a whole race caught in the grind of history. It is hardly an extrapolation from the text to ascribe the prologue directly to its author as a statement of his intention, to read it as defining in advance the purpose of the narrative Kourouma offers of the African experience. For *Monnè* is nothing less than an epic of African adversity, more focused in its intensity than Ouologuem's melodramatic *Le devoir de violence*, which covers much the same historical ground. In its character as testimony, Kourouma's *Monnè* offers us, in the exemplary form of narrative, a grave meditation upon the peculiar ironies of history.

An introspective quality thus informs Kourouma's novel, a quality that turns largely on the association of the historical vision it embodies with the forms of an indigenous orality, felt as a necessary dimension of the mode of expression of this vision. The novel illustrates the way in which there is often a double articulation of narrative in the historical and cultural context of contemporary Africa: the literate form of the novel is both the medium of an engagement with history and a creative transformation of orality within writing in its formal realization. The novel thus exemplifies a significant relationship between narrative art and the contingencies of African experience and its imaginative transposition in narrative form. It makes clear the fact that the association between theme and narrative mode represents an effort to create a new harmony of consciousness at the level of form, an effort motivated by the circumstances and the conditions of the emergence of modern African discourse.

The late Raymond Williams wrote: "The relation between 'writing' and 'reality' is a form of the relation between men and their history" (Williams, 1971, 30). If we substitute the word *narrative* for *writing* in this statement, we come, I think, to a better sense of its ineluctable implication in those large human transactions that constitute the living stuff of history, what makes for its animating principle. This view, it seems to me, is especially relevant to Africa, where a vivid sense of history is inherent in the ongoing and, one might say, quotidian process of transformation in our lives. For us, history is much more—or, perhaps, much less—than a matter of dramatic events and striking personalities; it manifests itself in the structural forms of collective existence, in the ruptures and strains that traverse almost on a continuous basis the fabric of social existence everywhere on the continent. Thus, in Africa today history takes on the character of a daily drama, of fiction, and fiction, in a quite natural reciprocity, takes on the character of history, so that in our modern literature we witness an immediate correlation of life and textuality. History is not simply a general reference or even a major theme of modern African expression; it represents the substance upon which the African imagination is called upon to work.

The colonial experience can be invoked as an explanation for this intense engagement of the African imagination with history, an explanation that draws attention to the polemical significance of all forms of modern African expression, whether these are imaginative or overtly ideological. Imaginative literature in particular has functioned side by side with historical writing in the African assertion of an indigenous historicity, in the challenge to Western discourse, which has sought to deny us true historical existence before our encounter with Europe. In other words, narrative has formed an essential part of the counterdiscourse of decolonization.

But it seems to me more meaningful to envisage modern African expression within a more comprehensive perspective, for these works do not merely answer to a limited ideological interest but fulfill a more profound historical need: the construction of a justifying narrative as a means of underwriting the modes of contemporary awareness in Africa. This point leads me to think that Lyotard is perhaps too hasty in proclaiming the end of narrative in providing operative systems of apprehension in the contemporary world. It is debatable whether his argument is fully applicable to the Western societies he obviously has in mind; to label these societies "postmodern" (or even "postindustrial") is to forget that they are themselves still confronted by the dilemma of modernity in its myriad manifestations. Be that as it may, the least that can be said, as regards Africa, is that the narrative genre continues to offer, incontestably, a vital and significant resource for the processing of experience.

In this regard, it seems to me that Fredric Jameson, in his one excursion into the field of so-called Third World literature (as far as I am aware), was in fact correct in his remark about Sembene Ousmane's novel *Xala* in sensing the general allegorical dimension of this literature (Jameson, 1986, 65–88). But if we bear in mind Raymond Williams's statement on the relation between imaginative discourse and historical experience, we have to extend Jameson's intuition to all forms of narrative that, in varying historical and cultural contexts, seek a connection with life. The relevance to these contexts of the colonial paradigm becomes evident here; the violence of encounters between bodies and forces on the ground that this paradigm evokes offers a heightened image not only of the agonistic relations in society but also of the clash of discourses that are involved in these relations and that characterize them as what Bakhtin has called the logosphere. The distinction between history as immediate experience and history as the narration of that experience also assumes significance from this point of view; the recollection of the past is also a form of relation to history and involves a process of self-reflection on the part of social groups and historical collectivities.

In this perspective, narrative presents itself as *metahistory*, not in the conventional sense of a second order of historical discourse but in a more immediate sense as a mode of meditation at the level of imaginative discourse—that is, regulated by form—upon immediate experience. This metahistorical import of narrative seems to be implied in Aristotle's *Poetics* in which history is considered as secondary to tragedy (to which we can now add fiction, as implied by Conrad's statement that serves as the epigraph of this chapter). For Aristotle, history is concerned with events in their singularity, with each in its uniqueness, while tragedy/fiction provides a total vision of all the events that constitute historical experience—in other words, the essence of the human condition.

In Africa today, the best of our literature has a metahistorical significance in this sense, especially as this literature represents an anxious interrogation of history as a function of the pressures of the collective experience. It happens to be the case that it is principally in fiction that this interrogation is today most forcefully dramatized, a development that gives interest to the novel as a medium of imaginative discourse in Africa. In the modern narratives of Africa, history is constantly being refigured as *allegoresis,* so that we can speak not only of a continuity of function but also of the impulse from the traditional narrative forms to the modern African novel in the European languages. Narrative, engaged with history and textualized in literate discourse that consciously integrates the forms of orality, enters once again and perhaps most fully into its character as "metacode" for the formulation of those representations by which the collective consciousness is structured. "In the beginning was the word"—thus begins the Gospel of St. John, which goes on to add; "and the word was made flesh." In the mystery of the incarnation, which this passage from the Christian Bible celebrates, the faith in the operative power of the word is conjoined to a sense of divine purpose, to a *telos*. We might recall here that Eric Auerbach had much to say about the reference value of this founding myth of Christianity for forms of narrative in the European Middle Ages (Auerbach, 1953). In a similar way, myths of origin predicated on the creative potential of the word animate African narrative forms, both traditional and modern.

In the modern context, the tension between retrospection and anticipation as inscribed in the vicissitudes of African experience and as figured by the African imagination is rendered especially acute by the facts of our recent past and the circumstances of our contemporary existence. The modern African novel, situated thematically and formally between an unfulfilled past and a problematic present, represents a mode of exploration of this tension in an imaginative endeavor to chart a course toward the future. Narrative, as a signifying dimension of the African imagination, presents itself today as nothing less than the effort by the African writer to discern for the continent, beyond the harsh realities of African experience in modern times, a principle of transcendence in history.

7

The Crisis of Cultural Memory in Chinua Achebe's *Things Fall Apart*

If there is any single work that can be considered central to the evolving canon of modern African literature, it is, without question, Chinua Achebe's *Things Fall Apart*. The novel owes this distinction to the innovative significance it assumed as soon as it was published, a significance that was manifested in at least two respects. In the first place, the novel provided an image of an African society reconstituted as a living entity and in its historic circumstance, an image of a coherent social structure forming the institutional fabric of a universe of meanings and values. Because this image of Africa was quite unprecedented in literature, it also carried considerable ideological weight in the specific context of the novel's writing and reception. For it cannot be doubted that the comprehensive scope of Achebe's depiction of a particularized African community engaged in its own social processes, carried out entirely on its own terms, with all the internal tensions this entailed, challenged the simplified representation that the West offered of Africa as a formless area of life, "an area of darkness" devoid of human significance.[1] Thus, beyond what might be considered its ethnographic interest, which lent the work an immediate and ambiguous appeal—a point to which we shall return—Achebe's novel articulated a new vision of the African world and gave expression to a new sense of the African experience that was more penetrating than what had been available before its appearance.

The second factor making for the esteem in which Achebe's novel is held has to do with the quality of his manner of presentation, in which the cultural reference governs not merely the constitution of the novel's fictional universe but also the expressive means by which the collective existence, the human experience framed within this universe, is conveyed. The novel testifies to an aesthetic project that consists of fashioning a new language appropriate to its setting, which serves therefore to give life and substance to the narrative content and thus to enforce the novelist's initial gesture of cultural reclamation. As a consequence, the manner of presentation became integral to the narrative development to a degree that must be considered unusual in novelistic writing. As Emmanuel Obiechina remarked, "the integrative technique in which background and atmosphere are interlaced with the action of the narrative must be regarded as Achebe's greatest achievement" (Obiechina, 1975, 142). It is especially with regard to this close imbrication of language and theme that *Things Fall Apart* can be said to have defined a new mode of African imaginative expression, hence Kwame Appiah's description of the work as "the archetypal modern African novel in English" (Appiah, 1992, ix).[2]

The work has acquired the status of a classic, then, by reason of its character as a counterfiction of Africa in specific contradiction to the discourse of Western colonial domination and its creative deployment of the language of the *imperium*; it has on this account been celebrated as the prototype of what Barbara Harlow has called "resistance literature" (Harlow, 1987).[3] The ideological project involved in its writing comes fully to the fore in the ironic ending in which we see the colonial officer, after the suicide of the main character, Okonkwo, contemplating a monograph on the "pacification" of the Lower Niger. Okonkwo, we are told, will get the briefest of mentions in the monograph, but we know as readers that the novel to which this episode serves as conclusion has centered all along upon this character who, as the figure of the historical African, the work endeavors to reendow with a voice and a visage, which allows him to emerge in his full historicity, tragic though this turns out to be in the circumstances.

Despite the novel's contestation of the colonial enterprise, clearly formulated in the closing chapters and highlighted by its ironic ending, readers have always been struck by the veil of moral ambiguity with which Achebe surrounds his principal character and by the dissonances that this sets up in the narrative development. As Obiechina remarked in an oral presentation I had the privilege of attending, the novel is constituted by "a tangle of ironies." For it soon becomes apparent that Achebe's work is not by any means an unequivocal celebration of tribal culture; indeed, the specific human world depicted in this novel is far from representing a universe of pure perfection. We are presented rather with a corner of human endeavor that is marked by the web of contradictions within which individual and collective destinies have everywhere and at all times been enmeshed. A crucial factor, therefore, in any reading of Achebe's novel, given the particular circumstances of its composition, is its deeply reflective engagement with the particular order of life that provides a reference for its narrative scheme and development. In this respect, one cannot fail to discern a thematic undercurrent, which produces a disjunction in the novel between its overt ideological statement, its contradiction of the discourse of the colonial ideology, on one hand, and on the other, its dispassionate and even uncompromising focus on an African community in its moment of historical crisis.

I will examine here the nature of this disjunction not only as it emerges from the novel's thematic development but also as it is inscribed, quite literally, within the formal structures of the work, in the belief that it is by undertaking a closer examination of these two dimensions of the work and relating them to each other that we are enabled to fully discern its purpose. For the moral significance of the work seems to me to outweigh the ideological burden that has so often been laid upon it. I believe the implications of the novel extend much further than the anticolonial stance that, admittedly, provides its point of departure but which, as we shall see, eventually yields to issues of far greater import concerning the African becoming.

We begin this examination with an observation that situates Achebe's work in the general perspective of literary creation and cultural production in contemporary Africa. The most significant effect of modern African literature in the European languages is perhaps the sense it registers of the immediacy of history as a sphere of existence, as a felt dimension of being and consciousness. Achebe's work is exemplary in this regard, in the way he captures in his fiction the inner movement of transition on the continent from an antecedent order of life to a new and problematic collective existence, this new existence contemplated as the outcome of an implacable historical development. Beginning with *Things Fall Apart*, his entire production seeks to take a measure, in its full range and import for Africa, of what Molly Mahood has called, in her study of the same title, "the colonial encounter" (Mahood, 1977). Achebe's explicit concern with the cultural dislocations provoked by the harsh circumstances of this encounter and their far-reaching consequences in human terms suggests at first a limited point of view, which appears to emphasize the primacy of an original identity owed to cultural and ethnic affiliations.

However, we cannot but observe that, as a writer, Achebe is in fact situated at the point of intersection between two world orders, the precolonial African and the Western or, more specifically, Euro-Christian, which impinge upon his creative consciousness. It is important to recall this defining factor of the total cultural situation by which Achebe's inspiration is conditioned and to stress the directing influence of his Western education and the sensibility associated with this education upon his fictional reconstruction of the collective traumas enacted by his novels and the comprehensive process of self-reflection they imply. Thus, an attention to its various inflections indicates that the narrative voice adopted by Achebe in his first novel has to be imputed in large part to his status as a Westernized African, the product of Christian education. This is a voice that speaks often, perhaps even primarily, from the margins of the traditional culture, as is evident in this passage from early in the novel:

> The night was very quiet. It was always quiet except on moonlight nights. Darkness held a vague terror for these people, even the bravest among them. Children were warned not to whistle at night for fear of evil spirits . . . And so on this particular night as the crier's voice was gradually swallowed up in the distance, silence returned to the world, a vibrant silence made more intense by the universal trill of a million forest insects. (7)[4]

The passage suggests that the perspective from which Achebe looks at the traditional world is that of an external observer, a perspective that implies a cultural distance from the background of life—of thought and manners—that provides the concrete reference of his fiction. We encounter the same stance in another passage where the narrator observes of the community to which the work relates: "Fortunately among these people a man was judged according to his worth and not according to the worth of his father" (6). Of these and similar passages, Nigerian scholar David Ker has commented: "Umuofia is simultaneously 'they' and 'we' and this subtle combination of detachment and participation helps Achebe to manipulate point of view" (Ker, 1997, 136). This is a plausible reading, which brings the novel's content into functional relation with its narrative codes, except that the personal testimony Achebe provides of his own education in a Christian household indicates clearly that his identification with the indigenous heritage was a later and conscious development. In other words, Achebe can be said to have undertaken the writing of *Things Fall Apart* out of an awareness of a primary disconnection from the indigenous background that he seeks to recover and to explore in the novel.

The point can be made from another perspective by observing that, as a modern African novelist, Achebe is hardly in the same position as the traditional storyteller, creating his stories un–self-consciously out of a full sense of coincidence with the culture within which he practices his art and that provides objective support for his imaginative projections. Moreover, Achebe is obliged to employ a newly acquired tongue, one that is at a considerable structural and expressive remove from the speech modes, habits of thought, and cultural codes of the historical community whose experience he undertakes to record in his fiction. Contrary to the claim by Romanus Egudu that Achebe's art in the novel is continuous with an Igbo narrative tradition (Egudu, 1981), the whole imaginative effort manifested in *Things Fall Apart* was called into play and given direction by a willed movement back to what the novelist regards as the sources of the collective self, which he has had to reconstitute both as a function of the ideological objectives of his novel and also, and much more important, as an imperative of the narrative process itself, a point to which we shall return.

We might observe, then, that the impression of the writer's familiarity with his material and the quality of authentic life registered by his language are in fact effects of this reinvestment of the self on Achebe's part, thrown into relief by the consummate art of the novelist. It is well to bear in mind these factors, which are attendant upon the process of creation from which Achebe's novel proceeds, for they are not without important consequences for its narrative development and, ultimately, for its aesthetic and moral significance. These are not merely entailed by the ostensible content of the work, its "propositional" ground, to echo Gerald Graff (1980), but also are inherent in its formal organization and language. It is to the relation among these various aspects of the work that we now turn.

Commenting upon his own work nearly forty years after its appearance, Achebe declared, "The story of Okonkwo is almost inevitable; if I hadn't written about him, certainly someone else would have, because it really is the beginning of our story" (Achebe, 1991).[5] Achebe's observation concerning his fictional creation draws attention to the allegorical significance that Okonkwo has assumed for the African imagination; he is not merely a character in a novel but the representative figure of African historicity. A determining element of the novel's structure and development is thus the way in which his story is embedded within an elaborate reconstruction of forms of life in the traditional, precolonial culture, specifically, that of Achebe's own people, the Igbo of southeastern Nigeria. The tenor and warmth of Achebe's presentation of the traditional world, especially in the thirteen chapters that form the first part of the novel, with their elaborate representation of setting and involving in the process an insistence in positive terms upon the cultural context within which his fictional characters have their being, leaves us in no doubt that a polemical intent informs his reconstruction. The Igbo tribal world emerges here in all of its specificity, its daily routines and seasonal rituals attuned to the natural rhythms of its living environment. The language of daily intercourse that Achebe lends his characters endows with a special force the mobilization of minds and sensibilities within the society and animates with its poetic resonance its modes of social organization and cultural expression. The even cadence that marks the collective life in its normal course is summed up at one point in a simple but telling way with "In this way, the moons and the seasons passed" (39). The elaborate account of the New Yam Festival that opens chapter 5 (26) takes on added weight of meaning in the light of this declaration of a natural order of the communal existence. We are made to understand that the extraordinary coherence that the organic rooting of the tribe guarantees to the social order in its natural environment is an immediate function of an established system of values by which the collective life is regulated. What is more, Achebe's depiction of the prescribed pattern of social gestures and modes of comportment creates an overwhelming impression of a collective existence that unfolds in ceremonial terms, punctuated as it is by a train of activities that enhance the ordinary course of life and serve therefore as privileged moments in a more or less unending celebration of a social compact that is remarkably potent and is in any case fully functional on its own terms.

It is this intense quality of life that is conveyed symbolically by the drum, which functions so obviously as a leitmotif in the novel that it generates a singular connotative stream within the narrative. The omnipresence of the drum in Achebe's image of Igbo tribal life seems at times on the verge of betraying him into the kind of unmediated stereotyping of the African by Western writers to which he himself has vehemently objected. The intrusion into his own writing of the demeaning idiom of colonial discourse is recognizable: "Drums beat violently, and men leaped up and down in a frenzy" (86). But such a drop in narrative tone serves ultimately to enforce the larger vision he offers of the community he is presenting, for we soon come to grasp the true significance of the drum as manifesting a vitalism inherent in and interwoven with the community's organic mode of existence: "The drums were still beating, persistent and unchanging. Their sound was no longer a separate thing from the living village. It was like the pulse of its heart. It throbbed in the air, in the sunshine, and even in the trees, and filled the village with excitement" (31).

Achebe presents us, then, with a dynamic framework of social interactions and interpersonal relations, which lay the affective foundation for what, in the language of Durkheim, we might call a collective consciousness, one that is properly commensurate with a sphere of existence and an order of experience that, by the fact of their being rigorously circumscribed, conduce to its institutional strength. It is instructive in this respect to remark upon the narrow range of the physical setting reproduced in Achebe's novel. This is established in what seems a deliberate manner in the novel's opening sentence and is associated by implication with the destiny of the central character who makes his appearance at the outset of the narrative devoted to him: "Okonkwo was well known throughout the nine villages, and even beyond" (3). The vagueness with which the narrator indicates the outer limits of Okonkwo's fame reflects the tribe's limited awareness of its location in space, of its specific place in the world. This accords with the curious vagueness of its name, Umuofia, or "people of the forest," a name that also doubles as the novel's locale and designates a community firmly situated within the natural world. The reduced spatial dimension of the tribe's sphere of existence enables a narrative focus on a world whose intimacy appears at first sight as a source of strength, the operative factor of an intensity of social experience that underlies an achieved state of equilibrium.

It should be noted that the contraction of the tribe's apprehension of space is closely associated with its bounded experience of time. The same opening paragraph of the novel in which we are introduced to Okonkwo provides us with a passing view of the tribe's myth of origin. It is not without interest to observe that this myth, in its evocation of a wrestling contest between the eponymous founder of the town and "a spirit of the wild," parallels the Old Testament story of Jacob wrestling with the angel, an encounter that, we are told, leaves him forever lame. The parallel suggests the way Achebe's mind is working through elements of his double cultural experience toward a unified conception of human destiny.

The tribe's myth of origin sets the tone for its entire mode of self-apprehension and structure of knowledge, what Gikandi has called "the Igbo epistemology" (Gikandi, 1991, 31–38; see also Nwoga, 1981). The prominence assumed by rituals of life in the culture, the tribe's periodic enactments of the various facets of its collective imagination, and its constant recall of foundations all ensure that time is experienced not as a static category but lived continuously and intensely, in the mode of duration. This consciousness of time permeates the collective life, so that the world view involves a ceaseless procession of a principle of life in an interpenetration of time and space that is ensured by the eternal presence of the ancestors:

> The land of the living was not far removed from the domain of the ancestors. There was coming and going between them, especially when an old man died, because an old man was very close to the ancestors. A man's life from birth to death was a series of transition rites which brought him nearer and nearer to his ancestors. (86)

The culture of Umuofia as depicted by Achebe functions through the immanence of its foundational myth in the collective life and consciousness. The immediate and practical implications of this myth and the system of belief derived from it are experienced at every level of the collective existence, for the mythic time of the ancestors serves as the measure of social control, as demonstrated by the role of the *egwugwus*, incarnations of the ancestors, in the administration of justice, a role that endows the laws and customs of the land with a sacred sanction. At the same time, the dialogue in which elders such as Ezeudu, Ezenwa, and Obierika engage with their own culture throughout the novel points to the process by which the principles governing the world concept and value system of the tribe are constantly debated, reexamined, and in this way, retrospectively rationalized. Thus, as represented by Chinua Achebe and contrary to the discourse of colonial anthropology, Umuofia, the primordial Igbo village, emerges as a locus of reflective civility.[6]

Achebe's attentive recreation of the processes of everyday living in the tribal society that he depicts in *Things Fall Apart* has led to the work being labeled an "ethnographic novel." The term may be taken as appropriate but only in the limited sense in which it serves to indicate a conscious effort of demonstration, aimed at presenting a particular society and its culture to an audience unfamiliar with its ways of doing and feeling, its beliefs about the world, and its strategies of response to the imperatives of human existence. The novel endeavors in this sense to create what Hochbruck (1996) has called the illusion of "cultural proximity" for the non-Igbo reader, who is confronted by the otherness, so to speak, of the human world that its cultural references are intended to designate or, at the very least, evoke.

We need to attend carefully to Achebe's handling of the ethnographic element of his novel in order to distinguish the varying modes of its integration into the narrative, for while several instances of authorial intervention intended to enlighten the reader on matters of cultural interest seem merely to provide orchestration for the bare outline of the plot and thus to lend it the richness of detail, others are indispensable for a proper comprehension of the narrative development itself and thus form an integral element of the novel's thematic unfolding. This is notably the case with the banishment of Okonkwo after his accidental killing of a clansman. The narrator points us deliberately to an understanding of the cultural implications of this episode: "The only course open to Okonkwo was to flee from the clan. It was a crime against the earth goddess to kill a clansman, and a man who committed it must flee from the land" (88). Further along, describing the organized destruction of Okonkwo's compound by the villagers after his departure, the narrator provides this insight into the mores of the land: "They had no hatred in their hearts against Okonkwo. His greatest friend Obierika was among them. They were merely cleansing the land which Okonkwo had polluted with the blood of a clansman" (88).

This last quotation illustrates the function that the novel's ethnographic content has usually been held to perform, its project of revaluation consisting of a comprehensive readjustment of viewpoint on a culture that had previously served as an object of Western deprecation.

Achebe's conscious effort to project a new light upon the precolonial Igbo world is evident at many points in the novel; there is clearly at work here a resolve to promote an alternative image to its earlier representations in Western discourse, one that affords an inside view not merely of its uncoordinated details as lived in the immediacy of everyday experience but also of its overall, functional coherence. Thus, the narrative process amounts to a reformulation in the mode of fiction of the "scientific" discourse of the ethnographic literature on the Igbo, a process by which Achebe seeks to reclaim a preexisting Western discourse on his personal background for a new and different ideological purpose.

But we must go beyond the documentary aspect of Achebe's novel to consider the relation it bears to a serious artistic purpose. We need to observe the way in which the language of the novel, the whole bent of its narrative development, gives expression to an imaginative impulse that functions in its shaping beyond the explicit revisionist intent, which we may suppose to spring from its ideological conditioning. It needs to be emphasized that this impulse derives in the first place from the formal requirements that Achebe as a writer knew he had to satisfy, those conducive to the quality of verisimilitude that have come to be associated with the rise and development of the conventional Western novel. In other words, Achebe's fictional reproduction of Igbo life must be seen in its immediate relation to the diegetic purpose and mimetic function of the novel as a genre.[7] The necessity to reproduce in his novel the context of life appropriate to its theme and external reference comes to govern the process of cultural reclamation to which his work bears witness. We can thus restate the connection between the two impulses at work in the novel by observing that it develops as a redirection—inward—of Western anthropological discourse, toward the true springs of life and expression in the African world, which have been obliterated by this discourse.

But it is evidently the primacy of art that predominates in Achebe's construction of his novel; this has a consequence for grasping its moral import, which we shall come to presently. For the moment, we may note that Achebe's novel is distinguished by an economy of style and a marvelous restraint in the presentation that endow it with a certain austerity. The novel's ethnographic freight is never allowed to weigh down its human interest nor to obscure its aesthetic significance. Every scene is vividly imagined and realized, and the more expansive moments of the narration offer us powerful descriptions, including the entrance of the egwugwus, or masked spirits, at the trial and the subsequent proceedings

(62–66), which give the novel dramatic lift at strategic moments. It is this process by which Achebe "naturalizes" his subject matter, to borrow Jonathan Culler's term (Culler, 1975), that also enables him to situate the narrative development and especially the cruel turn taken by Okonkwo's fate wholly and convincingly within the framework of the Igbo system of belief:

> His life had been ruled by a great passion—to become one of the lords of the clan. That had been his life-spring. And he had all but achieved it. Then everything had been broken. He had been cast out of his clan like a fish onto a dry, sandy beach, panting. Clearly his personal god or *chi* was not made for great things. A man could not rise beyond the destiny of his *chi*. The saying of the elders was not true—that if a man said yea, his *chi* also affirmed. Here was a man whose *chi* said nay despite his own affirmation. (92)

The passage hardly serves to inform us about the nature of the *chi*, a task that Achebe undertakes in a famous essay (Achebe, 1975); rather, it illuminates the ambiguous relationship of Okonkwo to his personal god, a relationship that exemplifies, in the specific terms of Igbo apprehension of the world, the grounded insecurity of the human condition that is the mainspring of what Unamuno has called "the tragic sense of life." The novel's imaginative scope thus extends beyond mere documentation to convey, through the careful reproduction of its marking details, the distinctive character of Igbo tribal life as experienced by its subjects, the felt texture from which it derives its universal significance. It is this that gives *Things Fall Apart* its power of conviction and validates the project of cultural memory attested by the novel.

But the effort of recall and recreation, linked as it is to the diegetic purpose of the novelist's deployment of form, also involves as a necessary implication of the fictional process a critical engagement with the internal dynamics and value system of the world that he presents; one that, in the event, goes beyond its placid exterior to focus directly upon its deeper tensions, to explore its cleavages, and uncover its fault lines. It is at this level of enunciation that the novel enacts what seems to me a veritable crisis of cultural memory.

We are alerted to this crisis primarily by the correlation that the novel suggests between the conditions of existence in the tribal society and the mental universe that prevails within it. Despite its admirable qualities in some important areas of human experience, the world that Achebe presents is one that is closed in upon itself, limited in its capacities, and hobbled in certain crucial respects by its vision of the world. We have already remarked upon the way in which Achebe's Western education and Christian background determine a narrative point of view marked by a certain detachment, so that his narrator stands back sufficiently to indicate an external regard upon this world, for it is not seldom that he adopts an angle of vision that lifts a veil upon the grave disabilities with which tribal life is afflicted. For the image that Chinua Achebe presents in his novel is that of a primary society, one whose low level of technicity leaves it with few resources beyond the purely muscular for dealing with the exigencies of the natural world. Because it is confronted with what is nothing less than a precarious material situation, it has perforce to accord primacy to manliness as a manifestation of being at its most physical, elevated into a norm of personal worth and social value. The valuation of physical prowess, in play as in war, the emphasis on individual achievement, considered as instrumental to social solidarity, appear then as strategies intended to ensure the security and permanence of the group. For, like most early societies, this is a civilization that is dominated by a passion for survival. On this point, Umuofia closely resembles these earlier societies, alike in their cultivation of the heroic ideal based on physical prowess, an ideal necessitated by their dependence on outstanding individuals for group survival.[8]

This defining feature of the tribe is highlighted by the centrality of the yam to the culture and the symbolic value with which it is invested, over and above its utility as a source of nourishment, a feature that provides a graphic illustration of the continuum from material existence to collective vision and ethos. Because of the intense muscular effort required for its cultivation, the yam crop comes to represent an annual triumph wrested from nature, the sign of the rigorous dialectic between the human world and the natural environment, which governs the communal life and conditions what one might call the social aesthetic—the festivals, rituals, and other forms of public ceremony—that infuses the tribe's collective representations with feeling and endows them with meaning for each consciousness within the community. Thus, the image of the yam gathers up the force fields of the culture and functions as a metonymic representation of the tribe's mode of relation to the world (Echeruo, 1979). The organicism that we have observed as a fundamental feature of the tribal community is thus related to the fact that it has its being essentially within the realm of necessity.

If then, from a certain idealizing point of view, we come to appreciate the values of intimacy and intensity of living denoted by the closed universe of the novel, such as Gérard Genette postulates for the Cambrai of Marcel Proust (Genette, 1972), the critical current that runs through the narrative soon reveals this universe as one marked by a profound contradiction between the powerful constraints of the social ideal, which privileges the interests of the group, and the truths of individual human yearnings and desires as embraced by a modern sensibility. It is on this basis that Achebe develops the theme of Okonkwo's struggle for recognition and the larger existential implications of this theme in its evocation of the universal human predicament. This theme, we ought to note, is framed by the triadic structure of the novel: Okonkwo's rise to prominence at Umuofia, which is interrupted by his banishment and life in exile at his maternal village, Mbanta, and his disastrous return to the scene of his early triumphs. The parallel between the story of Okonkwo and that of his society is thus made central to the narrative development, predicated as this is upon the interrelation between the rise and fall of Okonkwo, and the fortunes of the society and way of life he represents, and its unraveling by the forces of history.

It is useful at this point to consider the salient details of Okonkwo's story as recounted by Achebe and its bearing on the underlying theme of his novel. This story really begins with Okonkwo's father, Unoka; indeed, the elements of the singular dialectic that links Okonkwo with Unoka, on one hand, and with his own son, Nwoye, on the other, determine the temporal axis of the novel and indicate the succession of generations concerned by the action. This dialectic relates in a fundamental way to the structure of images and moral propositions contained by the novel. Unoka plays a double role here; not only does his fate and its effect upon his son provide the key to the latter's psychology, he also embodies the countervalues that stand in opposition to the inflexible social ideal of the tribe. For there is a real sense in which Unoka can be considered a rebel against the rigidities of tribal society. His unorthodox style of living is a conscious subversion of the manly ideal, to which he opposes the values of art along with a playful irony and an amorality that accords with his relaxed disposition to the world. It is true that his improvidence turns him into an object of general contempt and that he comes to a particularly disagreeable end, which seems at first sight to vindicate the severe reprobation of the tribe. But even his end in the Evil

Forest constitutes a triumph of sorts, a form of defiance that the narrator emphasizes with this significant detail: "When they carried him away, he took with him his flute" (13). In the end, he attracts the reader's sympathy by his unprepossessing attitude and by a certain humane simplicity, which is associated with his type, for the portrait we have of Unoka is that of a folk hero, whose insouciance stands as a constant rebuke to the vanities of the great and powerful of his world.[9]

In the immediate context of the novel, Unoka's refusal to conform to the prevailing ethos of the tribe is of course considered in wholly negative terms. More important, its subversive significance is forcefully repudiated by his son, Okonkwo, who wills himself into becoming the antithesis of all that Unoka represents, so that he comes to assume what can only be judged a fearful aspect:

> He was a man of action, a man of war. Unlike his father he could stand the look of blood. In Umuofia's war he was the first to bring home a human head. That was his fifth head, and he was not an old man yet. On great occasions, such as the funeral of a village celebrity he drank his palm-wine from his first human head. (8)

It is this portrayal of Okonkwo that prompted Thomas Melone to propose, in his pioneering study devoted to the first four novels of Chinua Achebe, an evaluation that both captures the essence of the character and exaggerates its import; he describes him as a "complex and unsettling personality" (*une multiple et déroutante personnalité*) (Melone, 1973, 64). Unsettling Okonkwo certainly is, but not exactly complex; given his delineation in *Things Fall Apart*, one would be inclined rather to consider him as a "flat" character, to use E. M. Forster's term. It is true that, in the particular context in which we encounter the character, the novelist nudges us to the edge of what could have been a powerful psychological portrait; considering his problematic relation to his father, who throws a long shadow over his life, Okonkwo's inordinate obsession with self has all the makings of a deep neurosis generated by a tenacious and consuming existential project, self-realization. *Things Fall Apart* can be summed up as largely the narrative of the process of self-fashioning by which Okonkwo is transformed into the somber inversion of his father. But the mental condition into which he falls as a result is not really explored, so that we are not led into the inner workings of his mind as a fully realized individual. Even at his moment of greatest mental turmoil (in the immediate aftermath of his killing of Ikemefuna) we are provided with hardly any insight into the happenings within his troubled soul. The point here is that, despite the occasional glimpses the narrative affords into states of mind, which are also occasions for introspection on the part of the character, the narrative narrows our gaze to focus upon what is presented as essential to his makeup: "Okonkwo was a man of action, not of thought" (48).

It is not therefore the pyschological depth of his portrayal that lends Okonkwo his power to fascinate but rather his physicality, all projected outward ("he was tall and huge," the narrator informs us [3]) in such a way as to constitute him as the incarnation of his society's ideal of manhood. This is the ideal that Okonkwo translates in his attitude and manners into an overbearing masculinity. Even then, we cannot but respond, at least in the beginning, to what we perceive as his immense vitality,[10] made all the more intriguing by its sexual undercurrent, an element of his total personality clearly indicated through the seductive power this exerts upon Ekewfi.

The allusion to Okonkwo's sexuality raises the issue of gender and its narrative implications for it is this element that seems to have inspired the most inattentive reading of Achebe's novel, especially by some feminists, who object to what they perceive as the work's undue focus on the masculine principle and a corresponding depreciation of the feminine. The feminist view is exemplified by Florence Stratton's negative interpretation of what she calls the novel's focus on "gender ideology" (Stratton, 1994, 164–70). More pertinent is the critique by Susan Z. Andrade, who remarks upon "the category of the masculine" in Achebe's novel, which, she says, "attempts to avoid the representation of colonial relations in gendered terms by inscribing an excessively masculine Igbo man." She goes on to observe:

> In the Manichean allegory of anti-colonial struggle . . . the colonial /European side is characterized as masculine, while the weak and disorderly native/African is necessarily feminine. . . . Paradoxically, Achebe's preoccupation with the implicitly gendered pattern of colonial relations means that he can only imagine a negative masculinity; he has no room for a celebratory feminism. (Andrade, 1996, 255–56)

It is plain that these readings and others of the same stripe ignore the evidence of the novel itself, which foregrounds the distortion of the communal ideal by Okonkwo in such a way as to suggest a narrative commentary upon the social and moral implications of this ideal. Far from endorsing what might be termed a cult of Igbo masculinity, Achebe's novel offers ample evidence of a narrative preoccupation with the less than reassuring features of what may be considered a "basic personality type,"[11] which is fostered presumably by the work's reference culture and exemplified so forcefully by the character of Okonkwo. We are more than once alerted to the fact that Okonkwo's adoption of the manly ideal is excessive and even wrongheaded, as when Obierika emphatically expresses to Okonkwo himself his lack of enthusiasm for the prowess in wrestling demonstrated by his own son, Maduka. Obierika seems to have been conceived as a foil to Okonkwo, serving as a kind of Menenius Agrippa to Okonkwo's Coriolanus, so that his attitude indicates the possibility of an alternative stance. This opposition enables us to discern a disavowal of Okonkwo at the level of the novel's system of connotations, a level at which we sense the imaginative direction of Achebe's novel and the moral sense it carries as it works toward a confounding of Okonkwo's exaggerated sense of self.

This critical focus is gathered up in the folktale that functions both as an interlude and as a narrative commentary upon Okonkwo's egoism, a device that is fully in line with the convention of storytelling in the African oral tradition. In this sense, it serves Achebe in formal terms as an intertextual resource in the construction of his novel within which it is deployed, through a process of *mise en abîme*, both as a supplement to its ludic function and as metafiction, in a redoubling of its narrative code (Obiechina, 1993). As a direct comment upon Okonkwo's hubris, it points beyond the immediate action to the moral problem involved in the tense dialectic between collective and individual. We must recall in this connection the function of the imagination as what may be termed the preconceptual foundation of the "life world" in traditional society, a function that gave to the art of storytelling its significance in the deepest sense—as a mode of critical reflection upon the vicissitudes of human existence (Towa, 1980).

The relevance of the folktale interlude to the imaginative discourse elaborated by the novel is that it affords a clear pointer to a critical preoccupation manifested explicitly as a distinct thematic cluster centered upon the issue of gender in the novel. As Solomon Iyasere has pointed out, Okonkwo is confronted at every turn by the female principle as it informs the organization of collective life and the communal consciousness of Umuofia (Iyasere, 1978). The female principle functions indeed as a major trope in *Things Fall Apart* and constitutes a significant dimension of its system of ironies. A striking instance of this is provided by one of the most dramatic episodes in the novel, the abduction of Okonkwo's daughter, Ezinma, by Chielo, the priestess of the Earth goddess, Agbala (70–77). Chielo detains the girl an entire night in her cave, while the great warrior Okonkwo is obliged to wait outside, unable to intervene to recover his daughter until the priestess is ready to return her to him in the morning. When we consider Okonkwo's affective investment in Ezinma, in whom he discerns the male qualities whose absence he bemoans in his son, Nwoye, Chielo's act, in its challenge to Okonkwo's manhood ("Beware Okonkwo! Beware of exchanging words with Agbala. Does a man speak when a god speaks?" [71]), presents itself as a pointed recall to his attention of the gender category to which Ezinma properly belongs and the possible calls upon her that the distribution of gender roles determines within the culture. More concretely, it is Chielo's way of designating Ezinma as her successor, of reclaiming the girl and restoring her to a realm of feminine mysticism from which she is beginning to be separated by Okonkwo's projection upon her of a male essence.

The reaffirmation of the female principle signified by the Chielo episode is reinforced by other indications that suggest a consistent undermining in symbolic terms of Okonkwo's masculinity throughout the novel. As Carole Boyce Davis has rightly observed:

> The Chielo-Ezinma episode is an important sub-plot of the novel and actually reads like a suppressed larger story circumscribed by the exploration of Okonkwo's/man's struggle with and for his people. In the troubled world of *Things Fall Apart*, motherhood and femininity are the unifying mitigating principles. (Davis, 1986, 245; see also Jeyifo, 1993b)

The second part of the novel, devoted entirely to Okonkwo's life in exile in his mother's village after his accidental killing of his clansman, can be read as an extended development of this secondary theme, which subtends the narrative at its primary level of development. For Okonkwo's refusal to reconcile himself to the turn of events that leads to his exile provides an occasion for another reminder of the significance of the female principle when he is instructed by Uchendu, his maternal uncle, in the culture's veneration of the mother as source of life, its association of femininity with the vital principle, which is enunciated in resolute terms in the dictum *Nneka* (Mother is supreme). Okonkwo's glum acquiescence contrasts with the enthusiasm that accompanies his return to Umuofia, where his loss of social standing soon reveals itself as irreparable, and a tragic fate awaits him. The irony that attends Okonkwo's embodiment of manhood is that, pursued by the feminine principle as if by the Furies, he is finally vanquished by a destiny that culminates in his committing what we are pointedly informed is a "female" fault, which leads first to his exile and finally to his downfall.

In its deconstruction of Okonkwo's masculinity, the novel also draws directly upon a significant feature of its reference culture for validation. For while it reflects, in its account of individual behavior and group attitudes within its fictional world, the reality of male dominance as an empirical fact of the social system—the order of precedence denoted by the seating arrangement at the trial scene provides a graphic visual demonstration—the novel also directs our attention to the ways in which this fact is controverted in other spheres of the collective life and imagination, especially at the level of religious belief and experience. Although the society upholds the notion of manliness as a fundamental social norm, it is also compelled to recognize the controlling effect of biology upon its life processes and the obvious bearing of this factor upon group survival. If the social dominance of the men is unequivocally asserted, the parallel valorization of women in the symbolic sphere, demonstrated by the cult of Ala, emerges as a presiding topos of "the social imaginary," one that sets up a countervailing cultural and moral force to the massive investment of the social sphere by the men. The male-female dialectic thus serves to maintain an affective and ideological balance in the group; in this, it corresponds to a certain primary perception of a felt duality of the cosmic order as a principle of the universal imagination.[12]

This conceptual scheme is crucial for an understanding of Okonkwo's psychology as depicted in Achebe's novel, for it is against the feminine term of the gender dialectic, as understood and expressed in the culture— the nurturing instinct as opposed to the destructive, the tender as opposed to the violent, the aesthetic as opposed to the practical, in a word, the diurnal as opposed to the nocturnal—that Okonkwo has resolutely turned his face. The terms in which his cutting down of Ikemefuna is narrated suggest that behind the gesture of confident affirmation of male resolve, which he intends his act to represent, lies a profound discomfort in the presence of femininity. We are told that he is "dazed" with fear at the moment of the boy's appeal to him, but it is a fear that has been bred in his unreflecting mind by the image of his father, fear of having to reckon with the nuanced reformulation of established social meanings by the symbolic values associated with the female principle. Indeed, for

Okonkwo to be reminded anew of his father's image by Ikemefuna's artistic endowments and lively temperament is to be impelled toward a violent act of repression.

As Keith Booker has remarked, the killing of Ikemefuna represents a pivotal episode in the novel (Booker, 1998, 70) not only as a reflection of Okonkwo's disturbed mental state but in its reverberation throughout the novel as a result of its effect upon his son, Nwoye. It marks the beginning of the boy's disaffection toward his father and ultimately his alienation from the community that Okonkwo has come to represent for him. We hardly need to ponder the cleavage between father and son to realize that it provides the most potent sign of the disintegration of Umuofia society, provoked by the introduction within it of the Christian religion. Over the three years of their companionship in Okonkwo's household, Ikemefuna has come to embody for Nwoye the poetry of the tribal society, which is erased for him forever by the young boy's ritual killing, an act against nature in which his father participates. The fate of Ikemefuna, its stark revelation of the grim underside of the tribal ethos, engenders the emptiness in his heart that predisposes Nwoye to Christian conversion. The terms in which his conversion is described make clear the conjunction between social and moral issues as the determining factor. It is not without significance that the conversion itself is presented as an inner drama of sensibility in which a new poetry takes the place of the ancient, fills a spiritual and affective void, and thus comes to satisfy a need to which the traditional order is no longer capable of responding:

> It was not the mad logic of the Trinity that captivated him. He did not understand it. It was the poetry of the new religion, something felt in the marrow. The hymn about brothers who sat in darkness and in fear seemed to answer a vague persistent question that haunted his young soul—the question of the twins crying in the bush and the question of Ikemefuna who was killed. He felt a relief within as the hymn poured into his parched soul. The words of the hymn were like the drops of frozen rain melting on the dry plate of the panting earth. Nwoye's callow mind was greatly puzzled. (104)

The purple prose is integral to the language of Christian evangelism that Achebe adopts in the passage, setting in relief the last sentence, which arrests its lyrical flight with the abrupt reference to Nwoye's "callow mind." The effect of the juxtaposition verges on bathos, but its purport is unmistakable, for we are left in no doubt that this phrase describes a condition for which Nwoye's tribal background is responsible. His conversion thus represents the prelude to the refinement of mind and sensibility that the new religion promises.

Nwoye's adoption of a new name, with the significance it carries of a rebirth, consolidates his sense of allegiance to the new religion. But the particular name he takes suggests an import beyond its immediate meaning of individual salvation, for the name Isaac recalls the biblical story of the patriarch Abraham and his substitution of an animal for the sacrifice of his son, an act that inaugurates a new dispensation in which we are made to understand that fathers are no longer required to sacrifice their sons to a demanding and vengeful deity. Nwoye's adoption of this name in effect enacts a symbolic reversal of the killing of Ikemefuna and gives its full meaning to his conversion as primarily the sign of his release from the constraints of the ancestral universe.

Nwoye's story closes a family history that revolves around the troubled relationships between fathers and sons.[13] Centered as it is on the personality and tragic fate of Okonkwo, this family history comprises the novel's narrative framework and functions as an allegory of the destiny of the society they inhabit and to which they relate in diverse ways. What this allegory signifies, in the particular historical and cultural context of Achebe's novel, is the state of internal crisis into which this society is plunged, a crisis that we have come to appreciate as intrinsic to its presiding ethos. This crisis is rendered especially acute by the arrival of the white man, so that a major irony of the novel is that this historic event provides a resolution, an outcome that we sense as highly ambiguous insofar as it marks the harsh intrusion of the outer world upon the tribal universe, leading to the loss of its autonomy as a sphere of existence and expression.

Achebe's understanding of the epochal significance of this turn of events represents the conceptual foundation of the novel's narrative development. Its burden of historical truth derives from its external reference, the large correspondence of the events it narrates to the internal history of the society and culture with which it deals, and the profound upheaval in the Igbo world and indeed the entire region of what is now southeastern Nigeria, which culminated in the imposition of British colonial rule.[14] The formal working out of this understanding consists of the way it determines a double perspective of point of view, which is reflected in the narrative devices through which the drama of events unfolds in the novel and by which its moral import is clarified. This is evident in what we have called the novel's diegetic function, which relates to the explicit realism associated with the genre, the imperative of representation to which it responds. On one hand, it enables a positive image of tribal society to emerge, with its coherence and especially the distinctive poetry of its forms of life. On the other hand, we are made aware that this coherence is a precarious and even factitious one, deriving from an inflexibility of social norms that places an enormous psychological and moral burden on individuals caught within its institutional constraints, imprisoned by its logic of social organization, and inhibited by its structure of social conformities. The split that this occasions within the writer's creative consciousness makes for a profound ambivalence, which translates as a productive tension in the novel's connotative substratum.

We come to some idea of this deeper layer of meaning in the novel by considering the complex of images through which it develops.[15] At the risk of a certain reductionism, it can be observed that the structure of images in the novel revolves around the theme of contradiction, which functions as its organizing principle, amplified through the structure of ironic reversals by which the narrative is propelled. This feature is well illustrated by the contradictory meanings assumed by the image of the locusts on the two occasions it occurs in the text. The first, which recounts an actual invasion of the village by locusts, provides what may be considered the high point of the novel; contrary to expectations, the normal association of this pest with agricultural disaster is reversed as the entire population goes into a festive mood, collecting locusts and feasting on them. The irony of this episode is deepened by the fact that it immediately precedes the account of the consultations among the elders regarding the disposal of Ikemefuna and the narration of his ritual killing. It is not without significance for the narrative scheme that Okonkwo's participation in this ritual marks the precise moment at which his fortunes commence their downward spiral. The connection is directly established between his reverses and the fall of the clan in the second occurrence of the image of the locust, which reinforces the dark irony intimated by this narrative scheme by returning us to the conventional meaning of the image of the locusts in Obierika's designation of the white men, whose appearance on the scene he interprets as the ominous event it turns out to be: "I forgot to tell you another thing which the Oracle said. It said that other white men were on their way. They were locusts, it said, and the first man was their harbinger sent to explore the terrain"

(97–98).[16] Within this scheme, the progression of events in the novel is organized around a system of dichotomies and their transformations. We move in particular from the preestablished hierarchy of values implied in the opposition between the village of Umuofia and the Evil Forest to a dramatic reversal of this hierarchy.[17] The binarisms by which the unfolding of events is plotted in the novel and the ironies entailed by the process are especially marked here, for it is in the Evil Forest, which starts out as the negative marker of social space in the community depicted by the novel, that the Christians establish their new religion, which is destined to triumph over the ancestral religion. It is here that they succeed in creating a new community cemented as much by the enthusiasm called forth in them by the new faith as by its rhetoric of liberation (112). It is pertinent to remark here that the pattern of reversals itself draws upon an eminently Christian trope, encapsulated in the biblical sayings about the last coming to be first and the meek inheriting the earth, a trope that, we may recall, prompted Nietzsche's repudiation of Christianity as the religion of the weak and powerless in the world.

With these reversals as they occur in *Things Fall Apart*, the Evil Forest gradually becomes invested with moral authority and thus acquires a new and positive significance. Furthermore, the historical connection between the Christian mission and the incipient colonial administration and their collaboration in the overthrow of the tribal system constitutes this new space as the domain within which a new social order is to be elaborated. The account of this connection in the latter part of *Things Fall Apart* propels the Evil Forest to a position of centrality in the novel's system of meanings, so that, in its association with Christianity, it comes to represent the source of new humanizing values and, in this sense, simultaneously becomes an image of a transformation that prefigures a new future. In short, the Evil Forest comes to signify a new and developing realm of being.

The future to which this transformation is projected is clearly intimated in Mr. Brown's exhortations to his wards, exhortations that provide a temporal complement to the spiritual justification of his missionary activity: "Mr. Brown begged and argued and prophesied. He said that the leaders of the land in the future would be men and women who had learnt to read and write" (128). The remarkable prescience ascribed here to Mr. Brown is of course the product of narrative hindsight, propounded *ex post facto* and thus anticipating the historical moment of the events depicted in the novel. It is an imaginative prediction of the modernity that rises on the horizon, which is determined by the nexus between literacy and the new cash economy and which is destined to flow out of the process of social reconstruction set in motion by the advent and diffusion of Christianity:

> Mr. Brown's school produced quick results. A few months in it were enough to make one a court messenger or even a court clerk. Those who stayed longer became teachers; and from Umuofia, labourers went forth into the Lord's vineyard. New churches were established in the surrounding villages and a few schools with them. From the very beginning religion and education went hand in hand. (128)

Achebe's novel looks forward self-consciously here to the formation of a new Westernized elite and the emergence of a new national identity enabled by literacy and predicated on an ideology of modernization. The nationalist project that in the general consensus would devolve upon the Westernized elite finds a discreet echo here within Achebe's novel and gives it a thematic resonance that, as we shall see, extends its range into the field of utopia.[18]

Thus, by a strange and unpredictable turn of events, the Evil Forest comes to gather to itself these various intimations, so that it functions as the marker of the historical consciousness that underlies the narrative development of the novel. The peculiar overlap of theme and imagery here enlarges the novel's field of reference and suggestion in such a way as to point up the deep intuition it expresses of the compelling force of history.

But it is especially at the level of language that the double movement of Achebe's imagination in *Things Fall Apart* is fully manifested. It is revealing of the novel's thematic direction to observe and follow the course charted by the language, which proceeds from the vigorous rhetoric of traditional life, which infuses its early chapters with their peculiar energy, to the bare discursiveness that predominates in the later chapters. It is primarily the language of the early chapters that endows Achebe's novel with an epic resonance. The impulse to a revaluation of Igbo culture is clearly discernible here, for we are left in no doubt that the language of Achebe's characters is one that is constitutive of the culture and woven into the fabric of social experience. This language, in which social life is "objectified," becomes expressive of its seamless whole, of its tensions as well as strategies for their resolution, a language that may be said to found a whole register of the collective being. It is to this interrelation of speech mode and communal life that Bernth Lindfors draws attention when he describes the language of Achebe's world as "a grammar of values" (Lindfors, 1968, 77).

We sense then, behind Achebe's handling of language, an ideological *parti-pris*, which is not without its aesthetic payoff. There is an obvious delectation in language in the early chapters, which betrays a large measure of complicity with his subject matter on the part of the novelist. This conditions the felicity of style that has so often been remarked upon as a distinctive quality of Achebe's writing.[19] And it is indeed this aesthetic dimension—as distinct from the novel's documentary or ethnographic interest—that qualifies it as creative endeavor, as a notable instance of *poiesis*.

But alongside what one might call the performative style reflective of oral discourse and as counterpoint to its expressivity, Achebe adopts the tone of objective narrative, a tone derived from the Western convention of literate discourse, whose impassibility reflects the distance that he is obliged to retain with regard to his subject. This tone is evident in the direct accounts of customs and beliefs and other notations related to the tribal way of life, passages in which the skepticism natural to the rational viewpoint is barely held in check and is masked only by the neutral tone of the narrative voice. We sense the way in which this skepticism is held back in the long description of the search for Ezinma's *iyi-nwa* (53–61), but it is reaffirmed in the matter-of-fact account of Okonkwo going into the bush to collect herbs that he will administer to Ezinma to combat her fever. This report of an eminently pragmatic behavior serves as a coda to the exuberance of the story of Ezinma's stone, dispelling the air of verisimilitude that seems to attach to this story with a sober notation of fact. Similarly, Ekwefi's reminiscence of her encounter with an evil spirit is juxtaposed with a realistic, almost banal explanation of her visions: "She had prayed for the moon to rise. But now she found the half light of the incipient moon more terrifying than the darkness. The world was now peopled with vague fantastic figures that dissolved under her steady gaze and then formed again in new shapes" (75).

These juxtapositions reflect the workings of the novelist's mind as it hovers between fascination and unbelief, between an impulse toward an embrace of the cultural values suggested by his imaginative exploration of setting and narrative elaboration of context and a positivist outlook inseparable from a liberated consciousness. We have no better evidence of this ambiguous subtext than the wry report of the *egwugwu* who is rooted to the spot for two days for daring to cross the path of the one-handed masquerade (86). And Obierika's expression of awe at the potency of a neighboring village's "medicine" indicates that even the intelligence of a wise elder like him can be preyed upon by the superstitions of the tribe. Thus, while it is evident that the passages in which Achebe reports these beliefs and the practices associated with them imply a certain measure of understanding of their ways, it would be clearly absurd to suggest that he identifies with them at any level of his intellectual makeup.

It is especially instructive in this regard to note the way in which the bewilderment of the villagers at the survival of the Christians in the Evil Forest affords Achebe scope for an indulgent satire upon their conceptual naiveté, as determined by the collective belief system. This naiveté takes on a more ominous character in Obierika's account of the killing of the white man by the people of Abame, who tie up his "iron horse" to prevent it from running away to call his friends (97). It is significant that later in the novel, as a demonstration of the inadequacy of the traditional world view, we are informed of the test of efficacy passed by the new medicine introduced by the missionaries: "And it was not long before the people began to say that the white man's medicine was quick in working" (128). The term *medicine* is now employed in the sense of a technology of healing grounded in verifiable science, in other words in association with an objectifying, instrumental rationality.[20]

The insistence of the narrative voice on the fundamental weaknesses of the traditional cognitive system is thus unmistakable, and it raises the issue of the skeptical distance that, as novelist, Achebe is obliged to maintain from this system and indeed the intellectual detachment from the world he presents, despite his deep sense of cultural involvement in and affective engagement with his material. The shifting perspectives we encounter in the novel and the varied tones of the narrative voice afford pointers to the fact that *Things Fall Apart* is written out of a consciousness that is no longer at one with the indigenous order of apprehension. We are constantly made aware that the traditional background functions for Achebe not as a reference for an objective structure of knowledge but rather for the novelist's narrative construction and imaginative purpose, as a touchstone of his aesthetic, as a stock of imaginative symbols endowed with an affective value that does not depend on belief nor devotional commitment for their force of appeal. The relationship of Achebe to his material is thus comparable in some important respects to that of the Western writer to pagan mythology and even to aspects of Christian belief that are no longer capable of commanding the writer's intellectual assent or even emotional identification.

The fact that Achebe's second, objective style is often marked by irony does not detract from its value as the instrument appropriate to the function of chronicler that, as novelist, he assumes in those passages when he turns to this style, moments when he is concerned above all with registering the facts as they present themselves to him as a dispassionate observer of history. The interaction between the evocative parts of his novel and the realistic mode of its thematic progression is thus expressive of the interface between the oral and the written, which is central to his double cultural awareness. In formal terms, this interaction marks the transition from the epic to the novel to which Bakhtin has drawn attention as distinctive of the evolution of narrative (Bakhtin, 1981; see also Ong, 1982; Goody, 1987). The significant point about this interaction is the tension produced in the novel between what one might call a Romanticism of its oral style, which derives from a personal attachment of the writer to his African antecedents, and the realism of the Western style, which corresponds to his awareness of their supersession in a new dispensation. The deep mechanisms at work in the novel thus come to the surface in the language, which enables us to grasp the full connotative weight and rhetorical direction of the narrative. This is a story that begins in the register of myth and ends on a note of chronicle, a transformation that is reflected in its narrative style, which becomes progressively "de-poetized," as Thomas Melone has rightly pointed out (Melone, 1973, 65).[21]

The "downward" progression of Achebe's expression thus charts the course of the depletion of language brought on by events in the community to which the novel refers, a process that is registered within the work by the transition from a textualized orality through which the characters and the world of the novel are not so much represented as evoked, called forth into being, to the passive record of events imposed by the conventions of literate discourse. For the interaction between styles, the play of language on which the narrative development turns, forms part of the movement of history traced in the novel. As the story advances, we witness a linguistic process that culminates in the triumph of the culture of literacy, a process that also signals the engulfing of the indigenous voice, which was carried exclusively through the oral medium, by the discourse of colonialism.

It is this latter discourse that finally calls attention to itself, at the end of the novel, in the total identification of the linguistic vehicle of the text with the actual language in which the thoughts of the colonial officer are formulated. The passage is remarkable in many respects, not least for the way it draws attention to the differentiated use in Achebe's novel of the device of indirect speech. For in its bare matter-of-factness, it stands in marked contrast to the remarkable stream of interior monologue through which, as he is led to his death, Ikemefuna's forebodings are translated—in a dramatic counterpoint between an immediate sense of personal danger, which is rendered through indirect speech, and the reassuring formulations of communal lore. The loss of the vivid quality of Ikemefuna's monologue in the colonial officer's reported speech indicates that we now have to do with the disembodied voice of history manifested through this faceless, nondescript character. The historic turning signified by the end of Okonkwo's personal story is thus registered at the specific level of language; from being subjects of their own discourse, Okonkwo and his people have now become the objects of the discourse of another, elaborated in a language foreign to them.

There is a sense, then, in which the advent of the imperial moment is developed in Achebe's novel as a linguistic experience, as more or less a misadventure of language, which unfolds through the discursive modes of its narration. In line with this development, the temporal scheme of the novel appropriately shifts from the cyclic plane, associated with a rich organicism and intense vitalism, to the strictly linear; the precipitation of events in the third part of the novel contrasts markedly with the unhurried pace of the telling in the earlier parts. At the same time, the spatial scheme itself becomes transformed, enlarged, and in the process impoverished: from the affectively charged compactness of the nine villages to the impersonal perspectives of the Lower Niger, evoked in the ruminations of the colonial officer that bring the narrative to its close.

Things Fall Apart displays in its own peculiar way what Frank Kermode has called "the ambiguous innocence of the classic text" (Kermode, 1983, 74). Kermode's phrase itself is a suggestive one, for we might conceive of the classic text in terms of its centrality to a tradition, either one that is fully established but must still accommodate new works for its reinvigoration—the sense of T. S. Eliot's celebrated essay "Tradition and the Individual Talent"—or one that is emerging, advertising itself by its novelty, as is generally held to be the case with modern African literature in the European languages. The poetics of *Things Fall Apart* seem in a curious way to unite both of these senses of the classic text. On one hand, its economy of style derives from what seems like a complete adherence to the norms of the conventional novel, exemplified by its strictly linear structure with a beginning, a middle, and an end, which leads inexorably to the final catastrophe, the progression clearly marked by the novel's three-part structure. Moreover, it achieves its effects by means that refuse to call attention to themselves. This makes for an austerity that places it alongside that other classic of the African canon, Cheikh Hamidou Kane's *Ambiguous Adventure*. At the same time, it has claims to a uniqueness that derives from its departure from the Western model in fundamental ways. As the discussion above indicates, a tension exists between the surface fluency that distinguishes Achebe's text and the resonances set up within it by its hidden places of signification. Although *Things Fall Apart* presents itself at first sight as what Roland Barthes has called a "readerly" rather than a "writerly" text (Barthes, 1970), the key elements of its internal features indicate that there is more to its transparent texture than is at first perceptible. These deeper promptings of the text indicate that its apparent simplicity is belied by the complexities of reference and suggestion that lie beneath its directness of enunciation.[22]

The tension that these complexities generate in the text proceeds largely from the relationship that obtains between theme and form, which reflects an ambivalence that informs the fictional inspiration and therefore structures its formal expression. Simon Gikandi has endeavored to address this issue by claiming that this feature of the work derives from the writer's cultural background, which recognizes a plurality of discourses and admits different points of view, varying formulations of the truth of experience or reality (Gikandi, 1991, 44–50). But the ambivalence in the novel is so profound as to carry much more weight than Gikandi seems willing to allow. Rather than a function of cultural habit, it seems to me that this ambivalence stems from the critical consciousness inherent in Achebe's recourse to the novel as a narrative genre. The point can be made directly by observing that Achebe presents Igbo society "steadily and whole," to borrow Matthew Arnold's expression. For while this society is indeed marked by an internal coherence of its organization and a poetry of its expressive modes, it also betrays profound inadequacies and grave internal contradictions, which account for the disintegration that the novel records. Thus, *Things Fall Apart* does not merely embody a willed recall of cultural memory but develops also as an exploration of the specificities of life within the universe of experience it unveils, an exploration that amounts ultimately to a reassessment of its nature and presiding ethos. In other words, Achebe brings to his task of historical recollection a critical and moral intelligence.

The moral issue in *Things Fall Apart* seems to hinge upon how far Okonkwo can be considered representative of his society, how far he can be held to be its embodiment. For William Walsh, the centrality of Okonkwo to the issue is clear, as he says, "because of the way in which the fundamental predicament of the society is lived through his life" (Walsh, 1970, 52). But any categorical answer one way or the other skirts the question, since in fact, in real societies, individuals only partially embody the values of the community even when these are presumed to have been fully internalized, for in the process of acting out these values, they can also be found to strain against them. It is this dialectic between the individual and the society, inherent in what Durkheim terms "social constraint" (*la contrainte sociale*) that is so well mirrored in Achebe's novel in its depiction of Okonkwo's relation to his society.

This is a dialectic that is of course very much within the province of the novel. Indeed, as Sunday Anozie has pointed out, Okonkwo as a character corresponds in some respects to Lucien Goldmann's concept of the "problematic hero"; in Anozie's reading, Okonkwo emerges as something of a romantic hero, the bearer of a cult of the self (Anozie, 1970, 41–54, 120–141). It is easy to see how this attribute can constitute a menace to the kind of society that Achebe constructs, a potential factor of disaggregation in a tribal community. For the assiduous cultivation of individual self can only disturb the system of obligations and solidarities on which the sense of community is founded. Okonkwo's personal attitude and social conduct amount in fact to an idiosyncratic interpretation of social rules and lead irresistibly to a state of moral irresponsibility, despite his apparent conformity to norms. His self-absorption is of such magnitude as to test the limits of the dominant ideology and thus to reveal its points of weakness. It is this paradox of his situation that is dramatized by his exile, which can be read as a symbolic expression of the necessity to rein in his passionate individuality by its exclusion from the social sphere. This aspect of his character is presented as directly related to the simplified and totally unreflective approach to the world by which he lives and acts, in striking contrast to his friend Obierika. The same unreflective commitment to the communal ethos in his killing of Ikemefuna is manifested in his cutting down of the court messenger. Okonkwo's blinding passion leads him to a final act of egoism, which marks him with a tragic solitude, rendered tersely in the line in which we last glimpse him: "He wiped his matchet on the sand and went away" (145).

Contrary, then, to Gikandi's contention, the ambivalence by which the novel is governed inheres in the text itself and emerges clearly in the portrayal of Okonkwo. We must go further to observe that the largely negative thrust of this portrayal comes close to undermining the polemical intent of the novel. For if Okonkwo's tragic fate marks him as a symbol of the passion of the African in modern times, the ironic devaluation of the character and the ethos he embodies suggests a profound sense of unease on the part of his creator regarding many issues of moral import raised by the habits of mind and social practices that define the traditional universe of life and expression. There is thus a sense in which the sustained imaginative reflection upon Igbo society in Achebe's novel begins to tend toward a subversion of its ideological premises. It is as if Achebe's intellect, sensibility, and sense of artistic integrity had entered into contention with his primary affections for his cultural antecedents, thus bringing into peril his conscious project of bearing witness to the poetic quality of the universe in which they are rooted. Although it would be extreme to read Achebe's novel as the expression of a repudiation of the tribal ethos, as a form of recoil from the tribal universe, to consider the text in the light of its ambivalence is to recognize it for what it is: nothing less than an uncompromising reappraisal of the tribal world.[23]

It is important to stress that this revaluation has nothing to do with the diminished conception of African humanity and capacities constitutive of colonial ideology but arises as an immediate factor of the historical process represented in the novel. We appreciate the intense feeling of insecurity of the Umuofia elders as they sense the world with which they are familiar going out from under them. We sympathize therefore with the claim to cultural integrity defended by Okonkwo and others, more so as the novel establishes a parallel between their attitude and that of Mr. Smith, whose intransigence on behalf of the Christian cause mirrors that of Okonkwo on behalf of the traditional world. They are the true protagonists, embodying each in his own way the logic of the cultural conflict enacted in the novel, the logic involved in the drama of the colonial encounter. Moreover, this conflict is situated within the perspective of a cultural pluralism that is at first rehearsed in a good-humored way in the theological disputations between the Umuofians and Mr. Brown, but which soon assumes an agonistic character in the confrontation with his successor, Mr. Smith; it is this later development that is voiced by one of the elders, Ajofia: "We cannot leave the matter in his hands because he does not understand our customs, just as we do not understand his. We say he is foolish, because he does not know our ways, and perhaps he says we are foolish because we do not know his" (134–35). But this balanced view of cultural relativism hardly represents the lever of the novel's groundwork of ideas nor the resting place of its ideological or narrative progression. *Things Fall Apart* complicates singularly the issues so often raised in the context of the debate within which it is usually situated: the tradition/modernity framework. It goes beyond the series of dichotomies so regularly invoked in this debate as to have become platitudes: established custom versus change; cultural loss versus reproduction; accommodation versus revolt; and acculturation versus cultural nationalism. These issues are obviously implicated in the total discursive range of the novel's narrative development, but they do not in the end, it seems to me, constitute the real heart of the matter. It is not enough to see *Things Fall Apart* as simply a statement of cultural and racial retrieval, as a novel that embodies a discourse of nativism. Rather than a unilateral revaluation of the past, the central preoccupation of this novel, as indeed of Achebe's entire production, revolves around the deeply problematic nature of the relationship of past to present in Africa. What is at issue here, in the most fundamental way, is the bearing of that past upon the present, fraught as this is with implications for the future prospects of the continent.

Kwame Anthony Appiah's summing up of the novel is pertinent to this question when he remarks, "Achebe's accounting includes columns both for profit and loss" (Appiah, 1992, xii). Given what we have seen as its ironic stances and the key of ambivalence on which the narrative is rung, it seems to me that if the novel translates a sense of loss, this cannot be overwhelming. *Things Fall Apart* can hardly be read as a wistful lingering over an elusive past; nostalgia is not a determining nor even constitutive element of its atmosphere. The intellectual disposition of the writer, if not his imaginative consciousness, operating at a level deeper than any ideological conception of his function, seems here to apprehend a decided lack of congruence between the past of the novel's reconstruction, reanimated as a function of cultural memory, and the imperatives of the present, even as the claims of that past to aesthetic significance are upheld, and its psychological value in countering the debilitation of the colonial situation is activated. We are made aware of the inadequacy of the overarching ethos by which the past was regulated, its limitations as embodied in historical forms, the inadequacy of this ethos and of these forms arising precisely from their mode of insertion in the world. Moreover, as Pierre Nora has pointed out, the phenomenon of memory exceeds the purview of history (Nora, 1989). In this particular context perhaps more than any other, the dynamics of cultural memory involve much more than reaching into a past; they also engage the present, insofar as the traditional culture upon which they are focused remains a vibrant contemporary reality. But while it continues to exert its force upon minds, the question remains how far the past can be invoked to legitimize the present, how far it is capable of functioning as a practical reference in the contemporary circumstances of African endeavor.

These, then, are some of the issues raised by Achebe's work. The point is that the novel genre serves Achebe as a mode of reflection upon the nature and significance of the African past and its relevance to the African present. In *Things Fall Apart*, this reflective tone is made evident in the conversations and dialogues he attributes to the elders of the tribe, who are thereby presented through the course of the narrative as minds engaged in a sustained deliberative process. The novel takes on a discursive character as it stages a running debate on customs and practices, on institutions and values, on systems of belief. This debate is in reality conducted as an interrogation of the human possibilities offered by the material world and mental landscape that together comprise the tribal culture and stamp it with a distinctive quality. Although this interrogation is presented as internal, it amounts ultimately to an objective scrutiny in the light of an alternative set of values that, in the nature of things, were not available to the subjects themselves. This scrutiny forms part of the implicit ideology of the novel, of the system of ideas presiding upon its organization, for which the Euro-Christian system of values begins to function as touchstone and measure. This is not to imply that the emphasis on Christianity as a factor of liberation authorizes us to read the work as a justification of the new religion, much less of colonial imposition, but rather we should view it as a mirror held up to African society, enabling a process of self-apprehension. In other words, a new African consciousness emerges through the mediation of the Christian/Western vision of the world.

The tension generated by the fundamental ambivalence of the novel's propositional content can be grasped most intensely at this level, for the process of self-reflection manifested in the novel is traversed by what one might call a deep cultural anxiety. This is nothing like the self-contempt displayed in Ouologuem's *Bound to Violence,* but it testifies to the way in which the need to validate the tribal culture in some emotionally satisfactory way runs up against the question of value, a question that is central to the order of meaning proposed by the novel. It is in this light that Obierika, who stands as the manifest antithesis of Okonkwo, can be said to function as the moral center of the novel. He comes closest among the novel's characters to a representation of what Michael Valdez Moses has called a "modern sensibility" (Moses, 1995, 113).[24] It is perhaps not farfetched to suggest that we have in Obierika not merely the one character with which, as Jeyifo points out, the novelist seems to identify but rather a subtle projection of the critical consciousness that Achebe himself brings to the imaginative conception of the novel (Jeyifo, 1991). The evidence of the novel lends enough weight to this view as to make it a matter of more than mere speculation.

Whatever the case, the debate enacted within the novel gives the work an analytical bent to which its initial ideological inspiration is ultimately subordinated, for *Things Fall Apart* testifies to a clear recognition of a decisive break in the African experience of history occasioned by the colonial fact. It hardly needs to be stressed that this recognition is far from committing Achebe to an acquiescence in the methods of subjugation employed by colonial agents, whether white or black, exemplified by the deception and humiliation described in the latter pages of the novel in which the historical grievance of Africa is vividly represented and dramatized in the martyrdom of Okonkwo and the Umuofia elders. The pathos of their situation resonates through the entire society, takes on wider meaning as nothing less than the suspension of the entire culture, the arrest of those activities that gave both energy and poetry to everyday life in Umuofia. All of this portends the stifling of the tribe's spirit by a collective trauma: "Umuofia was like a startled animal with ears erect, sniffing the silent, ominous air, and not knowing which way to run" (139).

The anticolonial thrust of the novel is unmistakable here, but it becomes evident as we reflect upon the novel as a whole that this is not all there is to the story of Okonkwo and of Umuofia. The novel ends with the hero's suicide, but there is no real closure, for the white colonial

officer's musings intimate a new and unpredictable future for the Umuofians and for the continent of which they form an integral and representative part. The import of the novel arises from this intimation, for
what *Things Fall Apart* registers ultimately is an acute consciousness of
the historical and cultural discontinuity occasioned by the colonial encounter in Africa and of its ontological implications—the necessity for a
new mode of being, of relating to the world.

It is one of the of the novel's peculiar traits that the historical realism
that directs the narrative progression harmonizes readily with the elegiac
mood that serves as its groundbase, a conjunction that is registered in
one of the most remarkable passages in the novel:

> That night the mother of the spirits walked the length and breadth of
> the clan, weeping for her murdered son. It was a terrible night. Not even
> the oldest man in Umuofia had ever heard such a strange and fearful
> sound, and it was never to be heard again. It seemed as if the very soul
> of the tribe wept for a great evil that was coming—its own death. (132)

The epochal significance of the passage is intensified and assumes cosmic
resonance in the lament that pours out of one of the characters, Okika,
at the final meeting of the clan: "All our gods are weeping. Idemili is
weeping. Ogwugwu is weeping. Agbala is weeping, and all the others"
(143). Okika's lament directs us to the heart of Achebe's novel: it is as an
elegy that incorporates a tragic vision of history that *Things Fall Apart*
elicits the strongest and deepest response.

Things Fall Apart inaugurates the imaginative reliving in Achebe's work
of those significant moments of the African experience, which he has
traced in his five novels to date. Given the comprehensive perspective of
inspiration and reference within which they are situated, these novels
compose a historical vision. Consequently, they pose the general theoretical question of the formal relation of the novel as a genre to the substantive fact of history, a relation within which the purpose of Achebe's
work can be said to inhere. Because of its unique place in Achebe's corpus
and in the African canon, *Things Fall Apart* presents itself as the indispensable point of departure for an examination of this question.

The transition of Achebe's style from an epic mode to one associated
with the novel provides an indication of the changing modes of this
relationship. This stylistic evolution of the novel may be interpreted as
the scriptural sign of a corresponding adjustment of the writer's vision,

reflecting his sense, as the narrative develops, of the pressure of history as it begins to exert itself upon the community that is the subject of the novel. This seems to accord with a Hegelian conception of history as the unfolding saga of modernity, with the modern novel as its imaginative equivalent. The received opinion stemming from these sources has tended to understand modernity as a historical phenomenon arising primarily from the Western experience and as the paradigm that commands the writing of scientific history and, as a consequence, the emergence of the novel, the literary genre that is thought to be most closely associated with modern culture. In this view, the novel as a specific modern genre affords a new medium for the construction in aesthetic and moral terms of a vision of a totality no longer immediately available to consciousness in the fragmented, reified world of modern civilization (Lukács, 1977).[25]

For the conception of history that underwrites the status of the novel alluded to above, the society depicted in Achebe's novel along with the culture it sustains appears as prehistoric, subsisting, as far as the record of its existence is concerned, on mythical narratives orally transmitted and therefore unworthy of the attention of serious historical scholarship. Consequently, it seems hardly appropriate as the subject of a novel in the normal acceptance of the term.[26] *Things Fall Apart* challenges this conception, for the whole purpose of Achebe's novel is to bring the existence of this culture into view as a historical reality, one that bears witness to the human world realized within it. The narrative mode, in both its epic aspect and at the novelistic level of articulation, affords Achebe the means of restating the grounded historicity of the African experience in a creative reconstruction of the stages of collective being.

It is of course true that the sequence of events narrated and the society and culture represented are products of an individual imagination, detached from any function of pure predication; the narrative unfolding of events conducted along a definite plot line is thus sustained by an aesthetic faculty that is fully engaged in Achebe's reconstruction. It is evident therefore that, despite their historical focus, *Things Fall Apart* and *Arrow of God*—the two novels need to be considered together on this point—are not only *not* histories in any ordinary sense of the word, they cannot be considered historical novels either, in the conventional or narrow sense of their dealing with real events in the past and featuring real historical personalities as characters.[27] But this sense is hardly satisfactory for an understanding of the narrative function, hence the need for a more inclusive conception, such as the one propounded by Hayden White, who posits a fundamental relationship between fiction and history as modalities of the narrative activity and process. The point is well clarified in the following observation regarding the significance of narrative as a universal phenomenon: "The affiliation of narrative historiography with literature and myth should provide no reason for embarrassment, . . . because the systems of meaning production shared by all three are distillates of the historical experience of a people, a group, a culture" (White, 1987, 44–45).[28] This suggests that the assimilation of fiction to history is authorized not merely in formal terms—what White calls "emplotment"—but also in content, insofar as in both cases, the real world of concrete experience features as a referent of the narrative. But here, we work with a special notion of referentiality peculiar to fiction, deriving from its enhanced value as symbolic representation of experience. To quote White again: "Thus envisaged, the narrative figurates the body of events that serves as its primary referent and transforms these events into intimations of patterns of meaning that any literal representation of them as facts could never produce" (45).

These remarks bear directly on Achebe's two novels, for they present themselves as acts of remembrance that entail an intense engagement of mind and sensibility upon a collective experience and thus move toward what White calls "an order of meaning." In specific terms, the two novels manifest an understanding of the essence of history as being bound up with momentous events that alter the collective destiny in ways that are unpredictable but prove ultimately definitive. These novels are informed by a profound sense of the radical contingency of history.

It is this deep intuition of history that, it seems to me, distinguishes Achebe's work from that of every other African writer. This distinction emerges clearly when we contrast the tone of *Things Fall Apart* with that of Francophone African writings roughly contemporaneous with it, especially the works of Camara Laye, Léopold Senghor, and Cheikh Hamidou Kane, all of whom have created in obedience to a paradigm of the self that privileges the ideal of wholeness. This accounts for the nostalgia for the past that pervades their work, an impossible longing for an earlier state of being denoted by Senghor's *le royaume de l'enfance*, a nostalgia further deepened by the religious/theological dimension it assumes in Kane's *Ambiguous Adventure*. It is not without interest to observe that a similar aspiration for an enhanced quality of being animates Soyinka's mythical evocations of origins (David, 1995).

Achebe's work registers a severe recognition of the compulsion upon the human estate of the historical process itself—what he has called "the power of events"—a compulsion that admits of only narrow margins for the play of human agency. It is this that I have called elsewhere "humane pessimism," which I believe Achebe shares with Joseph Conrad (Irele, 1987).[29] It must be understood, however, that this pessimism is not by any means a disabling one, for it does not imply a resignation born out of a passive suffering of events. It calls rather for a purposeful adjustment to those great shifts in the structure of the world that destabilize established constellations of thought, initiate a new historical process, and enforce therefore a new adventure of mind.

This seems to me the direction of meaning in Achebe's fiction, which, in its immediate reference, represents an imaginative remapping of the African experience within the space of history, the literary mode deployed as a means of shaping consciousness for the confrontation of the new realities on the horizon of African being. The ironies and the ambivalence that underscore the drama of cultural memory in his first novel emerge in a new light from this perspective, attesting to a somber consciousness but one resolutely oriented toward a future envisioned as pregnant with new possibilities. In other words, a utopian component underlies the expressive modalities and encompassing vision in *Things Fall Apart.*

In a limited sense, the utopianism of the novel is inseparable from the nationalist vein that, as I have suggested, informs the narrative and the project of modernity that is its concomitant. This is not to imply that Achebe's nationalism in this or other works advertises itself as a programmatic fixation upon an ideal future. However, the understanding of history that underlies his system of ideas implies, as its necessary complement, a vision of African renewal. Thus, a tacit correlation exists between Achebe's imaginative discourse in its utopian implications and what Arjun Appadurai has called "the mega-rhetoric of developmental modernization" of African and Asian anticolonial nationalism (Appadurai, 1996, 22). It is well to remember that Achebe continues to sustain in his fiction right up to the present moment this vision of new beginnings in Africa, as demonstrated by the conclusion of *Anthills of the Savannah.*[30]

But the utopianism of Achebe's fiction, as it begins to declare itself in *Things Fall Apart,* has a broader scope than is suggested by the materialist and utilitarian preoccupations of nationalism. It involves what the

Manuels have called "an idealizing capacity" as a defining property of the utopian imagination (Manuel and Manuel, 1979, 5). In this respect, it accords fully with the universalist interpretation of the utopian function of literature propounded by Fredric Jameson, whose reformulation of Lukács's categories of *conservative* and *progressive* expands their meaning in a new dichotomy between *ideology* and *utopia*. In this reformulation, intended to refurbish the terms earlier proposed by Karl Mannheim for historical and sociological understanding, the term *utopian* comes to designate the way in which literature, as a socially symbolic act, envisions the realm of freedom as a human possibility (Jameson, 1981).[31]

I will conclude then with the observation that what cultural memory delivers in Achebe's first novel is not so much a revalued past, recollected in a spirit of untroubled celebration, as, ultimately, the opening of the African consciousness to the possibility of its transcendence, to the historic chance of a new collective being and existential project. The sense of the tragic clings nonetheless to this consciousness, for Achebe is aware that this historic chance, if real, is at best limited and fragile. His vision is probably best expressed by the voice of the Oracle in his poem "Dereliction" (in the volume *Beware Soul Brother*) who invites his questing worshipers to a form of action, perhaps a collective affirmation, in the precarious space constituted by the strip of dry land between sea and shore at the ebbing of the tide:

> Let them try the land
> Where the sea retreats
> Let them try the land
> Where the sea retreats

Achebe's tragic vision of history is presented in these lines in tension with his utopianism. But to invoke the tragic dimension of Achebe's first novel is not merely to seek to uncover the full scope of its statement of the colonial encounter in Africa but also to reach for its contemplative character, the sense it contains of the general human condition.[32] It is this sense that is conveyed by Barthes's summation of the tragedies of Racine as "the aesthetics of defeat" (*l'art de l'échec*) (Barthes, 1963, 61). The description applies equally to all of the great tragedies of world literature, among which *Things Fall Apart* must now be seen to occupy a distinctive place. Beyond its reference to the personal dilemmas of Racine's characters, Barthes's phrase points to the apprehension by the tragic imagination of the essential fragility of our human condition. The deep insight that tragedy provides into this condition may well shake our being with fear and trembling, but it is the illumination and psychic release it generates that enable humanity to keep going. As a necessary component of its exploration of the African experience, *Things Fall Apart* embodies this fundamental truth of the imaginative vision.

Return of the Native

Edward Kamau Brathwaite's *Masks*

In his book *The Poet's Africa,* devoted to a comparative study of the poetry of Nicolás Guillén and Aimé Césaire, Josaphat Kubayanda moves from the general observation that "Africa is central to the Caribbean search for signification" to an examination of the ramifications of the African theme in the work of the two great Caribbean poets, not merely in its primary significance as a counterdiscourse to Western representations of the Black race but, more fundamentally, as a focus for an enlivening sense of antecedents beyond the degradation of slavery in the Afro-Caribbean consciousness. Kubayanda's analysis demonstrates that, for both Guillén and Césaire, Africa functions ultimately as a symbol of personal redemption and as a source of new poetic and spiritual values. In his final appraisal of the perspectives offered by the African vision in Caribbean literature as given expression especially in Guillén's redirection of the energies of Cuban *negrismo* and in Césaire's exultant *négritude,* Kubayanda singles out the work of Edward Kamau Brathwaite as the most significant extension of the expressive field defined by the poetry of the two older writers: "Of the contemporary Caribbean writers in English, the Barbadian Edward Brathwaite perhaps most effectively articulates the Negritude consciousness of 'race,' history, and language" (Kubayanda, 1990, 124).

Kubayanda's statement provides a first point of entry into Brathwaite's work, drawing attention as it does to the thematic connection between the earlier expression of Black racial affirmation, which was often centered on and colored by an African sentiment, and the directions of Brathwaite's poetry with its extensive and anguished exploration of the Black condition in the world system instituted by Western imperialism. Brathwaite's work thus represents a reformulation of the abiding preoccupations of Black literature in its most emphatic thrust; indeed, the fact that his poetry issues from the same climate of affective responses to a common experience and revolves around the moral preoccupations that the experience compels has determined an intertextuality reflected in the deliberate echoes of Guillén and Césaire, which amplify the tenor of Brathwaite's poetry.

We might infer from this conscious alignment of his work with that of his illustrious predecessors that Brathwaite has sought to give further resonance to a common theme of Black expression, pitched anew to the actualities of his own time and circumstance. But his poetry does much more than reformulate or even complement, by relocating its points of emphasis, an antecedent testimony of Black experience. Its importance resides in the fact that it offers the first and still the most comprehensive exploration of this experience in contemporary literature. With the publication of *Rights of Passage* (1967), Brathwaite brought a new dimension—as well as a new language—to a common theme, a dimension that consists of the expanded historical perspective that he projects upon the African experience in its full stretch from the Old World to the New. As is well known, this perspective was afforded him both by his professional training as an academic historian and by his personal experience of Africa as a material reality rather than as an imaginative or ideological construct.[1] It is primarily from this point of view that the volume *Masks* (1968), with its determined focus on the African foundation of diaspora Black history and consciousness, assumes its central significance for the poems from Brathwaite's first trilogy, *The Arrivants* (comprising *Rights of Passage, Masks,* and *Islands*), as indeed for the rest of his poetry.

Considering this significance, it is indeed curious that Brathwaite's second volume has so far received little critical attention. With the notable exception of perceptive essays by Samuel Omo Asein (1971) and Maureen Warner (1973),[2] commentary on Brathwaite's work has tended either to offer no more than perfunctory remarks on the volume or to ignore it altogether. Yet *Masks* represents the pivot around which the collective adventure recounted in *The Arrivants* revolves. The ritualized passage to some form of self-knowledge suggested by the title of the first volume only begins to take on its proper meaning in the second, in which the poet narrates in precise terms the phases through which he advances toward an integration of the self through a reconciliation with history. This process is merely hinted at in isolated passages of such poems as "Tom" and "Epilogue" in the first volume, but it receives its proper elaboration in the second, which lays the groundwork for the statement in *Islands* (1969) and in subsequent volumes of the moral imperatives dictated by the natural and cultural connections that bind the Caribbean to Africa.[3] What follows is an attempt to provide an explication of Brathwaite's *Masks* in its narrative movement, to indicate its principal points of articulation as well as its significance for the rest of Brathwaite's poetry.

The poems of *Masks* form a unified sequence centered on the African vision within the poet's articulation of the comprehensive historical awareness that informs all of his poetry, an awareness that takes root from an interrogation of the historical contingency of Black presence in the Caribbean and in the rest of the Americas. Brathwaite has explained in a lengthy interview the *primum movens* of his poetry in terms of this initial interrogative impulse: "How did we get into the Caribbean? Our people, the black people of the Caribbean—what was the origin of their presence in the Caribbean?"[4] In the sharp light of these questions, which Brathwaite put to himself, the inspiration for his poetry seems to be an effort to grasp the etiology, so to speak, of Afro-Caribbean experience. Brathwaite locates the essence of this etiology in the long history of voyages, which have shaped the adventure of his people. This fundamental perception, which presides over the composition of his first trilogy, provides the thematic and structural ground for all of Brathwaite's poetry. *The Arrivants*, in particular, is a sustained narrative of an African experience that originates on the mother continent and extends to the diaspora, an experience in which the marking elements of Black destiny have been brought together into a single existential perspective, each episode bearing upon the other and determining the direction and lived texture of the whole. The image of the voyage offers, then, a governing trope that organizes the poetic experience in Brathwaite's first trilogy; its implications are then pursued in his later work. This trope points to the apprehension of what one might call a "Black time," which involves a tragic and simultaneously dynamic conception of history in its immediate and forceful bearing not only upon African experience but also upon the processes of a universal history in which the Black race has been profoundly implicated.

The initial emphasis on the negative aspects of the historical experience that Brathwaite reconstitutes in *Rights of Passage* stems directly from the proximate circumstances of this history as seen from its provisional term in the New World, specifically from the poet's immediate grasp of its contemporary manifestations in the Caribbean. These are projected backward as the all-embracing determining context of the collective experience as in this passage from "Prelude," which opens *Rights of Passage*:

> Dust glass grit
> the pebbles of the desert:
> sands shift:
> across the scorched
> world water ceases
> to flow[5]

The trajectory of Brathwaite's historical imagination indicated in these lines is further detailed in the aptly titled poem "The Journeys," which reproduces the long unfolding of the African experience as a continuum apprehended as much in intellectual as in moral terms. Against this background, Brathwaite foregrounds, in "New World A-Comin'," the originating event of Afro-Caribbean existence, that of slavery and exile in America: "with the wind and the water / the flesh and the flies, the whips and the fixed / fear of pain in this chained welcoming port" (11). The bitter irony of the poem's title pervades the expression in this and other poems of the volume and is amplified in the concrete quality of the poet's evocations of the Black Diaspora on which the volume's keynote is steadily rung. These evocations build up—in the allusions, the imagery, and the manner of presentation—to an overwhelming sense of the fragmented consciousness and existential discomfort of the black populations in their American abode.

At the same time, Brathwaite's remarkable modulations of tone in *Rights of Passage* also register a range of perceptions of this existence in its quotidian particularities, the varied modes of its negotiation in the individual lives of its actors. This variable tonality of poetic voice enables the transition from irony to a focused moral concern in his delineation of the bleak magnitude of the historical predicament that commands his individual awareness. Moreover, a resistant imagination moves under the apparent despondency of Brathwaite's evocations, coming to the surface in the poem "South" in this forceful evocation of the Caribbean environment:

> But today I recapture the islands'
> Bright beaches: blue mist from the ocean
> Rolling into the fishermen's houses.
> By these shores I was born: sound of the sea
> Came in at my window, life heaved and breathed in me then
> With the strength of that turbulent soil. (57)

The density of Brathwaite's language in this passage breaks with the suggestive tentativeness of his idiom in the rest of the volume; here the lyric engagement with his native island looks forward to the self-constitutive and visionary import of the second trilogy, which begins with *Mother Poem* (1977). But although "South" ends with the prospect of "the limitless morning before us," there remains the insistent question related to what might be conceived as the Afro-Caribbean existential point of anchor, the question posed in these lines of "Postlude/Home," which, in its many variations, serves as the underlying refrain of the poet's song of exile in his first volume:

> Where then is the nigger's
> home?
>
> In Paris Brixton Kingston
> Rome?
>
> Here?
> Or in Heaven? (77)

With this question the archetypal figure of Tom, "father, founder, flounderer" (15), is confronted in his several incarnations in *Rights of Passage*. His portrait and the ruminations ascribed to him go to the problematic center of Afro-Caribbean experience; dissociation from the self as a result of centuries of harsh history and systematic denigration have instilled in him an enfeebled self-apprehension:

> For we who have achieved nothing
> Work
> Who have not built
> Dream

> Who have forgotten all
> Dance
> And dare to remember (13)

It is noteworthy that Brathwaite reformulates here Césaire's famous lines in *Cahier d'un retour au pays natal* as a paradox of historical being; he redefines the terms of existence of a constrained humanity as one that manifests itself in the act of remembrance, which is so essential to the vitality of his people's consciousness and historical will. In *Masks* the poet meets the challenge of his own reformulation of this integral humanity.

The six sections of *Masks* compose a narrative of the poet's pilgrimage—in the religious sense of the word—to the sources of the self; they adumbrate the *peripeteia* of the poet's reconnection with the physical and spiritual reality of the ancestral continent and with a universe of being that confirms the sacred compact between the poet as singular consciousness and the collective body of the race in its full historical personality. These two poles of awareness condition the poet's double register of address, the interaction between his two voices, the epic and the lyrical, which are inherent in the basic antiphonal scheme of the volume and highlighted in "Volta" and "The Golden Stool." These two voices, engaged in a dialogue with community and with self, correspond directly to that of the oral artist, the Akan *okyeame*, who recalls the drama of history before the dispersion of slavery and to that of the poet himself, who is involved in a reassessment of his personal relation to that history. In the counterpoint set up by these two voices, the process of rediscovery that *Masks* enacts is made palpable in the telling. The historical consciousness that the volume enunciates is not an abstract one; it is centered rather upon an experience that, in its poetic expression, entails a summoning of past deeds and events not only as historical markers of this experience but also as the affective traces they have imprinted upon the present moment of historical awareness.

Perhaps the most striking feature of *Masks* is the way its language is keyed to its theme of reconnection to the mother continent. The three poems that constitute the section entitled "Libation," with which the volume opens, establish the distinctive register of expression and sensibility to which the whole volume answers, a register consistent with its subject matter and its historical and cultural references. In these poems we witness the Caribbean poet becoming attuned to the specific modalities of the forms of expression through which a particular African community, the Akan, has long represented itself. The process implies, in the circumstances, nothing less than a reconversion of Brathwaite's poetic voice to the aesthetics of African orality, from which the poetic movement in *Masks* derives its essential impulse. This can be seen as a development of Brathwaite's radical approach to the Western poetic convention, already apparent in the invocation (in "Prelude") that opens *Rights of Passage* and repeated in the "Epilogue" that concludes the volume; an invocation in which Brathwaite transforms Vergil's opening formula of *The Aeneid (arma virumque cano)* into terms consistent with the theme and context of his own epic narrative:

> Drum skin whip
> lash, master sun's
> cutting edge of
> heat, taut
> surfaces of things
> I sing
> I shout
> I groan
> I dream. (4)

In its integration, then, of the poetics of the *atumpan* drum, Brathwaite's verse establishes a formal correspondence between the aesthetic and normative significance of African orality—to which he assimilates his poetic idiom in this volume[6]—and the diacritical convention of written literature, to which his poetic voice remains bound by reason both of its language of expression and of its material representation. The correspondence not only maintains throughout the volume a constant tension between the immediacies of orality and the inert textual reflexivity of literacy but also, and more significantly, dramatizes the performative impulses of the Caribbean poet's rite of initiation as he seeks to recover an ancestral domain.

The transformative potential of this rite as invested in the *atumpan* drum not only sustains an underlying epic tone in the transition from *Rights of Passage* to *Masks* (a tone heightened with singular effect in "Mmenson") but also constitutes the drum as analogue of the poetic word in its full compass of tone and signification:

> The Great Drummer of Odomankoma says
> The Great Drummer of Odomankoma says

That he has come from sleep
That he has come from sleep
and is arising
and is arising

like *akoko* the cock
like *akoko* the cock who clucks
who crows in the morning
who crows in the morning

we are addressing you
ye re kyere wo

we are addressing you
ye re kyere wo

listen
let us succeed
listen
may we succeed (98–99)

The terms of this invocation situate the poet at the dawn of consciousness and prepare us for the expansion this consciousness is to undergo
in the poet's reliving of his distant history. The section "Pathfinders,"
which immediately follows the invocation, constitutes the narrative core
of *Masks* and provides the emotional template of its development. In this
section, Brathwaite reappropriates and invests with imaginative life the
Akan myth of origin as preserved in their oral tradition: the violent up-
rooting of the original clan and its exodus from its early home near the
Red Sea (recounted in "Axum") and the ordeal of its members during
their long migration across the continent to their present site in the forest
region of contemporary Ghana. The purport of the three poems "Ouga-
dougou," "Chad," and "Timbuctu" (104–6) relates to the marking episodes along the route of this migration, but apart from the historic resonances of the place names,[7] the landscape they evoke by their titles is
constituted into an active agent in the poet's recall of the epic of his Akan
forebears. In a narrative involving mountain and plain, desert and forest,
the rivers emerge as the pathways of a relentless historical progression.
The reciprocity between the two voices constantly sounded throughout
the volume is given focus in "Volta" (107) to dramatize the questing spirit
that animates this progression, one that seems at first to allow for no
possibility of respite. In the event, the respite that does intervene, though
it is to prove ultimately a provisional phase in the collective drama of

the Akan people, serves as the principal point of historical reference for the poet's exploration of ethnic and cultural antecedents. This provides the theme of the next section, "Limits."

As *Masks* is pivotal to the thematic development of *The Arrivants*, so are the four poems of "Limits" central to the meaning of *Masks*. These poems focus on the tension between the creative energies that enabled the emergence of the Akan people as a nation and the ironies of history with which they have had to contend, the consequences of which form part of the historical legacy of the Caribbean. This tension is dramatized in the contradictory impulses suggested by the pairing of the four poems that make up the section. "The Forest" (112) narrates the settlement of the Akan at their present geographic location and their determined investment in a hostile nature ("the pistil journey into a moistened gloom") in the effort to fashion in their new location a distinctive mode of life, while "Adowa" (117), to which it is structurally linked, registers their triumphant achievement, even in the teeth of natural adversities and human perversities, of an ideal civilization, manifested by and celebrated in the life-enhancing art of the dance.[8] Both poems speak to the issue of rootedness, to the relationship between soil and people that informs the sense of community. "Techiman" (119) and "The White River" (121), on the other hand, emphasize the imponderables of history, which render this relationship an essentially fragile one. Brathwaite conflates past and present as he revisits the long slave route from the town of Techiman in the West African savanna to the coast and recaptures the agonies of the commerce in human beings, which is an inescapable part of his historical memory. At this point of Brathwaite's narrative, the image of the sea, at the very edge of the continent, incorporates the intelligence of history in which the entire narrative is grounded:

> This was at last the last;
> this was the limit of motion;
> voyages ended;
> time stopped where its movement began
>
> horizons returned inaccessible.
> Here at last was the limit;
> the minutes of pebbles dropping
> into the hourless pool. (122)

In its juxtapositon of moments separated in time, Brathwaite's imagination in *Masks* remains close to the details of place, which position these moments in the overall tapestry that his poems construct out of history. The "limits" of the general title of this section thus become expressive of the overlap of time and space in historical being. Lived out in the space between sea and desert at a moment of its most intense manifestation, at the same time they prefigure the subsequent abrogation of this being in a new dispensation (the "new world of want"), which has been inaugurated by the encounter between Africa and Europe—in other words, it is bounded in time.

The discontinuities in the African world that supervene upon this encounter set the context for the dilemma of identity that Brathwaite relates in the next two sections, which contrast with the tense but meaningful coherence of his previous evocation of the Akan world. The self-conscious stance that dominates the poems of the section entitled "The Return"—"whose ancestor am I?" (125)—stems from the displaced familiarity of the native son returning from a long exile: "you who have come / back a stranger / after three hundred years" (124). The perplexities that the encounter with Africa at first engenders in him, reflected in "The New Ships," and the discordances that he remarks in "Korabra," with its pointed allusion to the disruptive impact of Christianity ("Here Nyame's / tree bent, / falling before the / Nazarene's cross / Bells silenced the / gong-gong" [134]) lead to the pained realization of a depleted history, which is registered in the nodal poem "Masks":

> Your tree
> Has been split
> By a white axe
> of lightning;
> the wise
> are di-
> vided, the
> eyes
> of our elders
> are dead. (130)

In this powerful poem, the mask functions as the collective figure of the ambivalent impulses with which the poet grapples and to which the poems in the central sections of *Masks* offer open testimony. But if, in its primary references, the image denotes a fractured collective will that resulted from a disrupted history (of which slavery and colonialism are the evident signs) and the corresponding fissure in the Caribbean poet's consciousness as he regards what seems to be the inscrutable face of Africa

("Will / your wood lips speak / so we see?" [131]), it is also symbolic of the continent's inexpressible inner spirit, which lays upon the Caribbean poet the unavoidable burden of understanding. It is this burden that we watch him take up in the poems of the next section, "Crossing the River."

Brathwaite's pilgrimage as recounted in this section is as fraught with unresolved ambiguities as in "Techiman." In this section, however, the act of remembrance in *Masks* is most vividly realized through the poet's reabsorption into the myths of conservation, whose meanings are triumphantly deployed in the pageants of Ashanti royalty, pageants emblematic of an African culture in full and vital display:

> see the bright symbols he's clothed himself in:
> gold, that the sun may continue to shine
>
> bringing wealth and warmth to the nation
> mirrors of brass to confound the blind
>
> darkness; calico cloth to keep us from sin (141)

The measure of reintegration he achieves through his identification with the celebration of life represented by these pageants enables the poet to articulate his claim to a rediscovered lineage and thus to assume, with all of its contradictions, the common history it signifies, one that has determined his Caribbean existence:

> Can you hear
> Can you hear me
> blood's tissue
>
> curving tissue
> of cheek, bone
> wrapped with breath, eyes
>
> I remember so well?
> Why did our gold, the sun's
> *sunsum* safe against termites, crack
>
> under the white gun
> of plunder, bright bridge-
> head of money, quick bullet's bribe? (149)

No poem in *Masks* demonstrates as clearly as "Sunsum," from which the preceding passage is taken, that the volume is not so much a celebration of origins as a confrontation with history, an *excavation* of the poet's introspections, which lay bare the subterranean area of his Caribbean awareness, to which has been consigned its most conflicting affective symbols.

It thus becomes clear that, at the surface level of its meaning, Brathwaite's conflation of past and present in his poetry works to suggest that the Africa of his experience and imagination is not a continent envisaged from a range of pure detachment. Brathwaite's Africa is animated by a responsiveness to the vicissitudes of a collective experience that he discerns as formative of a historical baggage carried from the past into the present and, necessarily, by virtue of the cultural implications of this continuum, of a significant element of his condition as a sentient and reflective being.

Thus, *Masks* takes its place in the general scheme of Brathwaite's first trilogy as the record of his progression toward a renovated consciousness. The final section, "Arrival," takes the form of a recessional, which confirms the ritual of self-accomplishment to which the poems in the volume have been tending: "I am learning / let me succeed" (157). These final lines of *Masks* do not mark a closure, as we become aware from the sequel to the volume, *Islands*, which extends the "natural history" recounted in *Masks* into a social and spiritual vision related to the Caribbean condition and to which the third volume and Brathwaite's subsequent work are committed. If the general title, *The Arrivants*, which Brathwaite has given to this trilogy, is to be taken in its original sense of "to reach a shore," it remains the testimony of an uncompleted journey. With its revaluation of the folk, its validation of their cultural practices and especially their religious ceremonies as forms of life and as repositories of values, *Islands* inaugurates, within this trilogy, the denomination, even to the point of its dilation, of the Caribbean consciousness that Brathwaite undertakes in his second trilogy.[9]

The archetypal scheme of *The Arrivants*—with its tripartite structure around the themes of home, departure, and return—is thus significant as the record of the poet's movement of mind as he strives to keep faith with the historical principles of his Caribbean identity and is impelled to recover an original force that accords with the solicitations of his native environment. The point is articulated with an engaging delicacy in these lines from "Islands," the poem from which the stances in the volume are generated:

> So, looking through a map
> Of the islands, you see
> rocks, history's hot

```
lies, rot-
ting hulls, cannon
wheels, the sun's
slums: if you hate us. Jewels,
if there is delight
in your eyes.
The light
shimmers on water,
the cunning
coral keeps it
blue. (204)
```

The passage recalls the tone of "South," and its setting against the dep-
redations of time of an organic vision—the image of the sea, that constant of the Caribbean apprehension and imagination, serves to support
its full weight of implication—suggests a balancing of human history
against a more enduring natural history enacted by the environment.

The transient and the eternal are thus held in a metaphysical poise.
It is this thematic undercurrent of *The Arrivants* that comes finally to
receive due prominence in Brathwaite's second trilogy, *Other Exiles*,
Mother Poem, and *X/Self*. The convergence of the sense of location, which
commands Brathwaite's vision of the Caribbean, with the charged ancestralism precipitated by the African adventure enacted in *Masks* is registered in this passage from *X/Self* in which the image of the tree assumes
an eschatological significance:

```
there was a lull of silver
and then the great grandfather gnashing upwards
from its teeth
of roots. split down its central thunder
the stripped violated wood crying aloud its murder. the
leaves
frontier signals alive with lamentations

and our great odum
triggered at last by the ancestors into your visibility
crashed

into history[10]
```

The language here concentrates in its especial vigor the messianic intransigence of the volume. In its immediate reference to the Caribbean situation, it indicates the way in which the African vision enforces for Brathwaite that aboriginal intentionality that makes collectivities the true

agents of their history and so endows it with meaning for them. In this respect the poet's social function emerges in its full clarity not only as guardian of the collective memory but also as bearer of its informing energies and passions. Brathwaite's poetry invites us to consider the Caribbean in this perspective and suggests that, for all its having been the theater of a long and sustained negative experience, it must now be perceived as the site of possibility. His poetry is thus intended as the vehicle for the mobilization of minds for the project of renewal this perception entails, a project that is given vibrant expression in "Sun Song":

> i would leave dross
>
> i would say with césaire spark,
> i would say storm, olodumare's conflag.
> ration. I would speak twinkle
>
> spirit of the blaze
> red river of reflection
> vermilion dancer out of smoke and antelope
>
> i summon you from trees
> from ancient memories
> from the uncurling rust.le of the dead
>
> that we may all be cleansed[11]

The ritual imagery in this passage accentuates the religious connotations of Brathwaite's terms of dedication. It is a rite that connects him directly with Aimé Césaire, from whom he acknowledges his poetic descent and to whose voice he conjoins his own, in an invocation of a future that will register the urgent temper of an active collective consciousness.

9

A National Voice

The Poetry and Plays of
John Pepper Clark-Bekederemo

In considering the work of John Pepper Clark-Bekederemo, one of the most creative and forceful imaginative minds at work on the African continent today, it is perhaps best to start with a general observation, namely, that there are two distinct but related impulses behind his expression. The first is the necessity he felt to convey the uniqueness of his experience of place and time. It was not enough for him to write in an undifferentiated and falsely universal way; it was imperative rather to situate his expression so precisely, in terms of subject matter and specific references, as to impress upon it the mark of an individual consciousness in immediate and active relationship to its shaping environment. From this fundamental preoccupation derives the second impulse: to find the most adequate terms in which to capture the distinctive quality of his experience and thus to establish in his work both an individual vision and a personal tone of address. These impulses, as well as the particular circumstances in which Clark-Bekederemo's work has evolved, have imposed upon him the demands of a constant experimentation with language and form, so that the continuous adjustment of his expressive means to an unfolding pattern of experience represents an essential part of his creative project.

The problem of securing an original point of entry into literary expression raised by this preliminary observation is of course one that any individual contemplating a career of creative writing has to ponder. It is even more pressing in its implications for the would-be poet, who has to reckon with the peculiar demands of the genre in the necessary effort to make new meaning not only through the medium of the language he or she shares with the community but also within a literary tradition that designates a background of significance and valuations with which every new work has to contend in order to establish its own area of expressive being. In the case of the modern African writer, this problem becomes especially acute, complicated as it is by the language question. The creative process in this case has to proceed from an area of tension between the structures of expression of the two languages to which the writer is related: that of the writer's native environment, including the complex of symbols with which that language is pervaded, and the imported language, with the literary conventions that it sustains and that the African writer has been conditioned by Western education and all the other factors of the colonial experience to assimilate and to some extent internalize.

The evolution of modern Nigerian literature in English, of which Clark-Bekederemo's work represents both a major source of development and a significant instance, provides a specific illustration of the working out of this problem, of the challenge it has posed to our writers and the way in which this challenge has been met. Clark-Bekederemo's work derives its interest in part from this situation, and in order to fully grasp the nature of his achievement, it is useful to examine some of the factors that constitute the ground from which his work has issued.

We must start specifically with the problem of language, from what seems at first sight the anomaly of an African writer using a European language, in this case English, for a creative purpose. This is of course a situation that has been the subject of a long-standing debate in discussions of modern African literature. The range of linguistic, ideological, and critical issues involved in this debate need not detain us here, except to emphasize the point that English occupies a position that can hardly be considered peripheral to the social and cultural interests that constitute potent forces within the process of national integration in a country like Nigeria, engaged, like all new states, in an active quest for a binding mode of national identity.

The fact is that, for better or for worse, the English language has been bequeathed by history as a legacy to Nigeria. The random pattern of colonization that brought diverse ethnic and linguistic groups together within the confines of a single political entity, combined with the imposition of English as the reference language during the colonial period, accounts for the privileged position that the language still occupies today in the national life of the country. The extreme nature of the linguistic diversity of Nigeria has worked largely to reinforce this position, to such an extent that English serves not only as the language of government, commerce, and education but also, as a necessary extension of its function in these spheres, as the common medium of national discourse and, more important still, of cultural expression at anything beyond the restricted level of ethnic manifestations. There is thus a real sense in which English effectively worked its way into the fabric of the national consciousness as it began to take shape during the latter part of the colonial period and is still being constituted at the present time.

The internal role of English within Nigeria is complemented by the undoubted international scope of the language, for it must also be borne in mind that English, with its many variants, is not only a common language within Nigeria but is also a language that has become, in George Steiner's term, *extraterritorial*, and this in more than its purely utilitarian function. The significance of this fact for the African writer has often been stressed in terms of the widening of the potential audience for African literature that this situation promises. But it is by no means certain that this extrinsic factor is an important, or even a relevant, consideration in the use of English—or indeed of French or Portuguese—by African writers. The fact is that, for practically all of them, they have had no choice in the matter. What is more, the emphasis on the question of audience obscures the really decisive factor in the process of literary creation with which the language question is of necessity bound—the intrinsic one of form and modality of expression. The implications of this factor for the African writer have to do with the problematic relation that obtains among an African work in a European language, the established conventions of Western literature, and how this relation determines the modes of engagement of the writer with the African background. How does one formulate through appropriate metaphors an experience that is authentically grounded?

The gravity of the problem is highlighted in English-speaking Africa by the fact that education in English and the familiar acquaintance with the language that such education enables places the potential writer in direct touch with what has been codified as one of the most powerful traditions in world literature, a tradition that embraces the so-called authorized version of the Christian Bible and includes the works of writers such as Chaucer, Shakespeare, Milton, Bunyan, Wordsworth, Austen, Eliot, and Dickens (among many others) as its principal points of reference. It has to be borne in mind that the process of linguistic acculturation within the colonial educational system functioned in great measure through a managed encounter with the works either acknowledged or certified as classics within this literary tradition. The result was that the experience of literature itself was fostered in the educated segment of the African population by an almost exclusive reference to the literary tradition of English as it was represented by colonial education.

To recall these factors is to draw attention to the cultural repercussions of the colonial experience, in particular to its peculiar manifestations in the area of literary values and awareness. It also sets the background for the varying forms of approach to the use and domestication of the European languages, and in particular English, for literary purposes in the African context, especially for poetic expression. Thus, when Africans began to write poetry in the English language, they had before them as models the hymnal verses of Christian worship, with their traditional sentiments, standard rhymes, and regular rhythms, as well as the poetry of English Romanticism. The determining impact of a conditioning to this kind of literary fare is well illustrated by the productions of the first generation of English-speaking West African poets in the years before the Second World War and in its immediate aftermath; in the poems of writers such as Ralph Armattoe, Gladys Caseley-Hayford, and Michael Dei-Anang in Ghana, Abioseh Nicol in Sierra Leone, and Denis Osadebay and Mabel Imoukhuede in Nigeria. These writers, incidentally, are well represented in the historic anthology *West African Verse*, compiled by Olumbe Bassir and published by Ibadan University Press in the mid-1950s.

The term *pioneer* has come to be attached to this early phase in the development of West African poetry in English. It is a term that need not carry the somewhat patronizing connotation it now seems to have acquired, for although it cannot be said that these early poets were truly accomplished nor produced distinguished work, a good part of this early production offered what on any fair terms must be considered interesting material. If the language of Wordsworth, Keats, Shelley, and especially

Tennyson provided these poets with norms of expression, it did not by any means determine a facile imitation but served rather as the touchstone of a poetics that came readily for the expression of preoccupations that were fundamental to the self-awareness of the poets. These preoccupations were articulated mainly through the themes of cultural discomfort that led to self-discovery, on which much of this early poetry turned. Above all, the pioneer poets demonstrated that English could serve—indeed, *had* to serve—as a useful medium for the imaginative exploration of their lived situation.

It is now possible in retrospect to see how limiting in its possibilities was the idiom that was available to these early poets. It is not so much that this idiom had become outdated even as these poets were deploying its resources to address issues arising from their situation; the problem was that it could not sustain their expression beyond a certain range of perceptions and responses. It is this limitation that accounts for the rhetorical flatness this poetry evinces for us today, a limitation that the succeeding generation of poets knew it had to overcome if it were to produce work of more enduring value. This is the generation that arose in the late 1950s; having become conversant with recent developments in the metropolitan literature, these poets adopted in a deliberate way the new procedures offered for their expression in the African situation. In so doing, they were able to expand the scope of African poetry in English and thus to impart to it a wholly new temper.

Clark-Bekederemo's work stands out in this respect. What is more, it can be said to have assumed a specific historic significance in the evolution of Nigerian, and indeed, African poetry in English, for it is indisputable that his early efforts were central to both the thematic reorientation and profound transformation of idiom that led to the decisive advance that the new poetry came to represent. The context of development of Clark-Bekederemo's work in this new direction, which also accounts for the genesis of Nigerian literature in English, extends in its ramifications well beyond questions of literature. But it is with specific reference to his education in English literature at the University College of Ibadan, where he was a student in the late 1950s, as well as the singular nature of the cultural and social ambience of his experience there, that this development must first be viewed in order to understand the role he has played in the shaping of a poetic expression in English, which rendered the language properly responsive to the promptings of his particular environment.

Like similar institutions in British colonies in other parts of the world, University College, Ibadan, as it was known in its early years, was founded in 1948 with the aim of preparing colonial students for degrees from the University of London in a limited range of disciplines. It was perhaps to be expected that, in the circumstances of its founding, the institution was conceived essentially as an academic and intellectual outpost of the British empire, so that the curriculum was modeled closely, and in certain cases directly, on what obtained at the sponsoring university. It is therefore fortunate that in matters of literary study, London as an institution was relatively forward-looking, for the English syllabus devised for Ibadan, based on successive periods of English literary history beginning with the Renaissance, covered a range of authors and works, which extended to the writers of the 1930s and even beyond. The syllabus also took account of the critical revaluations that had occurred in English literary scholarship, so that it gave due prominence to the strong line of English poetry, which runs from Shakespeare and the metaphysicals through Robert Browning and Gerard Manley Hopkins into the moderns—Wilfrid Owen, W. B. Yeats, T. S. Eliot, and Ezra Pound—and right up to the work of the later generation represented by such poets as Dylan Thomas, W. H. Auden, and Stephen Spender. The tag "Spenser to Spender" seems appropriate to describe the syllabus and to provide a fair idea of its comprehensive scope.

In making a large place for modern poetry, the English syllabus at Ibadan offered in particular an extensive introduction to what, in his book of that title, C. K. Stead has described as "the new poetic." This new poetic reflected a profound change in sensibility, which was also manifested in other genres as a pervasive tone of vision and expression, one that defines the general character of modernism as a distinctive movement in twentieth-century English literature. The novels of Joseph Conrad, D. H. Lawrence, Virginia Woolf, and James Joyce, which form a significant part of this movement, therefore also received considerable attention in the course in English offered at Ibadan during this period. No less important than the primary literature was the criticism that developed alongside this movement, represented in particular by the theoretical work of I. A. Richards, the essays of T. S. Eliot, the criticism of F. R. Leavis, and the scholarship of William Empson. English studies at Ibadan thus reflected the results in the postwar period of the movement toward a reorganization of the discipline as an area of serious academic endeavor.

We might add that the syllabus also provided a perspective beyond the British literary scene. It afforded the possibility in particular of an encounter that was more than casual with American literature, especially the drama of Eugene O'Neill, Tennessee Williams, and Arthur Miller, as well as aspects of continental European literature. Apart from the corpus of classical Greek drama, which was read in translation, one could also make a productive encounter with other important texts of contemporary Western literature—the novels, say, of Camus or the plays of Ibsen. The drama of Bertolt Brecht in particular was a singular revelation, which has left a permanent impact on the Nigerian dramatic scene.

These references have an immediate relevance for a consideration of Clark-Bekederemo's development, for they indicate the immediate influences that shaped the tenor and determined the direction of his work. For there is no question that, but for his encounter as an undergraduate with European modernism in its dynamic relation to the tradition of Western literature and in its specific extensions as described above, his horizons would have been confined within the narrow limits prescribed by the conventional expression in English to which he had been conditioned by his previous education. The moderns, on the other hand, introduced him to a new and distinctive experience of literature. Their poetry in particular opened up perspectives of expression and new possibilities in the language. It is well to consider in this respect the way in which the dimensions of form, thrown into sharp relief in the more subtle exploration of the resources of imagery and the greater reliance on strategies of paradox and irony, on suggestive allusiveness, even at the risk of obscurity, came into new prominence in modernism. This made for a complexity of statement, which produced a more demanding kind of poetry, one that sought to formulate in language an expanded response to life in order to achieve the wholeness of experience envisaged in the fairly prescriptive terms of Yeats's definition of creative endeavor in language: "Blood, imagination and intellect running together." And one way in which the conjunction of these elements could be assured was through a recourse to myth, which came to be viewed as the deep foundation of the imaginative consciousness itself.

The impact of the new literature on Clark-Bekederemo can be measured as much by his conscious assimilation of the idiom of modernism, which can be felt in the movement of his work, especially in the early poems, as by the specific echoes that can be picked out from individual passages. The presence of such echoes further reflects a method that he took from the moderns, Pound and Eliot in particular: the deliberate deployment of literary references in one's own work as a way of enforcing one's own meaning, a constructive use of what has come to be known as *intertextuality*. Behind this method lay a conception of poetic practice, which he also came to embrace and which implied an acute consciousness of craft. The encounter with modern poetry thus entailed for him a serious apprenticeship of poetic technique, a heightened awareness of the process involved in fashioning words into an organic unity of form in order to reflect the full press and to convey the original tonality of his poetic experience.

Perhaps more than anything, Clark-Bekederemo's initiation into the new poetic also led him to the recognition that, in the African context, the question that confronts the writer with a serious creative purpose in English becomes more than the adaptation of the imported language to the realities of the new environment; it involves rather a total appropriation in order to bring African expression into a living relationship with the tradition of literature in English over its entire range of development, a gesture moreover centered especially upon the sharpest manifestations of this tradition. We might note in this respect that his attitude toward the use of English goes further in its implications than that of Chinua Achebe, who speaks of making the imposed language "carry the burden" of his African experience. Clark-Bekederemo on the other hand stakes out a more extensive claim to the resources offered by the English language and its literary tradition, as is made clear by the lead essay, "The Legacy of Caliban," in his collection *The Example of Shakespeare*. In the endeavor to make good this claim, the compulsion he felt to assume for his individual expression a linguistic and literary legacy that had become available to him, however indirectly, Clark-Bekederemo helped to inaugurate a new kind of Nigerian poetry in English.

The personal effort itself must, however, be related to the total context of Clark-Bekederemo's development for an appreciation of its wider social and historical significance—to the cultural and intellectual climate that defined the collective ethos at Ibadan during his student days and from which his early work emerged. The word *renaissance* is perhaps too elevated to describe this context, but my personal recollection of the prevailing atmosphere at the university at that time is dominated by the tremendous sense of excitement with which, as students, we lived our experience of university life. That we were a tiny handful meant that we not only formed a closely knit community, we were inevitably affected by the distinct character of privilege that access to higher education took on for us in our particular circumstances and that every aspect of life at the university was designed to emphasize.

If the excitement we felt had an essentially social basis, much of it also had an intellectual source, which arose from our introduction to the humanities in their Western formulation, and we approached our studies with an ideological innocence that was nearly complete. This attitude may appear in retrospect surprisingly naive and even inexplicable; the truth, however, is that many of us were struck with a genuine astonishment at discovering structures of knowledge and ideas to which we came with practically no previous background or preparation; their impact on our minds was for that reason all the more forceful. Moreover, the remoteness of the intellectual culture to which we were being diligently assimilated by our largely British mentors to the actualities of our environment and the conditions of our existence endowed that culture with nothing less than the appeal of an attractive ideal.

This state of mind induced by our experience at the university came to be embodied and to assume a peculiar character in the English Department at Ibadan. Although there was no organized movement with a well-defined program, there existed among students of English a self-consciousness that came to be crystallized around *The Horn*, the student poetry magazine that Clark-Bekederemo edited in its first year of publication, from 1957 to 1958. When his poems began to appear in the pages of this modest production, they made a strong impression in student circles, and the long poem "Ivbie" to which an entire number of the magazine was devoted, even provoked a storm because of the uncompromising boldness of its imagery. What was in evidence in these poems was their confident appropriation of the modern idiom. Their radical departure from the previous efforts at producing African poetry in English with which we were acquainted was immediately apparent to all. Moreover, the self-assurance that went with the manifested quality of his talent gave these poems a distinctive accent among the cluster of voices that found their first expression in *The Horn*.

The magazine eventually developed into something more than an outlet for new poetic talent; it came as well to function as a medium of intellectual reflection and in particular as a forum among the students for debate about the place of culture in the new Nigerian nation that we felt, as if in our very pulses, was coming into existence. The underlying issue in this debate was the idea of culture as the condition for the refinement of the individual spirit and even for a conception of a decent way of life; the influence of Matthew Arnold's *Culture and Anarchy* was decisive here. Though focused primarily on literature, our preoccupations concerned the place and transformative potential of the arts in our society.

The atmosphere at Ibadan in the late 1950s and early 1960s encouraged the cultural concerns and aesthetic inclinations the magazine highlighted. The university had become a focal point of cultural activities oriented exclusively toward Western forms; indeed, by the late 1950s, it was a veritable island of Western culture in a vibrant sea of native life. *The Horn* devoted a considerable part of its content to reviews of university productions of plays, concerts, and operas and thus reflected in its pages the intense character of this activity and its foreign orientation. In this way, and combined with its devotion to poetry, the magazine not only fostered a cult of literature but also promoted an aestheticism that came in the circumstances to be associated with the discipline of English.

Although the cultural orientation at Ibadan during this period can be said to have had its beneficial aspect, insofar as it favored the cultivation of a cosmopolitan awareness, it carried in the immediate context of its publication the grave implication of an exclusivity whose social consequence amounted to a narrow elitism. Moreover, the heady character of the atmosphere in which we moved tended to obscure for us the moral and spiritual risk involved in the process in which we were so clearly caught up: the active formation of an elite taking its intellectual and cultural bearings from the West and becoming disengaged as a result from its own cultural and human milieu.

It may seem therefore paradoxical to state that *The Horn* also provided a way out of this incipient drama of alienation. For while it reflected cultural and artistic preoccupations that were oriented by Western references, it also functioned as the vehicle of a cultural nationalism, which implicitly challenged the primacy of Western expressions in the modes of apprehension to which we were being conditioned by our education. Two factors seem to me to have been responsible for this possibility of its playing apparently contradictory roles. In the first place, the engagement with foreign culture, for all the genuine enthusiasm we brought to it and the unabashed satisfactions it procured for us, left us ultimately with the profound sense of being unhoused in the realm of culture. If therefore we were to achieve any degree of balance in our imaginative experience and in our intellectual and emotional life—in other words, any form of true integration—we had to create forms of expression that conformed as closely as possible to the genuine conditions of life within our society. These forms had furthermore to embody an originality of expression distinctive enough to exert a countervailing force to the inclination toward the simple mimetism to which we were subject.

The second factor provides an ironic reflection upon the literary culture to the promotion of which the English Department at Ibadan was committed. As a concession presumably to the African milieu in which they operated, our British teachers introduced into the syllabus some literary works written by European writers employing either wholly or in part an African setting, notably Conrad's *Heart of Darkness*, Graham Greene's *The Heart of the Matter*, and Joyce Cary's "African" novels, *Aissa Saved* and *Mister Johnson*. Our reaction against these works was predictable and was as much a function of the largely negative image of Africa we encountered in them as of the obvious inadequacies we could immediately identify in their depiction of human situations in the African context, the limited and even unfeeling grasp these works displayed of the true texture of life in the African environment they sought to represent. It is instructive to recall in this connection Chinua Achebe's testimony that his motivation for writing *Things Fall Apart* was the need he felt to contradict the image of Africa and of Africans in the novels of Joyce Cary. Although Achebe had left the university well before Clark-Bekederemo entered Ibadan, his classic novel grew in part from the same reaction to the European literary discourse on Africa for which *The Horn* provided an avenue of expression.

It is no exaggeration to affirm that the poems we published in *The Horn* represented in their own way a contestation of the literary deformation of Africa in European literature devoted to the continent. They were the signs of a movement toward a more authentic expression of the African milieu in literature than was afforded by these European works. There was an evident purposefulness to the efforts of the contributors to the magazine: to develop a literature in English that was a truer reflection of the context of life within which they were located.

Because, for imaginative expression, the format of the magazine could only accommodate poetry, it was in this genre that the creative among us responded to a need that had made itself imperative. It is easy to understand the way in which the new poetic of modernism was suited to the project implicit in these endeavors, for it facilitated a reworking of the language in order to make it conform to the requirements of an expression centered upon our milieu and experience. There remained, then, beyond the exhilaration of our discovery of modern literature the challenge of applying its forms to the expression of our particular situation, the challenge precisely that lies behind the impulse to innovation that inspired the poets of *The Horn*, none more so than Clark-Bekederemo.

No less important in the cluster of effects that helped to foster this new literary awareness was the appearance at this time of the early numbers of the review *Black Orpheus*, edited by Ulli Beier and published by the recently established Ministry of Education of the Western Region of Nigeria at Ibadan. Through this review, located at our doorstep, as it were, we made the acquaintance of Black literature in the diaspora and of the Negritude movement. The review brought to us in an admittedly thin but nonetheless impressive stream excerpts in English, translations of representative samples in other languages, and critical essays devoted to the major writers. The publication of James Kirkup's sensitive English translation of Camara Laye's *The African Child* came at this time as a further revelation of the possibility of an authentic literature of African inspiration. Although these writers could not feature in our academic program, we read their works as they came to us with a ready passion, so that Langston Hughes, Countee Cullen, Nicolas Guillén, Aimé Césaire, Léon Damas, and Léopold Sédar Senghor soon became more than names to us; they opened up new horizons of thought and awareness of immediate import to our status and existence as colonial subjects. Their example promised nothing less than a form of initiation, in the truest sense of the word, into a universe of the imagination that we could enter with a wholeness of response. We felt through their works a sense of connection to a wider community of sentiment, to an affirmative impulse in which we had a feeling not only of being participants but also of having the seal of validity placed upon our own humble efforts.

When, therefore, in 1958, a double bill of Wole Soyinka's plays *The Lion and the Jewel* and *The Swamp Dwellers* was produced by the student dramatic society at the University Arts Theatre, it came as a welcome justification of our expectations. The plays went to the heart of our enthusiasms, so that we experienced the production as a landmark event in our cultural experience. It was about this time also that Chinua Achebe's *Things Fall Apart* appeared, which confirmed most impressively the point of our reaction against the European fictions of Africa and our intimation of a gathering movement toward the creation of a national literature. It must be remembered that Amos Tutuola's *The Palm-Wine Drinkard* had been published a few years earlier, and contrary to the impression that has been given of its having received a hostile reception in Nigeria, the work was in fact regarded with genuine admiration by the discerning part of the reading public there, which was certainly appreciable. At all events, the appearance of these works indicated, albeit in a rather scattered fashion, the constitution of a new literary expression among us. This was a development that seemed to us at the time highly propitious, for it was closely linked in our minds with our political hopes; the genesis we were witnessing of a national heritage of literary expression original to us could only herald the advent of the national community of our vision.

Soyinka, who had earlier been a student for two years at Ibadan before proceeding to Leeds for his degree, returned from England the year after the Ibadan production of his two plays to take up a position as research fellow in the English Department. It was in the student room made available to him on the campus of University College, Ibadan, and against the background of the charged atmosphere of expectation in the months immediately preceding Nigerian independence, that Soyinka wrote *A Dance of the Forests*, the play with which he sought to mark, in his own individual way, the historic import of the impending occasion.

The formal end of Nigeria's colonial status to which we all looked forward duly took place on the first of October 1960. In the ten years or so before that event, Nigeria went through a process of transformation of such magnitude that the period can be considered a truly momentous one—possibly, from the social point of view, the most significant—in the country's history. Constitutional changes leading to internal self-government provided the political setting for a determined modernizing effort marked by extensive economic initiatives, an effort that was epitomized by the tremendous expansion of education in the Western Region, an example that was quickly adopted by the government of the Eastern Region (Krieger, 1987). The period thus witnessed a social revolution that has had far-reaching effects. But the most distinctive feature of the time was psychological in its nature and effect, marked by a powerful release of energies that contributed to the euphoria of the times, a distinct collective feeling that swept the country. We were keenly conscious of being engaged in a historic process; we were recovering the existential initiative that colonial rule had denied us.

It was inevitable that the larger political and social background of life beyond the university should have had a direct impact on the outlook and thinking of students at Ibadan. The confident progress the country was making toward independence tended to have a muting effect on anticolonialist feeling in student circles, but as the ideological stance of Clark-Bekederemo's "Ivbie" indicates, these feelings were not altogether absent; indeed they formed an undercurrent to the dominant mood of optimism that prevailed among the students. Although the privileged status conferred by our education induced in us a feeling of self-importance, this feeling went undeniably with a strong sense of responsibility for our own society, for we were also ardent nationalists, passionately committed to a vision of our country's future. It is true that the signs of ethnic tension presaging difficulties in the process of nation building had begun even at this time to be visible, and there was reason for a certain foreboding concerning the future. This did not, however, make any appreciable impression on our minds as we looked forward with enthusiasm to independence and to a new future for our country.

The fervid atmosphere I have evoked here was reflected in the pages of *The Horn*. It is not too much to claim, in relation to its immediate function as a channel of literary expression, that this modest student magazine had a part that was far from negligible in the education of sensibility that prepared the ground for the development and reception of a national literature in Nigeria. The early work of Clark-Bekederemo, which was for some three years the major animating force of *The Horn*, went on to exert in this development a powerful and enduring influence. But beyond this limited perspective of the magazine's role, the cultural assertion that took place under its auspices can now be seen, despite its limited scope, as the manifestation of a profound reconversion of consciousness among the new elite of Nigeria as it was being formed at the country's foremost intellectual center.

The literature that began to be produced in this period by this elite grew out of various pressures, which converged on the minds of its most articulate members and reflected the factors at work in their objective social and cultural situation. This initial immersion of Nigerian literature in the realities of the national experience has remained a prominent feature of its subsequent development, manifested by its steady reflection of the vicissitudes that have marked the course of Nigerian history in the postcolonial era. This fact places Clark-Bekederemo's work in a particular perspective, for his writing exemplifies in a remarkable way the interaction of literature with the determining factors of the Nigerian experience, their coming together to form an instructive narrative of African destiny in modern times. His work needs therefore to be viewed against the political, social, and intellectual background I have sketched here for an understanding not only of its beginnings but also of its evolution in terms both of theme and form.

Clark-Bekederemo has invoked, as the justifying principle of his creative work, an Ijo saying that applies to his own immediate situation in the Nigerian context: "Two hands a man has." The invocation has a primary significance, which derives from the intimate linguistic and cultural connections he enjoys to two of the most prominent ethnic groups in the Niger Delta, the Ijo and the Urhobo. The fact that he has devoted his energies to a scholarly presentation of the impressive tradition of oral poetry and performing arts of these two groups attests to the way in which this double legacy of his indigenous background has been brought into fruitful connection with the other large frame of reference established for his experience by his Western education. The principle of complementarity suggested by the Ijo saying also governs his creative work in English. This can be seen in the way his work conciliates the two planes of awareness and of realization—of theme and of expression— which enable a mutual reinforcement of their respective modes of significance. The fact that much of his work, in particular the plays, revolves around the life and lore of the Niger Delta suggests that this area of the country, with its distinctive landscape and the symbolic associations it generates, functions not merely as a setting for his work but as its informing spirit, opening for his imagination a singular perspective on the world.

The issue that seems to have confronted Clark-Bekederemo at the outset of his writing career was how to localize his expression by making the English language inhabit, as it were, the spirit of the Niger Delta as it communicated itself to his imagination. A clear progression can be discerned in his approach to this issue throughout the evolution of his work, a process that begins to come into view in his early poems. These poems are mostly set pieces, explorations of landscape and situation in an imaginative effort to establish a sense of place. They provide an insight into this initial direction of Clark-Bekederemo's inspiration, the way in which he began to work his way toward an active redeployment of the English language to serve expressive ends removed from its "natural" setting and thus to invest the adopted language with a new significance.

It is of particular interest in this respect to observe the way in which, in the poem "Night rain," we are led by the evocation and the imagery from one level of meaning to another, transitions by which its theme is dramatically amplified and its structure of imagery given an extension of reference. At an obvious level, it presents a vivid rendering of a concrete scene: a tropical storm and its effects on a humble household. The image of the mother filled with solicitude for her children intervenes at the central point in the movement of the poem to give focus to the descriptive details through which the poem's setting is elaborated; "roof thatch," "wooden bowls and earthenware," "roomlet and floor," and "loosening mat" all suggest an appropriate background to the enactment of specific life in the poem. The conventional metaphor in which the raindrops are first perceived as beads on a rosary gives way to another, which registers a more sharply perceived detail of indigenous life:

> She moves her bins, bags and vats
> Out of the run of water
> That like ants filing out of the wood
> Will scatter and gain possession
> Of the floor.[1]

The second level of meaning in the poem emerges from this background of acute apprehensions. The transition from concrete evocation in the first part to the symbolic import of the second part is marked in the transfer from the limited sense that the word *drumming* is given in the early part of the poem to the more comprehensive meaning it acquires, denoted by "over all the land" in the latter part. The word in effect receives a new value, which reflects the change in perspective that takes place within the poem. The transition it signals turns in the most natural way on the image of the mother, an image that becomes magnified in its implied association with the landscape, itself powerfully invoked at the end of the poem as its ultimate reference. The setting thus assumes a primal quality, which in turn lends due force to the telluric terms of the confident affirmation of the poet's sense of being in the closing lines:

> So let us roll over on our back
> And again roll to the beat

Of drumming all over the land
And under its ample soothing band
Joined to that of the sea
We will settle to a sleep of the innocent and free. (311)

When this structure of transitions in imagery and reference is properly considered, it is not difficult to read the entire poem as a reliving of the movement of consciousness from which the whole meaning of the poem proceeds, as a statement therefore of the poet's ambivalent cultural situation and as the working out of an imaginative mode for its resolution. In this reading, the progression from the confused awareness of the opening lines ("doped out of the deep") to the exultant accents of the poem's final statement can be seen to recount an adventure with a supremely personal significance.

What emerges at once in "Night rain" is Clark-Bekedermo's assured handling of setting, a quality that is displayed even more clearly in such poems as "Fulani cattle" and "Girl bathing." In "Fulani cattle," the evocation of the long march of the cattle as they are driven on the hoof from the North to the South across the vast expanses of the Nigerian landscape affords an occasion for a graphic presentation of contemporary life in the country over a wide range of social and economic manifestations, an evocation that is then given an arrestingly contemplative turn at the end of the poem. With "Girl bathing," the pictorial associations of the title alert us to the temptation to facile exoticism presented by the subject, a temptation deliberately confronted and avoided in this poem, which builds on a cardboard image of Africa in order precisely to complicate and to give it a fuller and richer dimension. The tone of sensuality in this poem, channeled through the play of imagery as well as through the effects of rhyme and verse design, is felt to attach as much to the bathing girl, who is the immediate subject of the poem, as to the visual frame of her presentation. Thus, although "Girl bathing" makes no overt ideological point, the theme of renewal, which the poem intimates, can be said to involve the poet himself, so that the imagery and the meaning it sustains become expressive of his project of intense valorization on a broader front of references and allusions. The fact that the poem brings to mind David Diop's "Rama Khan" and Léopold Sédar Senghor's "Femme noire" is not without significance for this reading.

The aesthetic foundation of Clark-Bekederemo's project is thrown into sharp relief by the impressionistic style of "Ibadan dawn," in which the atmospheric quality of the evocation becomes the condition for its realized sense of ceremonial, its urging of a vital relation between the communal consciousness and the immediate framework of life. The notations in this poem provide the background for the compacted imagism of the justly famous shorter poem "Ibadan." And the vitalism that is suggested in "Ibadan dawn" is elaborated into pansexualism in "The year's first rain," a poem remarkable for its density of statement and the scope of the energies it celebrates.

It becomes obvious as we consider the pattern of imagery in these and other early poems that they are more than nature poems in the usual sense of the term; they articulate rather an active engagement of the imagination with the poet's environment. And their essential burden is their intuition of a process of coming to birth, an element of the poet's expression that is directly evocative of his own developing awareness.

The self-recognition implied by this element of the poems is dramatized in "Agbor dancer." Here, the theme turns on explicit statements of the relation between the poet's two orders of reference: the self-description "early sequestered from my tribe" stands in inverse relation to the notation "ancestral core" associated with the female dancer; both serve as opposed terms in a dialectic of identities unfolding in the poet's mind. Thus, the poem presents us with self-reflection in a manner approaching that of the French-speaking Negritude poets. The querulous and agonized tone that pervades their expression is, however, absent here; the interrogation of the final stanza does not dramatize a sense of conflict but underscores rather the affirmative insistence, emphasized by the Yeatsian ending—comparison with the final lines of "Among Schoolchildren" is inescapable—upon the significance of the dance itself, its projection of the dynamic interaction of body and mind with the world of nature:

> Could I, early sequestered from my tribe
> Free a lead-tethered scribe
> I should answer her communal call
> Lose myself in her warm caress
> Intervolving earth, sky and flesh (311)

These lines suggest a "neo-Africanism" inherent in all of these early poems—inherent rather than advertised, an underlying foundation of ideas, perceptions, and responses from which the thought, the themes, and the imagery proceed. We might say that an essential African sentiment animates these poems, manifested in a traditionalism that is counterpoised against a threatening estrangement of the poet's consciousness. This element of the poetry is however not worried into significance but impresses itself on us forcefully both as the tacit recognition of an assumed background and as the effect of experience. In other words, it is not pursued as in Okigbo's *Havensgate* into a drama of cultural self-retrieval nor, as in Soyinka's *Idanre*, elaborated into a comprehensive mythology proposed as a reference of a collective spirituality. Clark-Bekederemo's neo-Africanism functions rather as an all-inclusive framework of immediate perception, one that serves first and foremost to *place* his expression and thus to establish its natural context of vision, an original perspective for a reappraisal of his universe.

This unforced way of relating to the traditional background makes for the poignant interest of the poem "Abiku." There is no attempt within the poem to explicate the concept on which its theme of deprivation and weary resignation is based, to elaborate upon its meaning nor to connect it with the belief system of which it forms a part. The comparison here with Soyinka's poem of the same title becomes inevitable in this regard. *Abiku* is a Yoruba word meaning literally "born to die" and, in the context of a high rate of infant mortality, of successive pregnancies and deliveries, it came to furnish the concept for what is believed to be the repeated reincarnations of the same child in the same woman. This is for Soyinka the starting point for the weaving of an elaborate conceit around the emblems with which the capricious child is associated. With Clark-Bekederemo's poem, the meaning issues directly out of the enacted moments of the evocation. Thus, the *abiku* concept does not feature as an object of poetic or speculative interest in itself; it is endowed rather with a deep relevance to the human situation that is the subject of this poem and is made to carry the burden of personal emotion. It appears less as an accessory than as the foundation for the poet's meditation upon a singular form of tragic predicament.

The point here is that in none of these poems does Africa feature in a direct or self-conscious way as the subject of Clark-Bekederemo's expression. There is no deliberate approach to origins in the grand rhetorical manner of Senghor, in the hieratic mode of Okigbo, nor in the mystical mode of Soyinka. Africa assumes a presence in these poems not as an abstraction but within particulars that make up a texture of life, as a natural environment peopled with a human existence that the poet endeavors to bring to imaginative life.

The long poem "Ivbie," with its explicit polemical intent, offers the one notable exception to this observation. "Ivbie" is a poem that deserves extended treatment for a proper clarification of its complex network of allusions and an appreciation of its deep impulses. But even a cursory reading cannot fail to point up its problematic nature. It is what we might call a protest poem, for its theme connects directly to the historical context of Black literature, as this bitter allusion to the devastation of slavery and colonial exploitation makes clear:

> Those unguent gums and oils
> Drawn in barrels off to foreign mills
> The soil quarried out of recognition
> As never would erosion another millenium
> The blood crying for blood spilt free
> From keels away on frothing sea
> The dark flesh rudely torn (322)

"Ivbie" lacks, however, the true vehemence of other works of Black protest literature that come to mind. Two reasons can be advanced for what appears to be the relative detachment of tone that we observe in the poem. The first seems to me to be a function of Clark-Bekederemo's adoption of Eliot's style for much of his expression here, a move that betrays him into the occasional solemn abstraction, which is at odds with the emotional requirements of his theme, as in these lines with which the second movement opens:

> In the irresolution
> Of one unguarded moment
> Thereby hangs a tale
> A tale so tall with implications
> Universal void cannot contain
> The terrible immensity
> Nor its permanence dissolve
> In the flux wash of eternity. (322)

It is not apparent that there is a vital progression from these lines to the poet's denunciation of colonial violations quoted earlier, yet it is to this denunciation that it is meant to serve as introduction. There appears to be, therefore, a discrepancy between the dry manner of Eliot's style, which is here coopted for Clark-Bekederemo's expression, and the inspirational ground of his poem. This discrepancy between matter and manner produces throughout the poem an impression of contrivance, which seems to me to detract from its overall impact. The introduction of the Ijo deity Oyin, who recalls the blind seer Tiresias in Eliot's *The Waste Land*, is a case in point; there is an arbitrariness to the device that is clearly more distracting in its effect than contributory to a proper organization of the poem's system of references and its general emotional tone.

The second reason is related to this last observation and has to do with the way the urgency of the theme of protest is diminished by the context in which we encounter the poem. The focused evocations of Clark-Bekederemo's early poems generate such a field of collected force that the song of lament that "Ivbie" aspires to be is undermined in its significance by the spontaneous vigor that these poems communicate. We come to feel that the overwhelming sense of personal presence in the other poems has become in the long poem little more than a gesture of self-dramatization. The nature of the cultural malaise to which "Ivbie" gives voice appears in this light to be somewhat factitious, too rhetorically presented (as in the echo of Shakespeare's *Macbeth*: "Sleep no more!") to come across with the proper force of conviction.

The reservations expressed here concern what appears to be the deliberate intellectualism of the poem, which results in an obvious derivativeness of its formulations. It remains true, however, that the poem's ambitious intentions are not only fully declared but are intensely realized at crucial moments in its development, as in this passage from the third movement:

> Now, where are the lightning-spokes
> That quivering should dance
> Ten thousand leagues into the limbs of things?
> Where are the broadways
> Of oriflamme that opening wide should lance
> Into the heart of darkness,
> As when trembling like a fresh
> Maid before her man,
> Moonlight distils flourescent submarine seas? (323)

The sustaining tension of the poem becomes manifest in this passage in which the charged irony of the allusion to Ariel's song in Shakespeare's *The Tempest* and to Conrad's well-known fiction of Africa is played against the poet's deep awareness of his own primary truths and developed into an expansive vision of their ultimate elemental significance. The double awareness that runs through "Agbor dancer" is here fully dramatized at the level of explicit thought as well as that of expressive means. "Ivbie" can be said therefore to articulate explicitly the theme of rediscovery that informs the other poems and is made palpable in their imagery. It charts the movement of the poet's mind toward a full response to the solicitations of the local environment, the "market murmur of assembled waves" (328), which that environment suggests to his imagination and which so powerfully resonates in his own expression in these early poems.

What is remarkable about these early poems is the intelligent effort to reorganize the adopted language to the poet's situation and circumstance. It is instructive to compare this effort to that of the white South African poets, who were the first to envision the possibility of a poetry that took Africa as its subject and whose preconceptions, tied as much to the European conditioning of their sensibilities as to their prejudicial view of Africa, proved ultimately disabling in their attempt to give credible expression to their encounter with and relation to a new landscape of human and natural life (Coetzee, 1988). It may be thought that, as one writing from the inside, Clark-Bekederemo enjoyed an indisputable advantage over these poets. Yet it is obvious from an examination of his versification that these early poems involved a strenuous testing of his medium, a conscious process of naturalization at the level of form and composition, through which he sought to bring his language into a state of expressive equivalence with his experience.

The results of the experimentation with language upon which he was engaged in these early poems are, of course, variable. Sometimes a straining after effect can be discerned as it seems to me to be the case with "The imprisonment of Obatala." At other times, the sense of rhythm is not always consistent with the tone and general movement of the poem as required by the theme, although it should be borne in mind that the interference from the indigenous background of voice may well constitute a value in itself for African poetry in English. As already noted, "Ivbie" suffers a softening of its tone from a self-consciousness that creates a dissonance between inspiration and formal realization. This is the kind of uneven quality that one can expect in a young poet making his way through a field of antecedent voices in quest of his own. Yet it has sometimes been used to discount the triumphs that Clark-Bekederemo is entitled to claim at this early period of his career. The rhyme scheme in "Easter," for instance, is so carefully woven across the broken rhythm of the verse that it participates in the progression of the poem's thought toward its ironic conclusion. And we can feel, in poem after poem, how verbal and formal effects collaborate to render an overwhelming sense of felt life.

We might observe that the wrestling with form and language in these early poems reflects the poet's determination to invest his evocations with such vivid energy as to get them well beyond the compass of a mere exercise in "local color." In this respect, Clark-Bekederemo's debt to Hopkins has proved largely beneficial, even if some of the effects on his poetry are sometimes as disconcerting as in the original source. The alliterative pattern initiated with "doped out of the deep" in "Night rain," the precision of the imagery, the visual notations, and the whole press of language in this and other poems makes this debt evident, even without its open acknowledgment in the subtitle to "Ibadan dawn." The authentic quality of Hopkins's idiom, of his vocabulary, verse rhythms, and verbal sonorities are so appropriate to the vibrant quality of these poems that the occasional jarring note seems of little moment when judged against their overall impact. And it is not only Hopkins, but also Wilfrid Owen and W. B. Yeats whose positive influences can be felt giving direction to Clark-Bekederemo's exploration of poetic language. "Fulani cattle," for instance, offers such a subtle variation on "Anthem for Doomed Youth" that Owen's poem can be considered to serve as its intertext as much in its theme as in its form; the resourceful use of near-rhymes and other features of Owen's idiom and technique contribute to the experience of Clark-Bekederemo's poem. As for Yeats, his influence is so pervasive that it can be said to have been wholly absorbed into the texture of Clark-Bekederemo's personal idiom.

It is worth insisting that the poet's appropriation of these models in his early poems often vindicates a method that may have proved damaging to his individual genius. The really important point is that, far from taking his situation for granted, Clark-Bekederemo took it seriously enough to ponder the lessons that the masters of the language he was obliged to use had to offer. His effort was bent toward refining his craft sufficiently to encompass an unprecedented creative purpose. That purpose was to reconstitute in language a specific field of experience pervaded by a developed sense of his location in the world and to endow that location with true poetic significance. It is this intention that lends to Clark-Bekederemo's early poetry its firm sense of conviction and its vitality of expression.

The achieved sense of place that *Poems* mobilizes affords the perspective from which to view *A Reed in the Tide*, the volume that follows. Poems such as "Flight across Africa," "Times Square," and "Cave call" are impressions of travel, entries in a mental diary, records of isolated moments in a widening experience of the world. They project the multiple perspectives that proceed naturally from a self-assured consciousness. A number of these poems relate to his experience during the year he spent as a visiting scholar at Princeton University, an acerbic account of which he has provided in *America, Their America*. The poet's attitude toward the materialism and consumerism associated with America, as it comes through in "Service," may seem conventional. However, when the sardonic tone of the poem is linked with the hedonistic connotation of the word *service* in the popular, urban culture of Nigeria, the connection with his sense of home and the meaning become clear as a willed distancing of the self. The poem is a repudiation of "the siren streets and afternoon" of a civilization with which he is unable to strike a spiritually satisfying relation and whose spread over the globe he therefore deplores. The context of these poems does not, however, fully account for their general atmosphere, for although they display a variation of tone and mood, they have in common an almost whimsical restlessness, which suggests that the poet is almost by temperament unsuited for the role of "the fortunate traveler," which the Caribbean poet Derek Walcott assumes in one of his best-known collections.

The juxtaposition in *A Reed in the Tide* of poems related to external experience with other poems dealing with the internal social and political situation of the postindependence era, which Nigeria had just entered at the time of their composition, sets up a thematic counterpoint between the private realm of the poet's inspiration and the public sphere of an emerging concern with national politics. The critical turn that the Nigerian situation began to take at this time imposes upon the poet's attention the claims of the social universe of his existence, which now begins to be featured as a primary focus.

The use of a natural image to depict the corruption in public life in "Emergency commission" establishes the moral perspective of the poet's concern and illuminates the import of the two poems that focus directly on political figures who played prominent roles in the unfolding drama of the Nigerian crisis. In "The leader" and "His Excellency the masquerader," the allusions to aspects of the traditional background bring home, so to speak, the human and social implications of the poet's preoccupations. Where in the former the agony of politics is expressed in the allegorical idiom of the folktale tradition—an idiom that the poet employs with great effect in his succeeding volume—in the latter, an ironic reversal of the normal healthy associations of traditional ceremonies provides the basis for a bitter satire of political behavior. These political poems more than foreshadow in theme, language, and their general atmosphere the poems of *Casualties*, his next collection, which is devoted entirely to the convulsions occasioned by the Nigerian Civil War of 1967–1970.

This continuity of poetic inspiration from one volume to the other is underscored in the dirge-like "Song" with which *Casualties* opens in its recall of an earlier age of youthful idealism contrasted to a present desolation, an age

> When but to think of an ill, made
> By God or man, was to find
> The cure prophet and physician
> Did not have. (340)

The sentiment of a shattered ideal mourned in this opening poem provides the emotional setting for the poet's stance toward the tragic course of events of which *Casualties* constitutes a searing record. The gloom that pervades the panoramic view of civil turmoil that he offers in "A photograph in *The Observer*" suggests more than a generalized feeling of emotional distress; the final refrain, "night falls over us," indicates a more comprehensive grasp of the essential pathos of history as exemplified by the unfolding drama of national events. The apocalyptic terms that characterize the plangent horror of the Nigerian Civil War in "The beast" and the harrowing realism with which it is detailed in such pieces as "Season of omens" and "July wake" confirm the extensive emotional range of the poems in *Casualties*.

Because several of the poems weave a tale around specific individuals, they require for their understanding some familiarity with the details of the Nigerian crisis. The effectiveness of the imagery in "The cockerel in the tale" depends, for example, on identifying the specific allusions in the poem to the role of Major Nzeogwu, one of the leaders of the January 1966 military coup, which unleashed the chain of events that culminated in the civil war. Similarly, "The reign of the crocodile" has to be read as the poet's personal commentary on the personality and style of government of General Ironsi, whose inadequacies proved a major factor in the subsequent slide toward the civil war, which broke out in July 1967. The poem appears in this light as an expression of the poet's personal indignation at the failure of leadership during a critical period in Nigerian history.

But *Casualties* is not primarily concerned with the abstract issues of the politics that came to a head with the Nigerian Civil War. It ranges much further into the ambiguous moral terrain where public events exert contradictory pressures on individual choices. The volume speaks directly to the personal dilemma this situation presents to the poet himself and is remarkable for the honesty with which he confronts this dilemma in the various poems as they weave their emotional and moral thread through the volume. Nowhere is this more evident than in the sequence of three poems devoted to his relations with Emmanuel Ifeajuna, another principal actor in the events of the Nigerian Civil War, who was also a personal friend. The composite portrait of Ifeajuna that emerges from "Leader of the hunt," "Conversations at Accra," and "Return home" is marked by a profound ambivalence, which attests to the poet's conflict of loyalties. The three poems do more than dramatize the confusion of two troubled minds, that of the poet and the subject of his poem; they are intended to discount the abstract heroics of the public square in a severe probing of private motives, as the poet gropes toward the duty of human understanding, which the moment and the demands of a personal bond require.

Where the Ifeajuna sequence involves some elaboration, "Death of a weaverbird," an elegy to Christopher Okigbo, a fellow poet and another close friend, who was killed on the Biafran side of the civil war, is keyed to understatement. Its refusal to dwell on the man but rather to invoke the claims of a common pursuit betokens a resistance to emotion, an appeal to the controlling power of art. The poem thus takes its poignancy less from the text than from its context; its departure from the conventions of the elegiac genre serves to enforce the statement it makes of a grief larger than words.

It is thus a willingness to go behind the headlines and the rhetoric of public stances to the conflicts generated within individuals that distinguishes this volume. Against this background, the rhetorical flourish of "We are all casualties" in the title poem dedicated to Chinua Achebe rings false, for it understates the emotional reach of these poems, the intimate thrust of the experience of the civil war for the poet himself and for many individuals, which he engages in such poems as "Dirge" and "Night song."

The obvious public reference of the poems of *Casualties* may seem to imply that the volume is confined to the circumstances of Nigeria and thus are limited in their significance. But they do not only comprise a narrative of the Nigerian Civil War, they organize themselves into a meditation upon the event. It is this aspect of the volume that accounts for its most striking formal feature: the predominance of animal imagery, which is developed throughout into a scheme of primal metaphors. The poet's construction of this scheme points to the suggestion it carries of Nigeria, the reference of the poems, as a kind of jungle and of the civil war as a drama of elementary and destructive passions. They derive in this sense a didactic function from the allegorical mode in which they are cast; this mode becomes in turn a means of displacing the public aspect of the theme in order to reinforce the introspective character of the poems.

The fact that the volume's scheme of metaphors is derived from the oral tradition becomes of the utmost importance from this point of view. It makes clear the poet's concern to address the immediate audience in terms with which it is familiar, which relate directly to its established structure of sensibility and response. Thus, while *Casualties* often documents the events and presents the characters involved in the Nigerian Civil War in factual terms, it also transposes these elements into an imaginative register with a highly ethical resonance. In other words, these elements assume their value within the framework of a comprehensive parable, which determines the didactic function of the volume by pointing to the necessity of moral values as a foundation for political and social life. The oral tradition thus serves as the formal and moral perspective for the poet's consistent angle of vision on the characters and situations that enter his meditation.

It seems fair to affirm that *Casualties* represents Clark-Bekederemo's finest poetic accomplishment. The stress of the historical moment that occasioned the composition of these poems called forth from him a "terrible beauty" of expression. It obliged him to a creative endeavor in the quest for a mode of address appropriate to the occasion, to the experience centered upon it, and to the audience it affected. It served both to sharpen the sense of responsibility inherent all along in his earlier work, as well as to inspire a new experience of poetic form, which enabled him to find an original voice. The paring of his idiom for the tale of desolation he had to tell brought a firmer temper to his poetry, gave it a new dimension in which language, emotion, and imagery became finely fused within a firmly grounded and coherent aesthetic framework. *Casualties* is indeed nothing less than the triumphant demonstration of the expressive potential of the African imagination.

It is perhaps no surprise that this achievement could not be fully matched in the sequel to the volume, *State of the Union*, which is devoted to the social and political malaise of Nigeria in the aftermath of the civil war. The dominant key here is related not so much to a mood of disillusionment as to a disengagement of the poet's feeling from his subject. The poems seem to develop on an even plateau of uncomplicated emotion, so that the language seems to shun the forthright rhetoric of a persuasive discourse for the indirections of a weary irony. This character makes for a subdued tone in most of the poems.

It is possible to argue that, in *State of the Union*, Clark-Bekederemo has carried the stripping of his poetic language, which he began in *Casualties*, to its limits. Already in the "Epilogue" to this latter volume, we began to feel that the spare, taut diction he had cultivated for his narration of the Nigerian Civil War had become too plain to move us with the telling power of genuine poetry. It may be reasoned that the need he felt to testify to the ills of society justifies the unadorned garb he chose to give to his expression in *State of the Union*, that his objective was to communicate in the most direct way possible with his audience, which called for a language immediately accessible to them. It may also be that the nature of the subject he took on, the failure of will in the national community, resulted in a depressed imagination reflected directly in his language.

State of the Union is not, for all that, devoid of interest. The note of disillusionment modulates into a more markedly personal mood of rueful dejection in some of the poems in the latter section of the volume and provides an insight not only into the overlap of the public with the personal in Clark-Bekederemo's poetry but also into a certain logic of development in all of his work, a point to which we shall return presently. For now, it is useful to remark upon the way poems such as "Autumn in Connecticut" and "Birthday at Wesleyan, Middletown" begin to dwell upon the theme of passing time and decay, a theme whose implications provide the key to the poet's reflections upon his individual condition in "The Coming of Age." The elegiac note that predominates in this section of the volume is struck with a simple but resolute clarity in the lines that conclude the poem:

> All under spell of day
> Moves on into night. (400)

The brooding note of the poems in the latter section of *State of the Union* runs easily into that of *Mandela and other poems*. The neat division into three clearly marked sections is of particular interest for a consideration of this slim but highly distinctive volume. The political subject in the first section, with its Pan-Africanist vision, recovers for us some of the motivating force of his early work and emerges in a tone of exasperation in "A Letter to Oliver Tambo." The two sections that make up the rest of the volume place this political background in something of a recessive light. The second section, composed of a series of elegies, is set off against the background of hope and continued aspiration mapped out by the opening section; the poems in this section comprise a somber quartet in which the enacted ritual of mortality sets the atmosphere for the extended contemplation represented by the poems in the last section of the volume. This connection makes the volume assume a retrospective significance; they are a preliminary summing up of life and experience as the poet moves into the uncertain climate of middle age.

The volume thus traces for us the transition from the exuberance of Clark-Bekederemo's early poems to a somberness that has been lurking in his previous expression (as in "Tide-wash") and now comes fully to the fore. The poet insists upon the elegiac note in this last volume to the point where it takes him over the edge of a morbid perception in some of the poems. However, if the starkness of "Death of a Lady" and "A Passing at the New Year" seems disturbing, they have something in common with a Romantic imagination; for all their bleakness, they represent less a gesture of despair than a reasoned activity of the poetic mind engaged in a sustained interrogation of accumulated experience, a seeking of the essential meaning of an individual life and its place in the world.

Mandela and other poems throws a sharp light from this point of view on the personal voyage traced by the progression of Clark-Bekederemo's themes, which take us from the delight in the world and sensuous excitement of his early poems to the pensive and measured gravity of his latest work. At one level, that of public reference, this progression runs parallel to his country's history and registers the descent toward a mood of social despair. But at a more profound level of consciousness, it involves the sober recognition of the inevitable scourge of time, the inexorable process of decay in the world of nature, which is at the same time the condition for its renewal.

It is no accident that the dominant image in his poetry relates to the tides of the Niger Delta, the manifestation in a familiar landscape of the idea of changeability, of the experience of transition, and of the natural phases that govern the movement of life. Nature in its closest guise to the poet offers here a dramatic illustration of all existence as a continuous flux, within which humanity itself appears as indeed "a reed in the tide." The conclusion to "Streamside exchange" is especially suggestive of this entrenched position in his imaginative thought. What seems like an awkward rhyme in the final lines of the poem acquires a singular force; it works perfectly to give a matter-of-fact tone to the bird's response and thus to underscore the grim finality of the apprehension it registers:

> You cannot know
> And should not bother;
> Tide and market come and go
> And so has your mother. (318)

We become aware, then, as we consider the development of his poetry, that a tragic vision is integral to Clark-Bekederemo's aesthetic consciousness. We might explain the thematic progression of his poetry by observing that this view of his imagination was at first obscured by the enthusiasms of his beginnings, but once he came into full possession of his language, it only needed the confirming effect of events and personal experience to uncover and bring this vein into stark prominence. Whatever our attitude toward the view of life that Clark-Bekederemo proposes to us in his poetry, we can have no doubt that it provides the theme that accounts for the direct power of his expression.

Clark-Bekederemo's plays provide an expanded framework for the expression of the tragic vision that runs through his poetry. There is a clear affective and aesthetic solidarity between the two aspects of his work, which is emphasized by the fact that the Niger Delta is the setting for all of the plays. This prompts a preliminary observation, which places the plays themselves in a general perspective. The natural environment of his native region assumes significance here as the theater in which the drama of the human condition is acted out. For while each play is self-contained, they tend to be structurally linked. This appears to be the playwright's way of insisting upon the essential unity of their inspiration. They represent in this light individual instances of a comprehensive structure of tragic apprehension.

Clark-Bekederemo's reputation as a playwright rests largely on the success of his first play, *Song of a Goat*. The play had an immediate impact when it was first produced in 1961; its theme of domestic tragedy, centered upon questions having to do with fertility and procreation, had appeal to a Nigerian audience, for whom such questions have a primordial importance. The play, which includes the ritual slaying of a goat as part of the dramatic action, was calculated to impress; its motivation, however, was not a crude sensationalism but the awakening in the audience of the sense of drama as communal rite. Besides its theme, the appeal of this play derives essentially from the playwright's robust vitality of language, its remarkable consistency of tone, his impressive handling of atmosphere, and the successful realization of the play's moral focus. The compactness of the play, the swift movement of its action toward a tragic climax, contributes to an overwhelming and tightly wrought tension.

Although the action of the play is not overtly concerned with the issue of culture conflict, which dominated African writing for a time, the two levels at which it develops—the psychological and the social—suggest an interpretation that places it squarely within the context of a breakdown of the rules of custom. The heart of the problem with which the play deals is quite simply the variable hold of social constraint on the individual. The Masseur speaks for the needs of society with his constant reminder of a convention that stresses the survival of the clan, appealing through this reminder to Zifa's sense of community against his sense of personal identity. His words, "The soil is sacred, and no one man may dispose of it," express an all-encompassing ethos by which the clan has given coherence to its collective existence. Zifa's reluctance to accept the dictates of this ethos, despite his disability, amounts to an insistence on the claims of the individual against those of society, an attitude that threatens the conception that his society continues to entertain of its organic life.

Ebiere's distraught condition is, in this view of the play, much less a function of her sexuality than of her husband's intransigence, which denies her the possibility of reconciling her personal physical and emotional needs with her instinctive adherence to the conventions of her society. Her sense of wrong on these counts comes through in a speech whose formulations derive their meanings from the context. When she refers to herself in these words—

> I who have suffered neglect and
> Gathered mold like a thing of sacrifice
> Left out in sun and rain at the crossroads (22)

—the imagery brings out a sense of frustration at more than a purely personal level. The life-enhancing properties of the sun and rain are in fact invoked as part of a religious consciousness, which links the ritual of sacrifice with the solidarity of the clan and the communal well-being. Her grievance comes down to the acute sense of marginality she is made to feel by being thwarted in her creative function and thus being denied a role with which she has wholeheartedly identified in maintaining the continued life of the community.

The fact that the character of Tonye is merely sketched within the drama has been seen as a failure of craft on the part of the playwright. This view cannot, however, be sustained, for the portrait of Tonye conforms entirely with the formal scheme of the play. Tonye's role emphasizes the imponderable nature of the drama in which all the characters are caught; he is merely the accessory to its tragic unfolding, the hapless victim of what is manifestly a dilemma of transition. The point is that the conflict enacted in this play transcends the two main characters; it revolves essentially around the norms by which their society will live in the new dispensation, hinted at if not fully established in the play.

Song of a Goat has been compared with Eugene O'Neill's *Desire under the Elms*, but as noted already, the theme of sexuality is not as central in Clark-Bekederemo's play as it is in O'Neill's. A more appropriate parallel is that between the theme of Clark-Bekederemo's play and Garcia Lorca's plays *Yerma* and *Blood Wedding*. Clark-Bekederemo has stated that he had not read Lorca when he wrote his own play, and we can give full credence to this assurance and accept that the observed parallel between his work and that of Lorca is purely fortuitous. A valid comparison between the Nigerian playwright's work and that of the Spaniard can easily be sustained without assuming an influence from one writer to the other, however. Both were writing about a community in which the harshness of the environment conditioned an ideological emphasis on communal survival and consequently determined a preoccupation, often anguished and certainly pregnant with tragic possibilities, with the fundamentals of life.

It is a preoccupation of this order that receives prominence in *Song of a Goat*, whose text is one long rumination on the idea of growth and vitality; a sense of the reciprocities between blood and soil becomes, as it were, a natural extension of this presiding idea, which emerges from the theme and action of the play. The close parallel between the imagery of "The year's first rain" and *Song of a Goat*'s first act alerts us to the interaction between the poet's habit of sensibility and his projections in the play as these are embodied in his characters. It is essential in this respect to attend closely to the formal design of the play as a verse drama, a feature that connects it directly to Clark-Bekederemo's early poem, upon which it expands within the scheme of a developed dramatic action.

This formal connection between Clark-Bekederemo's poetry and his dramatic work is perhaps most evident in *The Masquerade*. The lyricism of the courting scene in the first act effectively transforms this scene into one long poem, a paean to youth and to the land, an affirmation of life in the exultant spirit of "Girl bathing." The evocations in this scene take their place in the dramatic context of the play as the poetic background for the tragedy of star-crossed lovers. And it is the opposition between the welcoming attitude toward life natural to youth in its first bloom and the rigidity of the older people, the loss of their capacity for creative responses to life's promptings, that produces the tragic outcome.

From the point of view of structure and dramatic action, *The Raft* is certainly the most compact of Clark-Bekederemo's plays. There is a continuous flow of action, which contributes to the impression of restriction already determined by the reduced world of the raft, which serves as its scenic framework, and the unified temporal scheme—twenty-four hours from one sunset to another—within which the whole action of the play is enclosed. At the same time, the tight construction of the play is able to accommodate a full account both of the life of its characters, down to the technical details of their professions on which the play depends for its action and its symbolism, and of aspects of contemporary experience, which place the action in a wider perspective.

The Raft has been interpreted as a parable of Nigeria, its four characters representative of the four regions of the federation in the pre–Civil War era. In this interpretation, the play is seen to contain a clear message to a country adrift in a political storm and heading toward disaster. The allusions to the prevailing social and political circumstances in Nigeria at the time the play was written are many and specific enough to justify the view that the playwright's concerns as a citizen find a large measure of expression in this play. Thus, a reading of the work as direct commentary on Nigeria is indeed plausible, but it is one with which we cannot rest content. For one thing, the correspondence between the action of the play and the social and political situation it addresses is far from being as simple as this reading would allow. The expressionist tone is enough to preclude a hasty analogy of the play with any kind of univocal political or social statement. Moreover, the wider ramifications of the play are expressly indicated in the headings that the playwright has appended to the text in each of its four tableaux. These headings suggest a more elevated scope to the playwright's intention than is allowed by a narrow political interpretation of his play.

We come to an idea of this intention once again by way of the poetry. The far-from-idyllic tone of the poem "Return of the fishermen" anticipates much of the human and natural atmosphere of *The Raft*. The use of dramatic irony in the first tableau, entitled "Tide-Wash," is central to the drama; the enveloping fog that is given a simple mention in an early scene deepens in meaning later in Kengide's cry, "The fog is everywhere," which is prolonged in its anguish by the words "has shut up the world / Like a bat its wings." The ominous import of this cry is at once made explicit in the words "All is blindness and scales!" The scene in which this utterance takes place forms part of a consistent pattern in the play's dramatic movement; a good deal of comic business seems to go on, only to be punctuated at intervals by a sudden awareness by the four characters of their desperate plight. The parallel of this pattern to those moments of lucid insight that sometimes assail us within the random, uncharted flow of human experience hardly needs emphasizing.

The Raft strikes us as nothing less than a meditation on the precariousness of the human condition. There is nothing portentous about the way the play goes about what we may take to be its demonstration of this theme; indeed, the setting is appropriate to such a demonstration, founded upon a conception of the Niger Delta as a properly elemental environment, one that lends itself readily to a drama of extreme situations apt to test men's mettle and thus to wring from them a recognition of their true place in the universe. The straightforward symbolism of the whirlpool both features the actual menacing quality of the environment and figures the cosmic terror it induces. The play rings a series of variations on the expression of this terror. Kengide's cry quoted above is earlier voiced more trenchantly in Ibobo's morose reflection on his own existential situation:

> I try to shut my eyes, gateways to my head
> Which is one great cage where misfortune,
> Like an alligator trussed within, batters
> At my temples, forehead and back. (97)

When later in the play, Kengide alludes to the bitterness of the kola nut as a metaphor of life, it is to generalize from the particular experience of the characters to that of humanity at large, whose agony is presented in the play as a dramatic representation.

The Raft's pessimistic vision affords no place for a comforting view of life. The heading "Iron and Fire" for the third tableau establishes a grim equivalence between the malevolence of man and the destructive potential of machines, which the action illustrates. The deliberate ambiguity of the heading "Call of Land" for the final tableau alludes at once to the futile hope of the characters and the inescapable fact of human mortality, which provides a highly ironic comment on the vanity of worldly agitations. A desperate recognition of the absurdity of human existence thus runs through the play, summed up in these lines:

> No, each day some poor fellow is either
> Going out with a hiss or making his brief
> Entrance with a howl, and the women wail
> Going to bed and wake up wailing, for their seeds
> Are eaten up by the black beetle. (89)

It is not clear to what extent, in the writing of this play, Clark-Bekederemo can be considered to have been indebted to a certain tradition of modern European theater. What seems at one level of its development to be its loose structure—the seemingly rambling dialogue and unfocused action of the play—conforms to the tradition insofar as it affords a formal pointer to the conventions of what Martin Esslin has called "theatre of the absurd" (Esslin, 1961). But these elements are in fact highly organized toward a statement that is in immediate relation to the playwright's experience of background and handling of setting. For if *The Raft* is so profoundly concerned with the existential predicament of humankind, it is a function of a deep reflection prompted not so much by a nihilist vision as by a disciplined insight, the fruit of the playwright's contemplation of the immense vistas offered to his vision by the living framework of sea and sky, land and water in which human existence has its immediate location in the Niger Delta. The play is thus essentially an expression of a grounded awe of the obscure forces of the universe. In this sense, *The Raft* gives an original dimension of a properly metaphysical nature to the modern preoccupation with the absurd; by taking the measure of humanity against the scale of the natural world, which forms the background of his own experience, the playwright proffers his dread understanding of the human condition.

The total integration of setting into the dramatic movement of *The Raft* for a philosophical reflection points to its foundation in a coherent view of the world, in a cosmology that serves as the constant reference for the complex interaction of the lives that Clark-Bekederemo evokes in his plays with the environment. It was inevitable, then, that he would draw directly upon the dramatic resources offered by myth and legend among his own people for his next play, *Ozidi*, which is based on the Ijo epic he recorded, transcribed, and edited. Part of the interest of this play derives from its relation to its source in the Ijo oral tradition, a fact that prompts a comparison between the play and the original epic. It needs to be stressed, however, that the play is not a mere adaptation of the epic for the modern stage but is in fact a transposition of the traditional material, which makes it a separate and autonomous dramatic work. It needs therefore to be viewed as a restatement by the playwright, in personal terms, of the significance he attaches to the traditional epic.

Ozidi is without question Clark-Bekederemo's most fully realized play, the work in which he seems to have attained full mastery of his dramatic idiom. It is obvious that the conception of the play came to him fully formed from his living so long with the material in its original version. The full congruence of Clark-Bekederemo's genius with his subject becomes evident in the way the clear linearity of the action is orchestrated in a complex elaboration of the material he took from his traditional background.

As is so well demonstrated in the Elizabethan drama with which Clark-Bekederemo was familiar from his English studies, the revenge theme offers excellent prospects for effective theater. The heroic dimension that the theme receives in the national epic of his own people gave a pronounced lift to the playwright's imagination, which becomes fully attuned to the spirit of the Ijo story, to the tremendous energy of its original manifestation in the traditional epic. It is this quality that Clark-Bekederemo has endeavored to capture, as much in language as in the total design and movement of the play. The location of the action partly in the world of myth, similar in some respects to what we encounter in Tutuola's novels, gives the play a large dimension, which comes through in the following passage in which the Story-Teller reports the collaboration of the elements at the birth of Ozidi junior:

> In the seventh month of Orea seeing
> Her belly, she bore the dead Ozidi
> A son safe away in her mother's town
> Ododama. That day it rained barrels
> Of water through a sieve of sunshine. You
> Could say of the storm that a giant wind
> Had taken the sea as an orange by the mouth
> And sucking it, had spat in the face of the sun
> Who winced lightning, and then hurled it all back
> At earth as rain and bolts of thunder. (135)

Despite this mythic background, the play bears most directly on the moral dilemma of our human universe. An important factor that appears to be operative in the writing of the play is the profound fascination that the personality of the national hero of the Ijo people and that of his grandmother, Oreame, exercised upon the playwright's imagination. The appeal of these two characters served to stimulate what amounts to a personal reassessment on his part of their linked moral adventure. For *Ozidi* can be considered a modern morality play, concerned most essentially with the place of *hubris* in human affairs.

The play's focus on Oreame's formidable resolution serves as the playwright's mode of exploration of this problem. It is important to bear in mind in this respect that in most African languages, the connotation of the word translated as *witch* has a more positive ring than is suggested by its English equivalent. It designates quite simply one who happens to be endowed with extraordinary powers, which can be applied for good or ill. Oreame herself is presented at one moment in the play in her normal role as healer, so that what we witness is an inversion of the human function she fulfills in her community. It is not without interest in our consideration of this point to note the way in which her male counterpart and collaborator, the Old Man Wizard, is thoroughly humanized in the play:

> I am, oh,
> I am by the look of the setting sun.

My brain has frozen within the skull; it now
Knocks like a dry nut in its shell. (149)

Ozidi presents us with a character study of the utmost psychological and moral interest. Oreame's inflexible will makes her the embodiment of the driving principle of Ozidi's passion and, at the same time, the external-ized figure of his lack of growth in moral awareness. Despite his status as the ostensible hero of the play, Ozidi's immaturity is sufficiently dwelt upon to instruct us about the true character of his hubris; the awesome contrast between his unusual physical attributes and his undeveloped consciousness makes the point that the play is concerned with the de-structive course of an impersonal force to the point where, like a storm in nature, it has to play itself out for a restoration of order in the world. The public disavowal of Ozidi's frenzy occurs appropriately at the mo-ment when it reaches its highest peak, in the duel between him and Ofe, when he stands all alone with his grandmother in their victory. This scene, taken with the subsequent ones that illustrate the progressive cor-ruption of the moral purpose of Oreame and her grandson, highlights the ambiguous relation between the claims of justice they represent at the outset and the habit of violence they have adopted as their unfailing response to situations. Only when Ozidi is divested of his passion can he be welcomed back into the company of men.

As in the epic from which it is derived, the formal organization of Clark-Bekederemo's play serves to point up the human significance of the Ozidi story. The elaborate pageantry through which the plot moves in the epic is reproduced in the play in the context of a lively interaction between the text and the extratextual and paratextual effects, which both lend dramatic support to the action and contribute to its affective quality. All the indications are that, in his conception of the play, Clark-Bekederemo had firmly before him the operative principle of African art as a mode of total performance and that he sought to actualize this prin-ciple in his play within the framework of modern dramatic practice.

This observation raises the question of the technical demands of the play. It has often been an objection that these demands cannot reason-ably be met in the modern theater. But as anyone who has seen the film of the original epic made by Frank Speed soon comes to realize, there is nothing in the play as conceived and written by Clark-Bekederemo that is beyond the resources of a reasonably equipped theater company. For all its limitations, the film clarifies many of the technical issues raised by the play. Apart from the fact that the context is often presented directly in the dialogue, which takes on much of the burden of scene painting, it soon becomes apparent that the conventions of realistic drama are out of place in a work that relies primarily on the device of stylization for its most important effects.

The examples abound of the way in which, through its formal organization, the play aspires to the condition of total drama. The assignation to the drums of the "cauldron music" of Ozidi's bowels as they rumble in anger is only one instance of the various devices that tend toward this end. We might mention in particular the great scene of self-recognition by the young Ozidi, which depends for its dramatic impact less on dialogue than on stage business. Other scenes require particular effects and specific skills from the actors. The scene in act 2 in which Oreame takes Ozidi to the forest grove to be fortified by Old Man Wizard calls for choreographic skills that the playwright was well aware were well developed among the traditional artists of his own people and those of other ethnic groups in Nigeria, for instance, the famous acrobatic dancers of the Ishan people in midwestern Nigeria. He had no hesitation therefore in writing this scene as he did. For the rest, the use of mime and costumed masque is expressly indicated for many other episodes. All that is necessary therefore to bring the play alive is proper acquaintance with the principles and tropes of African artistic conventions and some imagination on the part of the producer.

These technical considerations are essential for an appreciation of the playwright's deepest intention, for the purpose of any production of the play must be to restore to full view of the audience Clark-Bekederemo's conception of his work as a form of communal celebration. *Ozidi* seems designed to provide something of a complement to *The Raft* in its immediate political significance as well as in its further metaphysical resonances; the bleak landscape of the earlier play becomes in the later one the cosmic backdrop for a drama of immense proportions. The outcome of this drama, in which the character of Ozidi attains an ironic but true form of transcendence, which is implied by his reduction to the level of ordinary mortal, gives the transformation an affirmative purpose, a celebration of the common humanity he shares with his people.

Clark-Bekederemo's *Ozidi* might be said to work ultimately toward a projection of the emblematic significance of the Ijo epic onto the contemporary national scene as a means of engendering the sentiment of a common bond in time and space. There is a real sense in which the play has meaning as the effort to convert a tribal into a national consciousness. If the Ijo saga enacts for its original audience a ritual of collective consecration through the celebration of a legendary figure and the invocation of the mythic imagination, the modern play seeks to enforce in secular form a collective consciousness in the new, urgent project of national integration.

This purposeful direction of the play's symbolism becomes explicit in the final scene, which seeks to involve the national psyche in its meaning. The final procession of actors and audiences takes on a wider significance from this point of view and must be interpreted both as the joyous acceptance of a restoration of harmony in the imaginative world of the play itself and as its symbolic anticipation in the real world of national coexistence inhabited by its contemporary audience. It is, moreover, a scene that underscores the playwright's sense of his artistic mission, the emphasis he places upon the function of drama as the means of a collective therapy.

There is a noticeable drop in dramatic pace and intensity as we move from this first group of plays to the three plays that constitute the Bikoroa trilogy. The return to the theme of domestic tragedy already treated in *Song of a Goat* gives the trilogy a simplicity of outline that makes for a certain concentration of effect. These plays seem to me ideally suited for performance over a three-day period, so that the pathos that runs through the trilogy can be more keenly felt as a continuous stream from one play to the next. Besides, their tripartite scheme virtually makes them into a single play in three extended movements, not only linked thematically by the working out through their development of an inexorable destiny in the fortunes of a single family but also unified by a reflective point of view. The fifty-year temporal span of the plays is projected across the rootedness of the community with which the play deals, which stresses the permanence of the human impulses operating within it against the background of developments in the wider world.

The real point of concentration in the trilogy seems to me to reside in the middle work, *The Return Home*, which displays all of the properties of ritual drama and thus functions as much more than a bridge from one moment of intensity in the cycle to another. The subdued atmosphere that prevails in the play has indeed its own intensity and seems designed to bring into focus the underlying moral and spiritual stress that the playwright explores through the three works. After the agitated action of *The Boat* and the meditative cast of this middle play, *Full Circle* can only fulfill our anticipation of a return in the trilogy to a definitive point of stasis.

Coming after the fairly standard format of the first three plays and the grand scale of *Ozidi*, the more withdrawn character of *The Bikoroa Plays* demonstrates the diversity of approaches to dramatic writing in Clark-Bekederemo's work. All of the plays present a number of problems, inherent in the innovative role they have played in the creation of Nigerian and African dramatic literature in English, which has meant a rethinking of virtually every point of dramatic style. But the principal problem with which the playwright was confronted remains as always that of language, more acute here than in the poems, given the presentational character and function of drama. For Clark-Bekederemo's task in these plays has been to devise in the English language and for immediate utterance a form of speech that is in character with the dispositions and mental universes of the men and women who people his plays.

His choice of verse drama as the formal framework of the first group of plays can be understood in this light, as he is compelled by the necessity to capture the exact register of indigenous speech in the dramatic situations his plays present. This makes for a distinctive rhetoric of which the extensive stock of proverbs, with their graphic imagery and terse formulation of thought, comprises a significant dimension, well reflected in the constant metaphoric turn of the dialogue ascribed to even the most humble characters. That the procedure is well matched to the context and atmosphere of the plays can be judged from this passage in *The Raft*:

> I have often heard
> It said you could see the street lights of Burutu
> Far, far out from stream. I thought it one
> Of their stories—like those about ghosts
> Who are never seen but by persons
> In distant parts who told it to a friend
> Who told it to another and so on till
> You feel in the endless coil of the guinea worm. (98)

It is not only that Clark-Bekederemo makes direct use of proverbs in the delineation of his characters in their normal, everyday habits of speech. The language of the plays is permeated by what we may term the proverbial dimension of African modes of discourse. The scene in *Ozidi* where Ewiri brings news to Ofe's compound of the arrival of the young

Ozidi at Orua provides an extended example of this characteristic manner of discourse.

It is curious that the playwright makes sparing use of outright transliterations; expressions like "Where God in heaven touches the ground" or "That's the bitter Ijaw truth," which are taken straight from the Ijo language, occur only occasionally. This indicates that his interest lay not in a mannered recasting in English but in exploiting the language's resources to convey the structure and tonality of indigenous speech. In the first series of plays, the use of blank verse enables him to approximate in English the peculiar cadences of his native Ijo, and he brings the pressures of this highly musical language to bear on his adopted medium of expression. Clark-Bekederemo's debt to the great master of English speech is in evidence here. Consider, for example, the Shakespearean accents of this extract from *The Masquerade*:

> Salt and sting, salt and sting, it's surfeit
> Of both that has ruined us. But look, there comes
> Umuko, a craft with none at the helm. (66)

If the eloquence of the passage sounds too close to the original source, becoming stilted as a result, it helps us demonstrate how the same accents contain the potential for producing the right dramatic effect, as in this simple but memorable passage from *Song of a Goat*:

> There will never be light again in this
> House, child, this is the night of our race,
> The fall of all that ever reared up head
> Or crest. (34)

English blank verse was admirably suited to Clark-Bekederemo's purpose, for its peculiar combination of strength and suppleness provided him with an expressive instrument he was able to manipulate for shaping the language of his characters. It enabled him to infuse much of the dramatic language in his plays with the contained power demonstrated by these lines spoken by the dim-witted Temugedege in his single moment of insight in *Ozidi*:

> But here is a boy, full grown, brought to me
> By mother of the wife who fled
> The homestead when lightning struck
> In broad sunshine. Did the bolt that splintered
> Our cornerstone till the soil as well,

Engendering by the one stroke the seed
That sprung this stem? (159)

Finally, we might note the transposition in these plays into the register of English of the sheer delight in language that is a constant feature of indigenous modes of linguistic interaction, a feature that is made evident in the dialogue of the characters. No better example can perhaps be found than in this strikingly visual presentation of swallows in *The Raft*, a passage that is also remarkable for its subtle play of alliterations:

> They are swarming all over the place. Look,
> They dive as if to plunge headlong into the swell,
> But even as their feet graze the wave crest, they
> Have swept steep back into the skies. (86)

It is in the simple felicity of such passages that we observe the way in which the poet joins hands with the playwright in crafting the language of these plays.

A survey of the kind I have provided here necessarily involves an evaluation, and I have said enough to suggest that if, as we consider Clark-Bekederemo's work in its totality, we observe the inevitable losses, we can have no doubt that the gains outstrip them decisively. His work is large enough to dominate the landscape of modern African literature. But it remains to point out his principal achievement, which for me consists of the signal contribution he has made to the development of a poetics appropriate to the requirements of a new mode of African imaginative expression. To stress this aspect of Clark-Bekederemo's achievement is to draw attention to two fundamental considerations prompted by the development of his work.

The first is in direct line with the formal implications of my remarks and is inherent in the elementary fact that the foundation of all literary expression is the structure of the words from which it arises. This implies that the writer's first duty is to attend to the particular quality of his expression and to match that expression to the context of his enunciations; text and context thus stand in a dynamic relation to each other. This seems a simple requirement, but it is one that has posed problems not only of an aesthetic but also of an ideological order to the African writer who has to employ a European language. Although Clark-Bekederemo has not involved himself in any elaborate theoretical formulations, his work demonstrates, in the deliberation with which he has worked out his idiom, a thoughtful approach to the problems of crafts-manship with which the combined pressures of his vocation and his situation confronted him.

The second consideration arises from the tense background of history from which all modern African expression issues and in particular the role of literature in the reconstruction of African consciousness. The Nigerian context of his work gives a special relief to Clark-Bekederemo's achievement in this regard. His work belongs to a stellar constellation that includes Christopher Okigbo, Gabriel Okara, Chinua Achebe, Wole Soyinka, and Amos Tutuola, who have planted the seeds of what has grown visibly into a national literature. The wholehearted involvement of this literature in the evolving destiny of the national community it represents gives it a social dimension, a live significance, in the difficult quest for cohesion in which that community has been engaged.

The personal role of Clark-Bekederemo in the genesis of this national literature has been mentioned. The precedent set by his early work was decisive in opening the way to much that is valuable today in Nigerian and, by extension, African poetry and drama, and his later work has been influential in the orientation of literary consciousness and creation on the continent. His poetry in particular has provided the sounding board against which the generation of Nigerian writers who came after him, especially those who have emerged since the civil war, have raised their voices and thus found the confidence of their own expression. For even where no conscious debt to him can be traced in the work of younger poets, such as Odia Ofeimun, Niyi Osundare, Harry Garuba, Tanure Ojaide, and Femi Osofisan, they have had of necessity to look to the foreground of Nigerian literature occupied by Clark-Bekederemo and other major writers in order to find their own space. It is no exaggeration to say that it is largely his legacy that they are in the process of consolidating, in the tumultuous climate of a society that has the strongest claim to being considered the most vibrant area of creative endeavor in Africa today.

10

Parables of the African Condition

The New Realism in African Fiction

It is not, I think, too much to affirm that in the new literature of Africa expressed in the European languages, the correspondence is a direct one between the themes and preoccupations that have governed the direction of the creative imagination and the distinctive aspects of modern African experience. Indeed those aspects that have gone into the shaping of the modern African consciousness, as much in its bold and broad configurations as in its more intimate manifestations, have also determined the lines of articulation of our contemporary literature. In the process of expressing the tensions set up in our modern awareness by the varied and often contradictory elements of the collective experience, the literature has come both to reflect that experience and to carry its imprint in the modes and particular accents with which our writers have sought to formulate its manifold character and to register its significant moments. This literature has served both as a direct and objective representation of our modern experience as well as a symbolization of the states of mind induced by that experience.

Given this background, it is easy to understand that in the colonial situation—which continues to stand as the significant reference for our modern experience—the response to the peculiar stresses of a problematic historical experience should have expressed itself in our literature as a distinct form of the Romantic imagination. There is no clearer illustration of this active implication of the processes of the imaginative creation in the facts of African historical experience than the literature of Negritude. Beyond its direct challenge of the colonial situation—through a documentary presentation of its political, economic, and social impositions as well as an anguished projection of its psychological and moral stresses—Negritude also involves necessarily the elaboration of a myth of self-justification for the Black race, a myth founded upon a revaluation of its African, precolonial antecedents. The African *mystique* in the literature of Negritude takes the form, as we know, of a celebration of the structure of thought and values associated with a pristine world of traditional society, which is identified with an organizing principle of the collective *ethos* of the entire Black race. The literature of Negritude is thus infused with a Romanticism that derives its sustaining force and value from what one might call a historical imperative. If, in an immediate sense, this literature represents an effort to redefine the terms of the colonial conflict as manifested in history, to reverse the meaning and implications of the historical drama in which the Black race and the African people in particular were involved, the process of self-affirmation also implies the elaboration of a nonhistorical scheme of reference for the Black identity, an appeal to an original principle of the collective being and experience outside the framework of the historical process itself.

The immediate correlation of the Romantic imagination in our modern literature to its historical and sociological determinants in the colonial situation makes clear the psychological function and positive significance of this form of our contemporary expression. At the same time, it is undeniable that in its strong ideological bent, it involves a simplification of the facts of the African experience, situated almost wholly within the perspective of an opposition between Africa and the West. It makes for a global, emotional perception of history, which leaves no room for a proper attention to the realities that constitute the actual, extensive fabric of an ongoing collective experience. Today, in the postcolonial period, those realities upon which the Romantic imagination in our literature understandably cast a shadow have emerged in their starkness; they dictate a shift of concerns on the part of African writers as well as a new perspective of vision.

I call this development "the new realism" to suggest that process by which African writers have begun to modify their stance and to adjust their angle of perception to take account of those political and social realities that began in the wake of African independence to impress themselves more closely upon the general attention through the entire continent. This is a development that stands in marked contrast to the earlier Romanticism, which was employed to affirm and to celebrate a specially projected sense of uniqueness. However, this Romanticism began to lose its point and pertinence as events on the continent began to take a new turn and to impose a more rounded, more *realistic* awareness of human experience than was permissible earlier.

The particular meaning I attach to the term *realism* relates therefore essentially to a new attitude toward the African experience in the more recent literature, a new apprehension of events, social forces, and human character as they interact to create the sense of a moral universe impinging upon the writer's consciousness. The term translates not merely a particular mode of formal presentation of the contemporary African situation but also, and principally, the awareness induced by the writer's new relationship to that situation and a corresponding urge to reinsert the African imagination within the total fabric of historical experience.[1]

This new realism of the African writer, which stands in contrast to the earlier Romanticism, reflects the mood of disillusionment that has invaded African minds as the hopes and expectations inspired by the general euphoria of political independence, taken as the signal for a new and positive phase of African development, began to fade.[2] This mood has determined the manner and attitude characteristic of what I have termed the new realism. The manner relates to the deployment within the imaginative work of a particular scheme of symbols, which register a negative apprehension of the African world and are represented as the objective historical reference of the imaginative text. The distinctive quality of this apprehension is a comprehensive somberness. The mood prevails in all forms of African writing at the present moment, but its features are most evident in fiction, which, by its nature, affords the writer the most convenient means of reporting upon life and underscoring such reporting with an expressive point of view.

I want to consider five novels representative of the new direction in African literature: away from the Romantic projection engendered by colonial domination and toward a more realistic engagement with the African situation in the postcolonial dispensation. These works present themselves as a series of statements upon our present condition and arise from an apprehension of the objective facts of our present experience. At the same time, as novels, they raise issues concerning the relationship between the aesthetic and moral values proposed by fiction and political imperatives in the real world. As Irving Howe has pointed out, these are issues that affect the process of imaginative creation and bear directly on the artistic choices the writer has to make in such a way as to transcend the immediate political and social focus of the work and thus connect with what he calls "some supervening human bond above and beyond ideas" (Howe, 1987, 24). The novels with which we are concerned need to be appraised from this critical perspective. For not only do the African novels of the new realism provide varied illustrations of a common theme, they also demonstrate the dilemmas it presents to each writer in his handling of this theme.

We begin our examination with a discussion of *This Earth My Brother* by Kofi Awoonor,[3] a novel that has received less attention than it deserves, largely, I believe, as a result of the striking parallel it offers to Ayi Kwei Armah's *The Beautyful Ones Are Not Yet Born*, a work that was for a time celebrated as marking in an original way, through the use of an insistent imagery and the deployment of a reflective prose, the new realism in African fiction. The parallel consists in the focus in the two novels on the postindependence situation in Ghana; at the center of Awoonor's work, we encounter this theme and setting, along with the political and social question as a factor for the mood of depression in which the whole novel is engulfed. The somber evocations of Awoonor's novel thus complement and confirm the apprehension of waste and desolation that also dominates in the meditation of Armah's hero: "Tonight, there is a deep silence in the land. Joe says it is the hush hour before the holocaust: it is the silence of death" (116).

Awoonor's novel displays, however, an originality all its own, an originality that is at once brought to our attention by its unusual structure, in which passages of narration alternate with interludes cast in the form of either reflections or poetic evocations. This technical feature of the novel would be merely intriguing if it did not turn out to have a point to it. In effect, the allegorical intention that Awoonor ascribes to his work is expressly carried through the interplay between the narrative passages and the interludes. The straight narration of the main chapters develops the novel in terms of the anecdotal, a main plot line composed of the casual progression of events, while the interludes explore the inner meanings of these external events. The distinction between the two resolves itself into one between experience and vision.

The theme of "experience" in a near-Blakean sense is given in the clearly articulated sociological references of the novel and handled with a realism directly centered upon social questions. The adventures of Amamu, the hero of the novel, is a typical story of social ascension and is employed to figure the contradictions and dilemmas of contemporary Africa. It exemplifies the remarkable openness created in African society as a direct consequence of the impact of colonialism, which fostered the emergence of an educated elite as a new social class. Amamu is a representative figure of that class, and in the descriptions of his various relationships, Awoonor offers an inside picture of that class—its way of living, its preoccupations, and its values. There emerges a satirical intent to the image he paints of the new African bourgeoisie, an image similar to that offered by Armah's *Fragments,* with the added point that the question of social inequality that arises from the emergence of the new elite is explicitly raised in Awoonor's novel. This is the whole point, it seems to me, of the alternation of episodes in which Amamu is made to journey between Kanda Estate, the residential area of the privileged, and Nima, the slum section of Accra. The contrast between the two localities signifies the opposition between the two social forces that confront each other in postcolonial Africa.

But it is not the drama of the class war in Africa that Kofi Awoonor's novel presents, and the documentary character of the social picture that emerges from the novel has no precise ideological significance, such as we find, for instance, in the work of Sembène Ousmane. The presentation of the new elite is offered simply as an indictment of the new masters in Africa:

> On the Liberty Arch the words are inscribed, "Freedom and Justice." The darkness of the black star lies in its square where immense appropriations are made to increase the striking force of the army of a starving, naked and diseased nation to march and wear its boots newly received from England under certificates of urgency—judging the state of depletion of the national coffers—the one who left stole all the money, the bastard, the b.f.—new epaulets, new strings, new crowns for newly appointed generals and brigadiers, and uniforms for latrine carriers. Fear death by guns. (30)

The twist of the final echo of T. S. Eliot's "The Waste Land" in the passage underscores with a grim note Awoonor's sarcastic summary of politics in postcolonial Africa. The corruption and inefficiency of the new masters is reflected in the material decay of the world it manages, and by a coincidence, which reveals a certain logic of the current fictional depiction of African society, the image that Awoonor employs to convey a sense of this decay is the same as in Armah's first novel, though handled with greater discretion. Thus the night soil that is carried through the streets of Accra comes to acquire the value of a metaphor connoting the moral squalor of the new society as determined by the disposition, attitudes, and actions of its new, indigenous rulers. In another evocation in the novel, the place of this metaphor in its overt system of meaning is unequivocally stated: "We will be caught on this mountain again, dying, screaming, our eyes on heaven. On this dunghill we will search among the rubble for our talisman of hope" (92).

Although the novel carries a distinct historical and sociological reference, as well as a clear critical intention, its real level of meaning has less to do with social experience than with individual fate and consciousness amidst the pressures of that experience. Amamu's adventure is intended to uncover the sense of an individual life as a pilgrimage through the vicissitudes of a concrete experience toward some kind of vision. The connection between the themes of experience and vision as they are presented here is developed principally in the relationship between the hero and Adiza, his mistress, who he identifies sometimes with a female cousin who had died young, and at other times with the mythical "woman of the sea," who functions as the spiritual reference of his adventure: "She was here, my mermaid sitting on my lap, dripping wet with water now crying now laughing. I stretched forth my hand to squeeze her breasts. They felt like flames, black blue flames of the burning of the spirit, bursting in my hand in gold" (4). The transformation of this figure into an object of immediate experience, her insertion into the course of Amamu's concrete life, is indicated in another passage:

> I found her among the dancers sweating on the floor in one of those wild new dances of youth. She is my woman of the sea. She is the one who appeared through the cleft sea in the slash of the moonbeam to come to me under the Indian almond. She led me then through all farmlands, she led me over the wide lagoon where the sprats sang a song from the salt basins, over bird island we flew with the gulls returning from sea. (60)

This female figure exists, then, at two levels of Amamu's consciousness and in the varied characters of other women to whom he relates. The conflation suggests the points of interaction in Amamu's awareness between a perceived and sentient order of reality and its movements within his deeper self. The interludes serve to develop the correlation between the two by providing the foundation of his spiritual growth, upon which is played out the story of his rise and fall against the background of an extensive knowledge of the world. The fragments of diverse religions, modes of sensibility, and ways of life become elements of a far-flung and disparate experience, which enters into the formation of his individuality and into the flow of an all-embracing consciousness, there to merge with an underlying current of the individual mind. It is as if these aspects of a comprehensive experience settle down to a primordial layer of that mind, where they are constituted into active functions of a second state of dream and imagination.

Of this profound layer of the hero's consciousness, Amamu's woman of the sea stands as a vital reference. She carries the suggestive force of mythical symbol in the novel and is associated, as its living principle, with what can only be considered an abiding spirit of the land. The purpose of the various degrees of correspondence between the facets of Amamu's life and experience becomes clear in this light: Amamu's constant response to the symbol confers on his adventure a sense of progress toward a restoration to the wellsprings of being. This sense of a movement toward fulfillment, toward a form of transcendence even, emerges readily from the evocation in the final interlude of the novel; because of its importance, it is worth reproducing at some length:

> My woman of the sea, I am leaving for the almond tree where I first met you. I shall be there when you rise, when you rise to meet me at our appointed hour. I am coming down from these mountains of dung from these hills of shame. I shall walk the steps of ancient war drums, I shall move to the beat of *husage, atrikpui* and *agbadza* in the twirl of my folded cloth you will read the sign of my coming. My lips will be sealed so I cannot sing those ancient songs. I will believe you when you say you will come into the same fields I rode with the ghosts the first memorials of my journey from the womb. For now believe me, the land is covered with blood, and more blood shall flow in it to redeem the covenant we made in that butterfly field, and under my almond. For you I renounce the salvation of madness and embrace with a singular hope, your hope. You will dance again in my time our time the same step you traced in the earth to the ancient drums, and through them reveal the eternal legend of your love. I shall crawl to your knees in the sand at the water's edge and retrace then the first syllables of my speech. . . .
>
> They are searching under the shrubs for the spirits of the departed priests of thunder. The drums themselves are muffled now by the anguish of the drummers lost in trance among the nims. . . .

It shall be the last and singular act that you will perform for her memory, the finite prostration shall signify one simple act of faith—that her return shall be proclaimed before the second cock in the land.

We will keep the faith that heavenly muskets shall sound her coming. . . .

Return the miracle return the miracle return the miracle. (165–66)

There appears to be a similarity here to the final integration in *L'aventure ambigüe* of Cheik Hamidou Kane's hero to the absolute, a movement out of the concrete life into a realm of mystical being. But in Awoonor's novel, that movement is determined by a failure of the hero to come to terms with the sordid realities of his world, and it does not portend exactly the sense of a defeated withdrawal as in Kane's novel, for Amamu's adventure assumes an exemplary significance for the collective life in a way in which Samba Diallo's does not.

The evocative writing in the passage serves more than an aesthetic purpose, for the imagery and references provide a lead into the meaning of Awoonor's allegory of modern Africa. Amamu's individual experience merges with the collective and lends a moral to it. The social references of the novel suggest the problematic nature of the African course in history and yield a somber vision of that course ("our sadness itself, based upon that distant sadness which is the history of this land, defies all consolation"[165]). There is a sense in which Awoonor's novel offers in extended and documented form a new version of his "Songs of Sorrow," a lament upon the state of Africa, seen as an enduring collective predicament. At the same time, it also proposes, in the contrast between Amamu's surface experience of life and its reference to a deeper principle of the collective being, an ideal of reconciliation with the self and of harmony with the world, which offers hope and consolation in this universe of desolation. There can be no question but that the particular nature of this ideal, as represented in Awoonor's novel, implies the recovery of an ancestral integrity of vision.

The moral of Awoonor's allegorical tale of Africa seems, then, to involve a throwback to an idealized African past as a reaction against an unacceptable present. For this reason, there is some paradox to the final Christian note on which the novel ends. But this paradox, this religious reference, points in its own way to the essential burden of the novel: its insistence upon the need for a wholeness of society as a condition for progress into a harmonious future. Again, on this point, Awoonor's novel complements Armah's first novel admirably; with both, we are made to respond through the movement of the narrative and of the imagery to a moral vision of human experience in its most general significance.

To turn to Sembène Ousmane's *Xala* is to encounter an altogether different world and atmosphere, although the novel espouses a similar vision as that of Kofi Awoonor in its focus upon the common theme as determined by the new realism, in this case as a variation upon the formal realism that has so far been central to Ousmane's work.[4] It must be remarked at the outset that *Xala* continues the steady development of socialist realism in his output and indeed brings this development to something of a high point. The critical exploration of the social scene in Africa in his writing receives in this work a new and sharp definition at the same time that the novelist's tone acquires a new mordancy. This continuity of Ousmane's inspiration links the theme of the short story "Un amour de la rue sablonneuse" in the collection *Voltaïques* to the more wide-ranging critique contained in the work under consideration. An even more significant connection is indicated by the use of sexuality both in the short story "Vehi Ciosanne" and in the novel *Xala* to paint a picture of a degenerate order within African society. Taken together, both works confirm in a striking way the comprehensive nature of Ousmane's ideological perspective, in which the old traditional class and the new bourgeoisie are seen to be banded together as reactionary forces and to stand as the antithesis of his socialist idealism.

Sembene Ousmane's reconstruction of the banal details of everyday life is essential to his committed idealism, which has found perhaps its most effective expression in the novella *Le mandat* (*The Money Order*). The picture he presents of the condition of the common people under the new post colonial dispensation is imbued with an uncommon sympathy, which flows directly out of what we feel to be the novelist's immediate understanding of the desperation that rules their lives, the same warm understanding that makes for the particular lyricism of Ousmane's first film, *Borom Sarret*. In *Le mandat*, the personal history of Ibrahama Dieng—possibly Ousmane's most memorable fictional character—is employed to provide an insight of intense topical interest into perhaps the most dramatic human aspect of the present-day social history of Africa: the massive process by which greater and greater numbers of individuals are being constituted into an urban *Lumpenproletariat* on the margins of the new civil society. Predictably, the sociological reconstruction also has an ideological significance, for the *peripeteia* of Dieng's humble saga in his efforts to cash his money order illuminate the marking phases of an experience through which, by a series of special judgments, he acquires a general consciousness of the common condition of individuals of his class. *Le mandat* is intended to provide insight into the formation of a revolutionary consciousness, one that leads to that state of commitment figured in the rather obvious symbolism that concludes the novel: "Dieng se redressa. Son regard avec celui de Bâ se recontrèrent" (Dieng rose to his full height. His gaze met that of Bâ) (219).

The narrative content and structures of representation in *Le mandat* have of course a firm anchor in a political orthodoxy, and I imagine that the novel will be considered an important contribution to the tradition of socialist literature and that, after the achievement of *Les bouts de bois de Dieu* (*God's Bits of Wood*), it will confirm Ousmane's honorable place in that tradition. But if *Le mandat* corresponds in its conception and execution to an orthodox formulation of the Marxist novel, *Xala*, while reproducing the vein in its essential texture, gives to this formulation a peculiar turn, for within its general framework of a realistic mode employed to serve a socialist moralism, Ousmane introduces elements that circumscribe that mode to give pointed effect to its didactic function. With its recourse to the notion of *xala* (that is, sexual impotence) as a basic device for the plot, the novel draws its inspiration both from popular belief and from the African tradition of the moralrity fable of which it can be considered essentially a modern transposition. In its extension of the folk tradition and its application to a contemporary situation, the novel *Xala* remains faithful to the spirit of the traditional form; here, the allegorical significance of the tale is enunciated through the sexual imagery that serves as the expressive channel of the novelist's critical intention.

It is pertinent to observe in this respect that the symbolism of *Xala* functions almost exclusively at the level of its collective significance. El Hadj Abjou Kader Seye, the principal character, is given just enough individuality to make him credible as a recognizable social type; he is really no more than a specific instance of the mercantile and bureaucratic bourgeoisie of postcolonial Africa and an embodiment of its life styles and values. The sudden access of impotence that frustrates him is just as obviously intended as a device for comment upon the weaknesses of that class: its lack of creative potential and its incapacity to offer to the society in which it has assumed a directing position an authentic system of sustaining values. The satirical presentation of the bourgeoisie—and its luxury (in every sense of the word), its narrow conception of its responsibilities, and its pretensions and vanity—is animated by a sense of outrage made all the more insistent by the suggestion that the impotence of the dominant class constitutes the significant inhibiting factor to growth and renewal in society as a whole. In *Xala*, we witness the opposite current to the flow of sympathy for the common people that runs so powerfully in *Le mandat*. It may be thought that the obvious partisanship of its social commentary makes for a certain thinness of the texture of human experience, which Ousmane presents at the realistic level of the narrative development in his novel. Indeed, his manner, as omniscient narrator, of intruding direct commentary that leaves us in no doubt as to his attitudes toward the milieu he depicts works toward depriving the novel of the full values of the fictional mode as a creative transposition of life in its density. However, given the theme and the earnestness that the novelist brings to its treatment, its single-mindedness may be counted an asset of sorts, for it does make for a concentration of interest. The unmistakable vigor of the narrative style and the fine sense for detail evident in the presentation also lend character to this aspect of the novel and give its evocations enough relief to carry conviction. Consider, for example, the terseness with which El Hadj's decline is narrated:

> Soleil après soleil, nuit après nuit, son tourment permanent corrodait ses activités professionnelles. Comme un fromager imbibe d'eau sur la rivière, il s'enfonçait dans la vase. Souffrant, il s'éloignait du cercle de ses pairs, où se nouaient, se scellaient les transactions. Alourdi, il perdait sa souplesse, son habileté à mener ses affaires. Insensiblement son magasin périclitait. Il devait maintenir son grand train de vie, son standing: trois villas, le parc automobile, ses femmes, enfants, domestiques et les employés. Habitué à tout régler par chèques, il en usait pour éponger d'anciennes dettes et pour l'économie domestique. Il dépensait. Son passif avait grevé son actif. (81)

> [Day after day, night after night, his torment ate into his professional life. Like a waterlogged silk-cotton silk tree on the river bank, he sank deeper into the mud. Because of his condition, he avoided the company of his fellow businessmen, among whom transactions were made and sealed. He was weighed down by worry and lost his skill and his ability to do business. Imperceptibly, his affairs began to go to pieces. He had to maintain his high standard of living: three villas, several cars, his wives, children, servants and employees. Accustomed to settling every-

thing by check, he continued to pay his accounts and his household expenses in this way. He went on spending. Soon, his liabilities outstripped his credit.] (Trans. Clive Wake, 52)

As with *Le mandat*, Ousmane demonstrates in this novel the virtues of a straightforward and racy fictional style. Moreover, both novels derive the force of their impact from their overwhelming relevance to our immediate social experience; we recognize that they place in the dynamic setting of fiction and thus in an appropriate objective light those issues with which any articulate conscience must be preoccupied in Africa today. Despite the barbed edges of its satire, therefore, *Xala* conveys a note of sincerity such that we come to accept its partisanship as arising naturally from the unequivocal and vehement involvement of the novelist with the questions he raises. The transparency of the text thus appears as something of a value; it becomes possible to see it as an indication less of a narrowness of vision imposed by the novelist's bias than of a forthrightness of statement.

This does not prevent Ousmane, however, from trying to give a special complication to his theme in order to enhance his statement. This particular dimension of the novel is related to what we have seen of its character as a morality fable in the African folktale tradition. Ousmane's use of the notion of *xala* as a reference for the belief system of the whole novel may at first sight appear curious, given its realistic framework and the habitual rationalistic outlook of all of his work. But the notion serves him admirably not only to express his critical view of the social class that is the object of his searching attention but also to convey a symbolism of subversion directed against the self-image of that class. This function of the notion as developed in the novel is particularly evident in the way it is used as a negation of the economic ideas of the new African bourgeoisie, which are represented as reducing themselves essentially to a mere quest for self-gratification. The acquisition of worldly goods and the appetite for consumption thus form part of a sensual inclination that finds its supreme expression in the ideal of sexual virility. The alienation of women becomes a natural consequence of this system of values; they are relegated to the status of objects to be possessed and enjoyed. The incidental critique of the abuse of polygamy by the men is joined here to a portrayal of the false consciousness of the women characters, who give their assent to the degradation of their gender in exchange for material benefits. In its immediate application to the bourgeoisie, *xala* signifies the factitious character of that class and represents a denial of its controlling values. The incapacities of the new African bourgeoisie as a class are measured against the vital tensions implied in the natural process, which culminates in begetting and creating.

By placing El Hadj Seye in immediate relationship to the bizarre figure of the beggar who puts the *xala* on him, Ousmane leads the action of his novel to a significant climax. If the relationship stresses the exploitative character of the economic methods of the bourgeoisie (somewhat ingenuously illustrated in the specific development of the plot), it also demonstrates that the class conflicts that those methods engender progress along a critical path, which leads to the possibility of alternative social arrangements and moral choices. The final confrontation between the two men, which culminates in the riot of the beggars, seems intended to be taken as an expression of the revolutionary potential of the present African situation; if that is so, its social message is made with a wonderful discretion, that of a symbolic mode of statement. For the scene in which El Hadj Seye is stripped and spat upon by the beggars cannot be taken merely in a unilateral sense as figuring the inevitable downfall of men of his class—nothing in the presentation suggests anything indicative of so confident an expectation, though such would indeed be consistent with the pieties of Ousmane's ideological affiliations—but rather as representing, more modestly but perhaps more profoundly, a moral proposition in which the debilitating appetites of the bourgeoisie would be supplanted by a new ascetism, as the outer form of an authentic creative endowment.

The final scene of *Xala*, reminiscent as it is of that of Luis Bunuel's *Viridiana*, cannot therefore be taken as a naive prediction of the coming African revolution; its departure from the norms of a formal realism is so clearly conditioned by its affiliation to the framing devices of the Spanish filmmaker as to make such an interpretation untenable. In the ritual reversal of situations and values that the scene depicts, it extends and deepens the realistic mode by which the social content of the novel is conveyed. In this final scene, the symbolism of *Xala* attains its level of greatest expressiveness and meaning.

No such symbolic function attends Mongo Beti's imagination in his conception and writing of the novel *Perpétue*.[5] Of the novels in what now appears to be Beti's second period, this work seems to me to maintain the closest link with the novels of the earlier, colonial period. It can be considered in particular a restatement in new terms of the theme of *Mission terminée* (*Mission to Kala*), whose general feel for the southern Cameroonian terrain it recaptures,[6] with the further dimension that the tragic vein that weaves a brooding counterpoint to the comic satire of the earlier work now comes fully to the fore. We recognize, for example, the same eye for ludicrous detail as in the earlier satires in this passage:

> D'abord, la mère, s'epoumona à souffler dans une poire végétale plantée entre les fesses de l'enfant couché à plat ventre sur ses genoux, la tête rasant le sol, le petit derrière pointé en l'air; puis saisissant les deux chévilles du jeune garçon, elle amena ses jambes dans la même ligne dangereusement penchée que le reste du corps; posant alors l'autre main sur les deux fesses de l'enfant, elle le maintint dans cette position raidie pour faire pénétrer le lavement plus avant dans le gros intestin. (45)

> [First, the mother strained her lungs to blow into a vegetable douche stuck between the buttocks of the child lying flat on his stomach upon her knees, his head nearly touching the ground, his little behind pointing up into the air. Then, seizing the young lad's heels, she brought his legs up till they were in line with the precarious slope of the rest of his body. Then she put the her other hand on his buttocks and held the child in this awkward position to make the enema penetrate more deeply into the large intestine.] (Reed and Wake, 31)

But the exuberance of Beti's writing which animates the evocations of *Mission terminée* and *Le roi miraculé* (*King Lazarus*) has given way in the more recent novel to a grimness and a darker apprehension of the same world. This determines the prevailing atmosphere of *Perpétue*, given right at the outset:

> Sorti de Ntermelen, on traversait un pays de forêts de plus en plus élevées de voûte, drues et ténébreuses, et de villages alignés des deux côtés de la route, dont plusieurs montrèrent à Essola le visage d'une mystérieuse désolation. (13)

> [They left Ntermelen and went through a stretch of forest country. Higher and higher the trees arched over the road, dense and shadowy. And both sides were lined with villages; many of these revealed to Essola an appearance of mysterious desolation.] (Reed and Wake, 4)

This desolation, we find out as the narrative progresses, refers as much to the material misery of the general population in the hinterland that the novel explores as to the moral tenor of their everyday lives. Thus, Beti's general point in the novel is the obvious one: the entire society has been corrupted and demoralized by the nature and methods of the regime that has succeeded the European colonizer. The figure of Baba Toura is proposed as representative of the dictatorial propensities and viciousness of the African ruler in the postcolonial situation. The political references of *Perpétue*—as of his *Remember Ruben* and its sequel, *La ruine presque cocasse d'un polichinelle* (Lament for an African Pol)—extend the explicit statement of the essay *Main basse sur le Cameroun;* they define not only the ideological orientation of the novel but also the whole tone, the peculiar blend of militancy, moral indignation, and despondency with which it is pervaded. This explains what appears to be the deliberate refusal of a controlled detachment on the part of Beti. As with Sembène Ousmane, the fictional world is intended as a direct restitution of a perception still close to the tensions in the real universe of social and political life of the novelist's understanding of events, unmediated by the distancing effect of the fictional mode. As we have remarked, this approach seems to work for Ousmane. With Beti, however, the disadvantage of this closeness to events is immediately apparent from the way it betrays him now and again into crude simplifications:

> Il y seulement quelques années, souvenez-vous, tout le monde pensait que les connaisseurs de book allaient bientôt tenir le haut du pavé. Oui, de temps en temps, on parlait aussi des commerçants et des transporteurs. Personne ne songeait aux musulmans du Nord, aux hommes à grandes robes. Mais voici tout à coup Baba Toura, et plus personne ne reconnaît plus le pays. Et voilà les connaisseurs de book précipités dans la fosse de la malédiction, comme des malpropres. (63)

> [Remember, just a few years ago, everyone thought the book people were soon going to be at the top. Yes, once a while, one spoke also of the traders and people in the transport business. Nobody gave a thought to the Moslems of the north, the men in flowing robes. Now suddenly, Baba Toura appears, and the country is no longer recognizable. And the book people are cursed and thrown into the ditch.] (My translation)

The point of view upon social developments in the Cameroons expressed in the quotation is attributed to a character who is possibly the weakest in the novel, but it also reflects Beti's' explicit position in *Main basse sur le Cameroun* and exhibits a churlishness that can only be considered incompatible with a serious critical purpose. In the specific context of the novel, the remark is intended to express the situation of general frustration, which the novel dramatizes in the fate of Perpétue, whose unhappy life forms the substance of the narrative. That fate is summed up in the remark of another character commenting upon Perpétue's protestations against her being forced by her mother into an undesired marriage, the act that begins her tragedy: "Trop tard, ma petite mère. Personne ne te consultera, n'y compte surtout pas. Ta mère t'a piegée. Nous sommes toujours piegés, et par les nôtres encore" [Too late, my little woman. Nobody will consult you—don't ever count on that. Your mother has trapped you. We are trapped from the start, and for that matter, by those closest to us] (110).

The remark underlines the significance of Perpétue's dilemma and her eventual sacrifice. It amplifies within the narrative itself the significance of the novel's title and its somber qualification in the subtitle: "ou l'habitude du malheur (or the habit of unhappiness)." The continuous pattern of unhappiness is inscribed in a long history of oppression and deprivation, which has come to determine a habitual collective response: dejected resignation. The confusions and frustrations depicted in *Mission terminée* have become accentuated into a deep moral abjectness in *Perpétue*.

There is therefore, as with Ousmane, a literal level of meaning ascribed to the story of Perpétue's humiliation and agony, for it is intended clearly as representative of the continent's betrayal by its leaders; her sacrifice to base interests and the novelist's partisanship implied by this ascription of meaning are emphasized by her forced marriage to the despicable Edouard, who is portrayed with bold, convincing strokes as the type of unscrupulous mediocrity who thrives best in the corrupt atmosphere of repressive regimes. In his position as the immediate local representative of Baba Toura, he personifies the moral emptiness of the general political life:

> C'est ainsi qu'Edouard eut la révélation de son pouvoir, vraiment illimité dans sa sphère de Zombotown, tout de même que celui de son maître sur la nation. Edouard était proprement la réplique zombotownienne de Baba Toura; c'était un Baba Toura en miniature. Voilà un homme qui avait su s'ajuster au cours des choses instauré par l'indépendance. (249–250)

> [Thus it was that the extent of his power was revealed to Edward. It was in his sphere of Zombotown as unlimited as the power of his master over the nation. Edward was precisely the Zombotown replica of Baba Tura, a miniature Baba Tura. Here indeed was a man who had known how to

adapt himself to the course of events set off by Independence.] (Reed and Wake, 179)

The poignancy of Perpétue's sacrifice is rendered more acute by the contrast between, on one hand, her sad acceptance of the sinister sexual bargain through which, after their marriage, Edouard delivers her to the Scarpia-like character, the police officer Mbarga Onana, and on the other, the spontaneous warmth of her adulterous relationship with Zeyang, the young football star. The understanding between Edouard and Onana stands out clearly as what it is—a perversion of the normal social code of marriage—and emphasizes the moral degradation that marks the political affiliation of the two men, the universe of corrupt values they represent. Against the sordid character of their understanding, Perpétue's liaison with Zeyang, for all its transgression of conventional morality, appears in a light all the purer. Her attraction to Zeyang springs from a natural impulse to health and vigor, to the promise of life. Our response to their liaison is thus conditioned by an implicit reordering of the normal valuations of the whole structure of social arrangements. Further, we connect that response to the larger meaning that we now attach to Perpétue's fate as the thwarting of that promise of life.

Although our sympathy flows naturally to Perpétue and Zeyang, it is not at all certain that we can accommodate Essola within its range, despite his identification with their cause, nor that our response to them will make for anything like a ready tolerance for the role he is made to play in the novel. Essola is a problematic character. Indeed, the change in the tone and temper of Mongo Beti's writing is most easily felt in the details and general effect of his molding of this character. In Essola, we have a somber reincarnation of Medza, the hero of *Mission terminée*. The play of parallels and contrasts between the two novels turns on the central position of the two heroes in the narrative structure of the works in which they each feature. The similarities are striking—their youth, their involvement in a quest that is also the occasion for an exploration of the milieu in which it takes place and finally, the culmination of the quest itself in an act of self-affirmation—similarities that establish clearly the continuity of Beti's inspiration.

The general vehemence of Beti's tone in *Perpétue* is indicative of the graver disposition of his hero in this novel as compared to *Mission terminée*. It prepares us for the grim determination of the particular form that Essola's act of self-affirmation will take. Essola's parricide is not only consistent with this new disposition but also fits in with the atmosphere of gloom within which it occurs. The sordid details of Perpétue's pathetic story as it unfolds in the course of his investigation comprise a dark canvas of characters and situations in which his terrible act may be thought to find, as it were, a natural setting.

Even when allowances have been made for all of this, the circumstances of the act itself, as depicted in the novel, are far from inducing an acceptance of the significance that the novelist invites us to attach to it. For one thing, Martin, the brother whom Essola kills, is precisely the kind of feeble but lovable character for whom we cannot but feel a strong pity. Essola's attempt to ascribe a kind of ritual significance to his act does not carry conviction. For although his act of parricide may be interpreted as an act of propitiation for the sacrifice of his sister,[7] his choice of victim reduces the value of this act considerably.

Much more serious is the disarticulation the episode causes to the relationship between the political theme of the novel and its moral implications. It derives quite simply from the fact that we are not made to feel a necessary connection between Essola's act of parricide and any broader political purpose. As we have the facts in the novel, his act springs much more directly from a personal vindictiveness than the considered imperatives of a mature political awareness. In the circumstances, it can only inspire a feeling of horror, for its value remains at best at the level of the character's individual psychology; it represents no more than a final release of a rage that has built up within an isolated and possibly damaged consciousness, rather than a gesture invested with the full energy of a collective will. Essola's attempt to put a political light on his act therefore appears awkward and patently contrived:

Vous avez assassiné Ruben ou bien vous vous êtes accommodés de ce crime pour que vos fils préférés, rendus irresponsables par votre excessive indulgence, continuent à festoyer impunément avec la rançon de leurs sœurs, à se repaître en quelque sorte du sang de ces malheureuses, comme des cannibales. (295)

[You killed Ruben or anyway you accepted the crime so that your favourite sons, whom you spoil until they become totally irresponsible, can go on making money with their sisters' ransom, in a way feeding on the blood of those wretched women like cannibals.] (Reed and Wake, 212)

The leaden quality of the writing and the impression of sheer posturing it produces reflect a fundamental flaw that mars the whole novel. We feel distinctly here that Mongo Beti is trying to manipulate our responses in favor of his personal sympathies and choices in the real world, rather than let those responses flow naturally out of the implications of the narrative scheme and the human interest of his novel. It is no wonder that so much of his text rings false. This judgment, it need hardly be said, concerns what appears as a real failure of Beti's art and has nothing to do with either the merits or the sincerity of his real-life commitment. The point here is that the extreme nature of Essola's act is not sufficiently justified by the action in the novel nor does it bear a conceivable relation to what one might consider a genuine political purpose. The arbitrary nature of Beti's contrivance becomes all the clearer when we compare Essola's gesture, which strikes us as resting on a confusion of political activism with a gratuitous terrorism arising out of the impulses of private passions, with that of Oreste in Jean-Paul Sartre's *Les Mouches,* in which no such confusion arises and whose moral value derives from its immediate social and political determinations. Mongo Beti's novel fails to suggest a comparable moral implication.

We might conclude, then, by observing that the failure of Beti's novel arises from the novelist's difficulty in giving to the world of his fiction the proper measure of impersonality it required to achieve a representative significance. This failure is all the more regrettable in that it was avoidable. Beti could well have done without Essola's parricide, for the novel is often charged with such pathos, and its evocations are rendered with such vivid realism that we need no further prodding to make the appropriate associations, in such a way that the moral of Perpétue's tale emerges with the necessary force and clarity.

If in Mongo Beti's novel we are made aware of a "palpable design" to relate the human interest of the work to an arbitrary political meaning, Wole Soyinka's second novel, *Season of Anomy,*[8] seems to suffer from an opposite weakness in the diffusion of its political theme within an exploration of the private sensibilities of the hero. The novel seems to indicate a curious ambivalence compounded at once from a sense of profound interest in politics as a phenomenon and an instinctive recoil from its immediate implications.

There are indeed interesting parallels between Beti's novel and Soyinka's, which make the differences between them somewhat paradoxical but instructive of the divergent approaches of the two writers to the imaginative handling of public issues. Behind each novel stands a political statement from which it draws its theme and the dominant quality of its emotional tone: *Main basse sur le Cameroun* in the case of Beti and the autobiographical essay *The Man Died* in the case of Soyinka. *Season of Anomy*, for its part, is a fictional transposition and interrogation of the events related to the Nigerian crisis that erupted in the early 1960s, which culminated in a civil war. The novel springs from Soyinka's personal involvement in these events, which also inspired the reflections contained in *The Man Died*. This work is accordingly much more a personal testimony of history than is Mongo Beti's equivalent text. Where the emphasis in Beti's essay is on the critical documentation of the objective operations and effects of the political situation in the Cameroons, marked by a neocolonial dependence on France, Soyinka inclines more toward a general meditation upon the inward significance of the relations of power and the tensions of history, upon their repercussions on the individual as well as the collective sensibility. Both works contain diatribe of a particularly virulent kind, but Beti's invectives arise out of a particularized sense of indignation, whereas Soyinka's are mediated and superseded in the long run by a more comprehensive and deeper introspective purpose.

It is precisely this mood of introspection, this inwardness, that pervades Soyinka's novel, most remarkably as regards his conception of Ofeyi, the principal character. Ofeyi is the antithesis of Essola; the contrast is made even clearer by the different effect in each case of the quest motif on which the structure of both novels is based. Where with Essola's journeyings in the course of his investigation into the death of his sister we have a real progression of facts, with Ofeyi we are presented with nothing more than an accumulation of impressions and sensations. There is no real definition at the level of the novel's political reference to the purpose of his quest, and even the political meaning ascribed to the novel does not involve an active participation of the character in any form of concrete political gesture.

This vagueness of the political theme of the novel accords with what we have observed to be its overwhelming reflective character but is nonetheless surprising. For it is not as if Soyinka came to the writing of this novel without a definite experience of political life or without a clear idea of the responsibility of the writer in the present African situation. In 1967, in an essay that was for a time much discussed, "The Writer in a Modern African State," he had deplored what he saw then as "the lack of a vital relevance between the literary concerns of writers and the pattern of reality that has overwhelmed even the writers themselves in the majority of modern African States." (1967, rpt. 1988, 15). The essay reflects a clear awareness of the social and political issues that determine the context of individual lives, as well as an acute sense of the critical function of the writer in a critical engagement with the "pattern of reality" in postcolonial Africa. This realization is fully echoed in *Season of Anomy:*

> The situation, social or political, the situation overwhelms, fouls, corrodes even the most intimate sensations. In such a situation, one is only half a man, no matter how superhuman his woman swears he is. The sentient sensitive totality of the man recognizes that he is only a mangled part of his human potential. (135)

If Soyinka seems in this passage to be speaking for himself through the reflections of his hero, he endows his realization with a general relevance in another passage, which extends the sense of Ofeyi's musings:

> The real death that the people were called upon to die was the death from under, the long creeping paralysis of flesh, and spirit, that seized upon them as the poison tuber might spread through the bowels of the earth. (129)

It seems clear, then, that *Season of Anomy* was written from the same sense of moral affliction from which much of Soyinka's work has proceeded. We might go further and say that the sense of responsibility it engenders leads to some kind of commitment to a revolutionary ideal, so that the novel is inspired by the dream of a radical transformation of the social and political situation: "The pattern could be reversed, the trick of conversion applied equally to the Cartel's technical facilities not merely to effect restitution to the many but to create a new generation for the future" (19).[9]

It is precisely at this point, in the logical development of the novel's political discourse that the center falls out of it. For the problem that has to be faced, which Soyinka never truly confronts in this novel, is that the revolutionary project implies more than mere moral injunctions; it calls for organized movement, sometimes involving the use of violence. The part of Soyinka that perceives this truth is projected in the character of the Dentist, who makes fleeting appearances in the novel and who may be presumed to represent Soyinka's fascination with the ideal of action. At the same time, Soyinka's deepest inclination appears to be toward contemplation, the introspective mode that seizes upon the poetic and moral ideal and gives it brilliant elaboration. It is this side of himself, "the man of images," that is expressed in Ofeyi, about whose spiritual adventure the novel revolves. Soyinka is not far from presenting revolutionary violence in this novel less as the means to a concrete social objective than as a method of psychological liberation and purgation of the individual consciousness. The terms of Ofeyi's reflection on the subject are revealing:

> There was something a little unnatural in this process of resolving the ethics of assassination, preparing oneself to accept or reject the cold-blooded necessity with a minimum of feeling. Demanding in return only the residual sensation of a freed conscience, exhilarated, a dreamless sleep. (136)[10]

Given this peculiar disposition of the central character, it is easy to understand that the novel does not move from this kind of quietism to an active confrontation of the ethical problem raised by political violence in the manner, say, of Albert Camus's *Les Justes*. It provides in fact no more than an outline of the concrete framework of political experience to which Ofeyi's reflections refer and in which the problem itself could have been dramatized. The manner in which the broad issues of political life are raised or even suggested conveys an impression of casualness, without any vital relation to a connected scheme of social or political ideas. The result is that the novel lacks the essential tension required to reflect a focused point of view on the questions of real life. It is as if the precise and articulate intelligence of the 1967 essay had lost its edge in the fictional enactment of those very issues upon which it was brought to bear.

If, therefore, *Season of Anomy* fails to satisfy, it is primarily because it does not offer a cogent elucidation of its ostensible political theme. Further, coming from a writer whose dramatic works convey so vivid a sense of specific life, the vagueness of the novel's references—as indeed the inadequate organization of the elements of the narrative—cannot but appear as something of a disappointing performance.

It takes, of course, more than a literal turn of mind to respond properly to the associations that the densely laden texture of the writing and its characteristic profusion of images suggest of a meaning beyond the immediate social reference. As D. S. Izevbaye remarked in a penetrating study, "At various points in *Season of Anomy* social problems blend with spiritual meanings and allegory with symbolism" (Izevbaye, 1976, 155). This feature of the novel is related to what we have observed as its introspective purpose. In other words, it is a poetic sensibility that Soyinka brings to his treatment of social and political questions in this novel. The vision behind the work is not that of a limited program of social transformation but rather of a renewal of the wellsprings of the collective life and sensibility. The vision receives an embodiment in the figure of Iriyise. As Ofeyi puts it:

> Vision is eternally of man's creating. The woman's acceptance, her collaboration in man's vision of life results time and again in just such periodic embodiments of earth and ideal. It was not a question of beauty or perfection. It was simply that, however briefly, with that transience that was a seal of truth on its own nature, Iriyise would reveal within her person a harrowing vision of the unattainable. (82)

There is a certain parallel, in this identification of a female figure with a spiritual principle, between Amamu's relation to his woman of the sea in Awoonor's *This Earth My Brother* and that of Ofeyi to Iriyise. The parallel is strengthened by the fact that Iriyise's attributes are also shared with a second female character, Taiila, through whom the moral import of the ideal she represents is made immediate to Ofeyi's practical life and options. There is, however, an important distinction: Soyinka is concerned less with the affirmation of a collective spirituality, as is the case with Awoonor, than with the vindication of a poetic ideal. We follow Ofeyi as he journeys through the horror of events, his mind and whole being firmly set upon this ideal. It is a journey toward a certain form of awareness, as the character declares in the novel: "Perhaps deep down I realize that the search would immerse me in the meaning of the event, lead me to a new understanding of history" (218).

But beyond the immediate grasp of the significance of the events of which he is a witness, of the social and human problems of communal life, and of the moral implications that they reveal to the sensitive intelligence, Soyinka takes his hero through an adventure whose symbolic meaning transcends the historical. The antithesis between life and death is given a literal and thoroughgoing expression and is dramatized in the opposition between the intensity of Ofeyi's visionary quest and the massive scale of the carnage that takes place around him, an antithesis that assumes an elemental significance through the transposition of the historical references of the novel into a mythical register. The events to which the novel alludes thus take on a dimension as a significant instance of the enduring tension between the fundamental polarities of human experience. This dimension gives a special emphasis to the representation of Ofeyi as a poet, as a type of contemplative personality; he is the man of feeling and insight on whom devolves the responsibility for upholding the claims of life.

As can be seen, Soyinka returns in *Season of Anomy* to what I have called elsewhere his myth of the artist (Irele, 1975), which is illustrated in the novel through an appropriation of the Orpheus and Eurydice motif. It is important to note his turning on this occasion from the image of Ogun, the Yoruba god of iron and archetype of the creative energy—and hence, for Soyinka, of artistic endowment,[11]—to the great European exemplar of the myth. In the study already referred to, Izevbaye points to the ambivalent nature of Soyinka's embodiments of Ogun in some of the characters of his first novel, *The Interpreters,* which contrasts with the clearer denotations he gives to those of the second. The simultaneous association of Ogun with both destruction and creation—with both chaos and harmony—suggests the tense dialectic of the essential movement of the human mind, which is attested in the collective representation of the Yoruba, a realism moreover that accords with the objective experience of history. But the association has as well a doubtful moral connotation, which is manifestly at odds with Soyinka's purpose in *Season of Anomy*, in which, as Izevbaye remarks, "Soyinka seeks a less ambiguous resolution" to the problem of violence and its role in human affairs. The novel does not in fact provide a sufficiently pointed enactment of the problem, and in terms of its political meaning, this is clearly a disadvantage. On the other hand, it seems clear that Soyinka's real purpose is to seek a spiritual meaning in the reality of history, a purpose made urgent by the novel's reference to a moment of stress in the evolution of his own national community, which corresponds to the state of functional disorder to which Durkheim has lent the celebrated sociological term *anomie,* adopted in the title of Soyinka's novel. In its exploration of the national situation of crisis, Soyinka's novel offers a counterpoise to what Henry James has called "the imagination of disaster" in its vision of spiritual regeneration. The image of Ogun remains relevant to this scheme and recurs indirectly in the novel, for Ofeyi and the Dentist are also differentiated embodiments of the terms in that other dichotomy by which the god is characterized in the collective consciousness of the Yoruba. Ofeyi's reenactment of the myth of Orpheus is in this light really a means of giving a deliberate preeminence to the attribute of Ogun by which he has attained the status of a cultural hero; he is a pathfinder and an artist of primordial harmony. Soyinka's turning to the image of Orpheus becomes therefore understandable, for this image represents a pure and uncomplicated illustration of the restorative potential of the poetic ideal. We might say then that Soyinka reinforces his habitual Yoruba frame of reference with the European myth in his plea for the necessary relation to the collective life and awareness of the poetic imagination.

Season of Anomy offers a special expression of the new realism in contemporary African fiction in the way its mythological register gives a deep and wide resonance to the common theme. The novel prolongs and brings to a head Soyinka's meditation upon the African and general human condition begun in *A Dance of the Forests*. In that play, the historical perspective exists primarily as a provisional angle of vision rather than as a substantive reference for the foundation of a radical skepticism, which is modulated in its immediate expression in the play into a strong sense of premonition. Each work that has succeeded has reflected a feeling that "the pattern of reality" in Africa has done nothing but confirm that premonition. To this feeling as well as the unhappy circumstances of his personal experience of events must be attributed the bitter tone of all of the writings directly related to the Nigerian crisis.[12] In *Season of Anomy*, the last work in the series, we have a final working out of the bitterness. It now appears as if the sloughing off process was crucial to achieve a new poise, the quality that distinguishes the work that stands today as Soyinka's masterpiece, *Death and the King's Horseman*.

If Soyinka's novel may be said to represent an intensive interrogation of a particularly charged moment of African history, in his controversial novel, *Le devoir de violence*,[13] Yambo Ouologuem seeks to embrace the entire course of Africa's recorded experience in a long, single glance in order to achieve a comprehensive intelligence of its import. What he perceives can be stated quite simply: the African experience represents nothing more and nothing less than the unfolding of a fundamentally rooted plight. The pertinence of this view derives essentially from its dramatic opposition to the Romantic vision of the African past and from the way it takes the present reaction against that vision to its extreme point. For if Ouologuem's novel does not deal with the African situation in strictly contemporary terms, its reassessment of the past leads directly to the present, insofar as it is intended to shed a light upon the anxieties and preoccupations of the moment. *Le devoir de violence* also has a special significance for the new direction in African fiction in the peculiar character and vigor of its statement, which makes for a provocativeness that accounts in large measure for the strong reactions the novel has elicited and especially for its enthusiastic reception in several quarters. That the enthusiasm was not confined to a certain Western current of critical opinion, which might be suspected of having an interest in the matter, is attested by the following African comment: "This novel, more than anything ever written, marks not only the end of Negritude's rosy image of ancestral Africa, but also the dawn of a liberal imagination on the continent" (Mpondo, 1971, 141).

The quotation, especially in the overstatement of its second part, illustrates, unfortunately, what I believe to have been a confusion in the general critical reception of the novel. It seems to me that there has been a certain hastiness in attributing to Ouologuem a candor and a generous disposition—a "liberal imagination"—simply on account of his presentation of a disagreeable point of view on Africa, qualities that a close examination of the novel does not support. There is the further question of the undeniable force of the writing, which again seems, by its sheer virtuosity, to have carried the responses of many commentators—African and non-African alike—beyond the point where it was possible for them to ponder with a stern and impersonal intelligence the ominous implications of the novel.

Certainly, Ouologuem's novel has an element of headiness to it that is calculated to arouse strong impressions, and its provocative character may be thought to constitute an essential attribute of its disturbing vision of African development in the past and of the shadow cast by this development over the present. Furthermore, the novel seems to unfold a perspective that reflects, more faithfully than previous African representations of history, the complex interaction of impersonal forces and human impulses that constitute the felt movement of historical development. In a passage that sums up the action of the novel, the French bishop, who seems curiously to speak with the voice of his creator, offers what appears at first sight to be just such a dialectical conception of history:

> Hier j'ai marché, commença l'évêque Henry au bout d'un moment. Cinq minutes. Un cinéma. Un film, Zamba; inspiré de l'histoire du Nakem-Ziuko. Je m'avance. J'entre. La séance avait commencé. J'arrive en pleine tuerie: un coup de feu à l'écran. Non. Il n'est pas mort: c'est le héros.
> Je ne comprends pas. Je cherche à renouer l'histoire. D'un coté, je sens confusément l'intrigue, et de l'autre, la boucherie. Au beau milieu, quelqu'un tirait sur les ficelles. Quand il tirait trop fort, cela puait le traître de mélodrame, et un grognement s'élevait dans la salle. Je regarde l'écran: tous les moyens y sont bons—qui biaisent, silencieux, aigus, jamais laïques, exaltants de la guerre secrète. Mais pour tous, la force de frappe reste essai sur soi-même, bien moins pour exprimer une vision sanglante du monde que pour parvenir à un accord imminent entre la vie et le monde. Ici, ce qui importe, c'est que, toute vibrante de soumission inconditionnelle à la volonté de puissance, la violence devienne illumination prophétique, façon d'interroger et de répondre, dialogue, tension, oscillation, qui, de meurtre en meurtre, fasse les possibilités se répondre, se compléter, voire se contredire. Incertitude.... La frénésie vibre dans les images, gardant la nostalgie des hautes époques et de la clandestinité. (199)

[Yesterday, said Bishop Henry after a while, I went for a walk. Five minutes. A movie house. A picture, *Zamba*, inspired by the history of Nakem-Ziuko. I go in. The picture has started. I arrive in the middle of a masacre. A shot is fired. No. He's not dead: he's the hero.

I don't understand. I try to piece the story together. On the one hand, I get a vague idea of the plot; on the other hand, carnage. Someone at the center of it all pulled the strings. When he pulled too hard, everyone could smell the melodramatic villain at work, and the audience grumbled. I look at the screen: anything goes—all the tortuous, silent, insidious, exalting and fanatically religious methods of secret warfare. But for all those people, the driving force is a self-testing, not so much to express a bloody vision of the world as to arrive at an immanent concordance between life and the world. The crux of the matter is that violence, vibrant in its unconditional submission to the will to power, becomes a prophetic illumination, a manner of questioning and answering, a dialogue, a tension, an oscillation, which from murder to murder makes the possibilities respond to each other, complete or contradict each other. The outcome is uncertainty.... Frenzy vibrates on the screen, preserving our nostalgia for heroic periods and clandestinity.] (Trans. Manheim, 173–74)

It is indeed instructive to place the agitation of this passage, as Soyinka has done in his essay "Ideology and the Social Vision," against the serene historical vision of a writer like Cheikh Hamidou Kane (Soyinka, 1976, 98–99). When Kane makes one of his characters in *L'aventure ambigüe* declare: "La vérité se place à la fin de l'histoire" (Truth is to be found at the end of history), it is plain that he is casting an idealist veil over the concrete body of enacted events and social facts that make the living process of history and holding aloft the mystical abstraction so attained for Romantic reverence. Ouologuem's novel brings a refutation and challenges the comfortable attitude toward which Kane's tragic calmness tempts us by insisting that the truth of history is revealed within the historical process itself and not outside or beyond it. The insistence upon the fact and significance of history as the actual experience that is known eliminates the kind of metaphysical conception that is obviously inimical to a meaningful confrontation with the realities of the collective experience.

The problem, however, concerns not the general validity of Ouologuem's conception of history as movement and drama but the particulars and the deliberate slant of his demonstration. If we return for a moment to the words he gives to his fictional bishop and examine them more closely, we realize that their dramatic quality is more apparent than real. It is true that the words press upon each other and create a swirl of different and rapidly changing directions of meaning as if to produce an effect expressive of the breaks and discordances that form the massive swell of history. But the words fail to convey a steady meaning, for it is not a sense of the concentrated drama of history that they render but of its grotesque agitation. We come to feel behind the peculiar rhetoric what amounts to a cynical vision of history, in its own fashion as unilateral and as *simplified* as Kane's idealism. By an unconscious irony, Ouologuem supplies in this very passage the terms that serve best to describe the whole tenor of his novel: "Au beau milieu, quelqu'un tirait sur les ficelles. Quand il tirait trop fort, cela puait le traître de mélodrame" (Someone at the center of it all pulled the strings. When he pulled too hard, everyone could smell the melodramatic villain at work.) In other words, in the eagerness to give an unusual impact to his work, the novelist proceeds by a deliberate method of exaggeration. This abandon in its manner gives more than a touch of crudeness to his statement and detracts in my view quite seriously from the value of the novel as expressive work.

I make this observation with considered deliberation, in full awareness that it goes against the current of critical opinion the novel has
elicited. It seems to me that opinion has so far succumbed to the powerful
talent manifested in the novel, as to lose sight of the overbearing nature
of its discourse, and met with a blind eye its obvious defects. The point
is that the novel as we have it does not possess the quality of vision
claimed for it. This is not to say that Ouologuem does not possess the
genius to sustain a work that deserves unqualified acclaim—I believe that
he does—but *Le devoir de violence* is not, to my mind, that novel. As I see
it, the novel's scale of conception and the brilliance of much of the writing original to Ouologuem are defeated in the long run by the display
throughout of a shallow sensibility. The relationship is indeed a curious
one between the recognizable robustness of the style and the effect that
it creates, but it is the same relationship that we have in all melodrama,
which is nothing but the expending of considerable means for small and
often grotesque ends. The rational view of this novel is that its remarkable
virtuosity is at odds with the immaturity of feeling it is made to serve.
The genius is there, but it is sadly misapplied.

We only need to consider the unevenness of the novel's structure to
realize the truth of this observation. It is significant that it fails to sustain
to the end the broad sweep of the narrative style announced in the early
parts, so that we feel a distinct drop of the tone in the middle, which is
only partly redeemed by the intense register of the final section. This
unevenness results from the abrupt change of voice after the first two
sections. The epic tone of the beginning, modeled on the manner of the
griot reciting a narrative of great and momentous events or of the chronicler composing a *tarikh* in the same vein—both suitable for an elevated
mode of presentation toward a serious purpose—is progressively abandoned for the more relaxed manner of the omniscient narrator of the
conventional Western novel, who is preoccupied with the banal details
of a realistic representation. The change may be explained by the passage
from a distant to a more recent past, but it introduces a distortion whose
only object seems to be to allow the novelist scope to indulge in realistic
effects of a dubious value. For it never, as with the last section of Achebe's
novel, truly signifies a new key of expression, in tune with a new mode
of apprehension. When one places such uncertainty of touch beside the
steady quality of the authorial voice that Ayi Kwei Armah maintains
throughout his novel *Two Thousand Seasons*, one sees it for the failure it
is. Armah's voice is able to sustain in a single powerful key a full range

of variations in tone to express a comprehensively organized order of sentiment and vision.

But leaving aside this unevenness of the novel's structure, what are we to make of the sheer wantonness of many of the scenes with which its outline is filled out? There is the incident, for instance, in which Tambina is raped by the diviner and murdered on her way home by Saif's henchmen, who throw her body into a cesspit. Or there is the scene in which Raymond Kassoumi discovers that the prostitute he has just slept with in a Parisian brothel is none other than his sister, who dies later in the novel from wounds inflicted upon her genitals by a blade hidden by a customer in her soap. I cannot see what these and similar scenes of gratuitous pornography and violence add to the novel; they only lend it an element of salaciousness that is, at bottom, puerile. It must not be imagined that objections to these parts of the novel can only be motivated by prudishness or, worse still, critical obtuseness, for such a view surely begs the question of the *artistic* value of these scenes or their function in the complete design of the novel. These incidents, which I can only qualify as wanton, may well appeal in themselves to a taste conditioned by the current revaluation of the marquis de Sade—and Ouologuem seems to have deliberately pandered to such a taste[14]—but not one of them evinces the controlled irony that makes Sade challenging, at least passably so, for a mature intelligence.

The effect of this indiscriminate piling up of atrocities is the damage done to the conception of the characters, who exist merely as cardboard figures, especially Saif ben Isaac El Heit, the protagonist in Ouologuem's tale of horrors. Saif as depicted in the novel is not even a worthy villain, he is neither a Machiavelli nor a Judas, as the bishop refers to him, but resembles rather a sordid Mafia *capo*, so that the kingdom of Nakem, which he controls, seems more akin to an underworld of desperate gangsters than to a historical stage on which a grave destiny is being determined. The excesses in the novel—and they cannot be considered anything else—have the effect, ultimately, of giving an air of triviality to a theme that requires serious treatment.

This is why I suspect Emmanuel Obiechina of a serious lapse of his usually sound judgment when he comments on the nature of Saif's violence: "The quality and subtlety of it raises the act to an artistic undertaking which adds an extra dimension of narrative realization to the novel" (Obiechina, 1978, 55). The claim of "subtlety" and "artistry" for the acts of violence perpetrated by Saif is made simply on the grounds of their purposefulness, which contrasts with what Obiechina recognizes as the "numerous examples of ugly uncharged violence" in the novel. It ought, however, to be plain from a reading of the novel that the distinction is really a specious one. And when we try to draw out a general proposition from the claim made for Saif's violence, we realize quickly its unsoundness. When Obiechina states on the same page that "the principle of violence as elaborated in this novel derives from Frantz Fanon's *The Wretched of the Earth*," one is forced to object to the injustice to Fanon's thought evident in the statement. For the simple truth is that Fanon's humane conception of violence as a liberating force for the oppressed finds no illustration whatever in Ouologuem's novel and bears no relationship to an imagination that would endow with significance the order of violence he offers. Given these qualifications, there is, it seems to me, a serious misunderstanding of the implications of the novel in Soyinka's assessment when he writes:

> Ouologuem pronounces the Moslem incursion into black Africa to be corrupt, vicious, decadent, elitist and insensitive. At the least, such a work functions as a wide swab in the deck-clearing operation for the commencement of racial retrieval. (Soyinka, 1976, 106)

Unfortunately, the novel provides no evidence for this positive appraisal. There is no gesture in the novel toward any form of "racial retrieval," for its negative representation is not reserved for the Moslem rulers but is general and includes in particular "la négraille" (the nigger trash, in Ralph Mannheim's brilliant translation).

It might be held against my view that *Le devoir de violence* is a satirical novel and that its extreme form of iconoclasm may justifiably include cynicism in its frame of reference as an essential element of its critical purpose. But even satire in its attack on human weakness must imply, to be effective, a positive moralism and a deep response to the real possibilities of human nature, without which it risks degenerating into a vacant misanthropy, as Leavis has pointed out in the case of Swift. I do not find for my part any such response coming through in Ouologuem's novel to measure his retrospection upon the African past nor the perspectives he seeks to uncover on the present and the future. A cynical view of history may well appear as a legitimate apprehension that conforms to its real nature. But it is a view that has nothing to do with the liberal imagination, if we are to understand by that term the meaning intended by Lionel Trilling when he associated it with the function of literature as "the human activity that takes the fullest and most precise account of variousness, possibility, complexity and difficulty" (Trilling, 1957, xii). Ouologuem's novel makes no gesture toward anything like a positive scale of values, not even "as an implication from an implication," as James Olney puts it (Olney, 1973, 213). The single implication of the novel has nothing involved about it. For Ouologuem, history is merely the temporal frame for the expression of the will to power of the Saifs of this world, which, by its nature, cannot offer any meaningful prospect of redemption for the multitudes of ordinary mortals who have to suffer its implacable grind. This implication is expressly applied to the African case: "Souvent il est vrai, l'âme veut rêver l'écho sans passe du bonheur. Mais, jeté dans le monde, l'on ne peut s'empêcher de songer que Saïf pleure trois millions de fois, renaît sans cesse à l'Histoire, sous les cendres chaudes de plus de trente Républiques africaines" (207) (Often, it is true, the soul desires to dream the echo of happiness, an echo that has no past. But projected into the world, one cannot help recalling that Saif, mourned three million times, is forever reborn to history beneath the hot ashes of more than thirty African republics [Mannheim, 181–82]). Violence is thus essential to the African being-in-history, according to Yambo Ouologuem. It is not, then, just a question of whether Africans of today have a usable past to which to refer for the needs of the present but whether they have any future at all.

Le devoir de violence betrays a disturbing and dangerous restriction of that responsiveness to life in its fullness and its rich possibility that, surely, ought to be the privilege of the writer. When Soyinka in the essay cited tries to excuse Ouologuem with the observation that "the positive does not engage his re-creative attention," we cannot but sense a note of special pleading, which cannot prevail against our natural recoil from so total an adherence to nihilism. His demonstration of the fundamental rootedness of the African plight in a heritage of blood is so gross an overstatement of his case that it becomes not merely anti-African but antihuman. To say, then, that his is a thoroughgoing iconoclasm is really to say that Ouologuem has no reverence, not merely for a constituted order of historical references and functional myths in contemporary Africa but for the sense of life itself.

The five novels I have been considering as representative of the new realism in African fiction evince a general, pervasive African concern related to what is felt as a contemporary dilemma. Like other novels that have revolved around this theme, they present a drama of the African consciousness, beset as it is today by the realities of the postcolonial situation, which imply not simply immediate problems of creating viable national communities but a comprehensive acceptable order of life and values on the African continent.

In their direct representation of contemporary political and social tensions or, as is the case with Ouologuem's novel, the transposition of these realities onto a scale of historical vision, these novels rest, for their effect, upon an assumed reciprocity between the imaginative life and the facts of the real experience of the community as perceived by the writer. The state of consciousness that they translate derives from the sharp particularity of the African experience at the present time as that experience presents itself to the discerning mind of each of these writers and touches the deepest reaches of his human conscience. These novels can be said to represent a variety of individual forms of response to a lived reality, and these responses vary not only in scale and intensity but in the depth of the perception to which they lead each writer. But whatever the quality, they all afford parables of our present condition in Africa, the sum of whose meanings amounts to a negative appraisal of that condition and a judgment upon the human impulses that are behind its making.

To the extent that a political consciousness is central to each of these novels, they continue a tradition of protest writing, of committed literature, which prevailed in the course of development of modern African expression during the colonial period. There is no little irony to this fact, an irony that proceeds directly from the circumstances in which, in the postcolonial context, this protest writing is directed against the African inheritors of the colonial legacy of oppression. Even where it is evident, as in these five novels, that this oppression is not perceived in the light of a clear ideological perspective, such as is afforded by the Marxist concept of the class struggle, the critical intention to which they give expression assumes the force of an indictment of the political and social elite in Africa.

The imprecision of the ideological postures revealed in these novels raises the issue of the effects they can be expected to produce in the general society, which forms both the reference for their fictional constructions and the object of their meditations. Beyond the attention it forces upon us regarding an adequate correlation between content and its aesthetic embodiment, this issue is complicated by other factors in the African context, which bear upon the production of literature and its relation to an indigenous audience. These concern such questions as the choice of language (whether to write in a European language or an African one), the choice of modes and genres (which of these corresponds most closely to the African sensibility as conditioned by cultural institutions and practice), and even choices that have to do with the material conditions of publishing. These questions enter into the whole sociological context of cultural production and are of direct relevance to any consideration of literature from the point of view of its political and social significance.

Against this background of interrogations regarding the place and purpose of writing in postcolonial Africa, it may be argued that the novels we have been considering, and all the other works that fall into this category, have hardly more than an immediate personal significance for each writer. The novel in each case is intended not merely as a documentation of reality but as an active confrontation of it, as a mode of involvement in that reality. In other words, imaginative expression is taken by each of these writers as a form of action, which is mediated by the fictional mode but expressive, essentially, of a mood of dissidence, which has begun to gather force as a defining feature of the collective life in Africa. In that sense, they signify a movement of consciousness within the larger society to which the writer's creative impulse is responsive and of which it provides an active formulation. This gives all of these novels a general significance that is inestimable, one that points to the passionate quest for a new order in contemporary Africa.

Notes

Preface

1. The conceptual implications of the Western image of Africa to which Achebe objects is strikingly illustrated by the way Jürgen Habermas derives from the anthropological studies of Evans-Pritchard a simplified representation of the Azande. It is instructive of his method and its entire ideological grounding that, in the preliminary specification of rationality to his theory of communicative action, the Azande serve as the very prototype of an unreflective mode of mythical thought, placed in sharp opposition to what Habermas calls "occidental rationalism" (Habermas, 1984, 55–66 and 152 et seq.).

2. Said's observations are so germane to my point here that they need to be quoted at some length: "On the one hand, there has never been so much attention to and debate about criticism; on the other hand, rarely has there been such a removal of criticism and critical attention from the ongoing production of society and history. . . . To read an 'advanced' critic today is often to read writing that is essentially a highly rarefied jargon. The historical sense, the rudiments of scholarship and curiosity (which in the past have always characterized even the most abstract of serious theorists) seem no longer to have much to tell a new theorist. Above all, in much of the New New Criticism the issues debated do not involve values or social and cultural questions or urgent philosophical questions; they most often are about 'texts' (so that one is made to feel that there are only texts), they deal in complex abstractions whose main reference is to other complex abstractions, their dense language belies a thin texture of ideas, experience, history" (Said, 1980, ix). The following comment by Murray Krieger sums up the point: "Any literary

text consists of language; and how can any language function without its being informed by the historical moment in culture that creates it?" (Krieger, 1994, 27).

3. In a remarkable obituary essay on F. R. Leavis, Michael Black, quondam Publisher of Cambridge University Press, stresses this point at the outset as essential to Leavis's conception of criticism: "In the last resort, literature is about life, or it could not have the importance Leavis attributed to it" (Black, 1978, 293). The view of literature as a source of moral intelligence espoused by Leavis may be said to inform Richard Rorty's remark that "novels rather than moral treatises are the most useful vehicles of moral education" (Rorty, 1998, 12); we can be sure that, coming from a philosopher of his stamp, this remark is far from being intended as whimsical. Bruce E. Fleming has described this view of literature and the critical practice associated with it as "the wisdom paradigm," as opposed to the "knowledge paradigm" that has come more recently to dominate criticism and literary scholarship as a whole (Fleming, 2000).

4. The enviable reputations established in recent years by some of the major African writers have helped to draw attention to Africa as an important area of literary creation. The continent now counts three Nobel Prize winners (Wole Soyinka and Nadine Gordimer writing in English, and Naguib Mafouz in Arabic), and African writers have also been recipients of other major literary prizes in the Western world: in France, the Prix Renaudot has gone to Yambo Ouologuem (1968) and Ahmadou Kourouma (2000) and the Goncourt to Tahar Ben Jalloun (1987) while in Britain, the Booker Prize was awarded in 1992 to Ben Okri for *The Famished Road*, and in 1994 a novel by another African, Abdelrazak Gurnah's *Paradise*, was preselected for the same prize. Before this, the Nigerian Festus Iyayi had won the Commonwealth Prize for Literature in 1988 for his novel *Heroes*. Apart from writers who have been honored with prestigious literary prizes, the roster of major literary figures from Africa whose works have received some form of consecration or another includes Léopold Sédar Senghor (elected to the French Academy in 1983), Birago Diop, Mariama Bâ, and Kateb Yacine and Assia Djebar writing in French; Chinua Achebe, Ngugi wa Thiongo, and Nuruddin Farah in English; and Agostinho Neto, Marcellino dos Santos, and Luandino Vierya in Portuguese.

5. It is not without interest to observe in this connection that the study of women's literature has been central to the recognition of gender as a functional category of social interaction and cultural dynamics, a recognition that lent impetus to the development of Women's Studies as an academic discipline (Stimpson, 1980; Brantlinger, 1990, 140–46). There have of course been other issues, some of them ideological, involved in the establishment of Women's Studies, as Bernard Bailyn has pointed out with regard to women's history (Bailyn, 1994, 67).

6. The bane of jargon that marks this scholasticism is addressed in

Said's remark quoted in note 2 above. It is illustrative of the problems caused by this factor that when two members of the audience at a session at which I gave a conference paper remarked to me later that they had no problem in understanding me, so ambiguous was their tone that I couldn't decide whether they were expressing their disappointment at my paper—since incomprehensibility is now regularly taken as a sign of profundity—or just pleasantly surprised. This issue has been dramatized by Terry Eagleton's severe comments on Gayatri Spivak's critical idiom in his review in the *London Review of Books* of her collection of essays entitled *The Postcolonial Critic*.

7. In their comprehensive survey of southern African oral forms (1991), Landeg White and Leroy Vail have challenged the very basis of the oral-literate dichotomy inherent in Western scholarship as it relates to the study of African and other Third World cultures. However, orality has now become a central concept of folklore and cultural studies, as well as comparative literature and literary theory (Zumthor, 1983; Foley, 1988, 1990). Moreover, as is well known, the oral tradition is now an established reference of African historiography (see Ki-Zerbo, 1981). It must be stressed, however, that orality exists within an extensive fabric of social practice and cultural expression in which narrative forms enter into relation with other forms of embodiment of memory, including the visual arts (see Roberts and Roberts, 1996).

8. It is typical of the misconceptions that surround the question that, in his response to Witi Ihimaera's defense of the oral tradition of the Aborigine populations in New Zealand, Tabish Kamir insists that writing has superseded spoken communication even in the contemporary cultures of the non-Western world, suggesting thereby that orality and literacy are mutually exclusive modes of communication. He thus fails to grasp Ihimaera's point, that the oral tradition of his people continues to serve as a cultural resource for his own writing in English (see "Debate," *Wasafiri*, no. 31, Spring 2000, 81–83).

Chapter 1

1. This point is suggested by Ong's term *noetics*, by which he designates the relation between the mental landscape of a cultural community and its modes of cognition.

2. It is in this sense that Trilling has employed the label the "liberal imagination" to denote a general quality of the work of the writers he discusses in his book of that title. We are also familiar with terms such as the "romantic imagination," the "dialectical imagination," and the "female imagination."

3. We can more easily conceive of the textual nature of oral discourse by analogy with the computer, in which the material is generated and

subsequently stored in the memory of the machine as in the human brain, although without a visible material vessel for its perpetuation. The one condition for the continued existence of the text so generated in both cases is that it can be retrieved in one form or another.

Chapter 2

1. I say "until now" because, as Marshall McLuhan foresaw, the electronic revolution seems destined to create a new order of language for the representation of reality.

2. I am using this expression here in a sense slightly different from Walter Ong's usage.

Chapter 3

1. The third collection in the series is entitled *Contes et lavanes;* all three collections are now published by Présence Africaine, Paris.

2. It is worth pointing out that the westward extension of Islam from the plains of Arabia and Persia across the Middle East to the Atlantic coast takes in a considerable part of West Africa, especially the region that lies within the savanna belt. The fact is well illustrated by the experience of Arthur de Gobineau, who is reported to have spent days discussing points of Islamic theology with the local *ulemas* at Dakar during a stopover in 1869 on his journey to Brazil to take up his post as French ambassador. He was thus able to connect his earlier experience of Islamic culture in Persia with its "black" version in West Africa. Although he never retracted the ideas on race set out in his *De l'inégalité des races humaines* (in the manner, say, of Lévy-Bruhl in *Carnets*, with regard to his previous work), one might speculate that the ethnocentrism displayed in his book would never have developed had he not written the book *before* his encounter with the Orient and Islamic culture. The deep-rooted nature of this culture in West Africa is amply demonstrated by the Islamic revival inspired in Senegal at the turn of the century by the writings of Cheikh Bamba, founder of the powerful Mouride sect, a revival that relied for its effect on literacy in Arabic, which pre-dated by centuries literacy in French in Senegal and its environs. On the evidence of the vast amount of literature in Arabic that still circulates in this region, which can be verified on the streets of Dakar, especially around the central market of Sandaga, it is fair to observe that, even today, Arabic is a more influential literary language in the region than French; the same observation applies to Nigeria and Ghana in relation to English. These observations have more than a passing interest for our subject. It is now well established, for instance, that historical research pertaining to these areas cannot be considered adequate without recourse to the manuscripts in Arabic that are still being

collected at research centers such as the Institute of African Studies at the University of Ghana and the Africana Library at the University of Ibadan. (The best known collection in the United States is presently under the direction of Professor John Hunwick at Northwestern University.) The contemporary importance of African letters in Arabic is further emphasized by the political legitimacy and the social and moral standing exercised by the elite in these areas on the basis of literacy in Arabic and grounding in Islamic culture. This is the background from which the narrative action derives in the two best known "Islamic" novels of European expression in West Africa, *L'aventure ambigüe* by the Senegalese Cheikh Hamidou Kane and *The Last Imam* by the Nigerian Ibrahim Tahir. There is a sense in which these two novels can be related to modern African literature in Arabic, for example, the works of the Nobel laureate Naguib Mahfouz and the Sudanese Tayeb Salih. (For general presentations of Islam in West Africa, see Trimingham, 1959, and Monteil, 1983.)We must not forget either the other long-standing tradition of African letters represented by Ethiopian literature in the ancient liturgical language of Ge'ez and in modern Amharic, a tradition indigenous to the continent, with its own script and its own conventions, which flourished at least until the overthrow of the imperial regime of Haile Sellassie in 1974.

3. The intellectual history that serves as the background for Eagleton's observations is provided more fully in other works, notably Gay, 1966.

4. The most serviceable modern edition of this work is by Paul Edwards, published in London in 1969 by Dawson. Edwards has also prepared two editions in abridged form, *Equiano's Travels* and *The Life of Olaudah Equiano*; the latter edition contains a useful bibliography on Equiano and eighteenth-century African writers, to which must be added Abbé Grégoire's *De la littérature des Nègres*, published in Paris in 1808.

5. I owe this expression to Sarah Suleri, who employs it to characterize a significant element of Naipaul's inspiration in her essay "Naipaul's Arrival."

6. See also Gates's reference to Phillis Wheatley in his general foreword to the *Schomburg Library of Nineteenth-Century Black Women Writers* published by Oxford University Press. In the concluding peroration to his work (cited in n. 4 above), Abbé Grégoire specifically advances the literary creations of the black writers he has been presenting as testimony to the humanity of the black race in general.

7. Blyden's attitude on this point emerges clearly from his correspondence, especially his letters to the American missionary Venn (see Lynch, 1978). The Senegalese *metis* Abbé Boilat was even more insistent on this point in his book, *Esquisses sénégalaises,* first published in Paris in 1853, and now reissued in a new edition (1986; see also July, 1968, and

Cohen, 1980). Abbé Boilat's work represents an important precedent for Senghor's reflections of the cultural question in Africa and in a curious way, as a reference for his theory of Negritude.

8. See Ajayi, 1965, for a historical and sociological account of the formation of the Nigerian elite in the latter half of the nineteenth century. Wole Soyinka's reconstruction (from his father's personal papers) in *Isarà* of the cultural atmosphere in colonial Nigeria in the years between the two world wars is also of considerable interest here.

9. This connection seems to me to confirm the validity of taking the term colonial situation in the broad sense, a sense reinforced, moreover, by the New World origins of both the Pan-African and the Negritude movements, in the latter case through the influence of the Harlem Renaissance and its derivation from the Haitian Renaissance in the years before the Second World War. These affiliations are well documented, especially in Garrett, 1963, and Kesteloot, 1963. The special relationship between the Senegalese Senghor and the Martinican poet Aimé Césaire, to whom we owe the term *Negritude* (first employed in his now-classic long poem *Cahier d'un retour au pays natal*), highlights the overlap of ideas and sentiments between diaspora black and African intellectuals generated by a common historical condition.

10. A parallel can be observed between Senghor's manner of putting a novel construction on Lévy-Bruhl's anthropology and that made explicit on a more elaborate and aggressive scale in the propaganda used by the National Socialist regime under Hitler of Tacitus' ethnography of the primitive Germans in *Germania*.

11. The unmistakably Nietzschean accents of Soyinka's essay "The Fourth Stage" suggests this particular direction of his thought; the essay is included in his *Art, Dialogue and Outrage*.

12. The title Achebe chose for his 1988 collection of essays is eloquent on this point: *Hopes and Impediments*.

13. See chap. 1; also Obiechina, 1990.

14. For an especially illuminating analysis of this play, see Gates, 1981.

15. For a more extended critique of Soyinka, see Appiah, 1985, 250–63.

Chapter 4

1. Shakespeare's play has understandably served as a reference for reflection on this theme by Caribbean writers, notably the Cuban Roberto Fernandez Retamar (1989) and George Lamming (1960). Aimé Césaire's play *Une Tempête* is a polemical reworking of Shakespeare's play that emphasizes its continuing relevance to the Black situation. For a fuller discussion see Nixon, 1987.

2. For a radical effort to call into question the Western conceptual system by an African, see Pathé Diagne's *L'Europhilosophie*, 1982, a work that, despite problems of organization and formulation, deserves to be better known; see also Outlaw, 1987.

3. For a broad discussion of these issues, see the essays collected in JanMohamed and Lloyd, 1990.

4. The historic significance of the Bandung Conference has been summed up as follows: "the national movements of Asia and Africa gradually developed into a universal revolt against the West, a rejection of Western domination which found expression in the Afro-Asian conference at Bandung in 1955. The Bandung conference symbolized the newfound solidarity of Asia and Africa against Europe" (Barraclough, 1967, 159).

5. The historical, sociological, and cultural factors that give a specific character to Third World anticolonial nationalism are examined by Anderson, 1983, esp. chap. 7, "The Last Wave" (104–28). See also Brennan, 1990, and the three essays by Said, Eagleton, and Jameson in Deane, 1990.

6. Stanislas Adotevi's acerbic critique of Negritude in *Négritude et négrologues* (1972) is essentially a denunciation of what he takes to be the complicity between Senghor's ideas and the propositions of European racist ideology with regard to the Black race.

7. Nkrumah's utopianism is in full evidence in *Africa Must Unite* (1964), published while he was still president of Ghana. For an excellent presentation of Nkrumah's career and political ideas, see Rooney, 1988.

8. This dilemma as it relates to Africa and the Third World has been well summed up by Paul Ricoeur: "On the one hand, the developing world has to root itself in the soil of its past, forge a national spirit, and unfurl this spiritual and cultural revindication before the colonists' personality. But in order to take part in modern civilization, it is necessary at the same time to take part in scientific, technical and political rationality, something that very often requires the pure and simple abandonment of a whole cultural past" (quoted in Brennan, 1990, 46).

9. These issues form the core of Michel Foucault's work; see in particular his broad formulation of them in *L'ordre du discours* (1971), his inaugural lecture at the College de France. Bakhtin's concept of the "logosphere" in its designation of the social sphere as a site for contending discourses is equally fundamental to the issues highlighted.

10. Consider, in France, the tradition of pro-Black literature that runs from Abbé Grégoire in the eighteenth century through Schoelcher down to Sartre in the twentieth.

11. The prime example of what I call here ideologies of progress is of course Auguste Comte's positivism, to whose spirit much of

nineteenth-century Western thought, including Marxism in its elaboration by Marx and Engels, can also be related. See Pollard, 1971.

12. That this system of valuations underlies Romantic literature is made clear by its theoretical formulations, notably in the writings of Coleridge on the imagination; for an extensive discussion, see Abrams, 1953. Terry Eagleton (1990) offers a more recent consideration situated within a resolutely Marxist perspective of the relation between historical and social factors and theories of art.

13. See Kumar, 1978. Both Leo Marx (1970) and Edward Shi (1985) have traced the same development and concern in American literature and thought. This Romantic strain is resurfacing today more generally in the ecology movement, of which Ernest Callenbach's *Ecotopia* (1976) is perhaps the best known literary expression.

14. Consider the forceful critique of Luc Ferry and Alain Renaut (1989) of the trend represented by these philosophers and others associated with them. An especially lucid and also critical appraisal of the same trend is provided by Sim (1986). My remarks are prompted by what I see as an uncritical and possibly disabling fascination with these French philosophers on the part of a new generation of French-speaking African intellectuals, particularly Valentin Mudimbe, on whom the pertinence of Foucault's analyses and the power of his intellect seem to have made a profound impression. By comparison, Edward Said's more circumspect endorsement of Foucault in *The World, the Text and the Critic* (1984), while allowing for these qualities in his work, proceeds from the kind of intellectual vigilance I am recommending.

Chapter 6

1. The founding text of Yoruba historiography is Samuel Johnson's *History of the Yoruba*. Johnson was a Westernized Yoruba who undertook in the late nineteenth century the composition in English of an account of the origins, development, religion, and traditions of his people. The work, posthumously published in 1921, has attained the status of a classic in Yoruba studies and remains a reference text of indigenous African historical literature. This pioneering effort was followed in the years after the Second World war by the work of professional Yoruba historians, the most prominent among whom are Saburi Biobaku, J. F. Ade Ajayi, and Akin Akinjogbin, all educated in European universities and trained in Western methods of historical research. Set against *Itan Eko*, this later historical writing among the Yoruba illustrates the distinction made by Hayden White between history as pure narration and history as "dissertation" (1987, 28).

2. Karl Marx, in his characteristically forceful way, makes clear the meaning of *history* in the sense of real experience when he writes: "His-

tory does *nothing;* it 'does not possess immense riches,' it 'does not fight battles.' It is men, real living men, who do all this, who possess things and fight battles. . . . History is nothing but the activity of men in pursuit of their ends" (1975, 93).

3. White's *Metahistory* provides perhaps the most comprehensive examination of the issues outlined here. White postulates a formal and functional relationship between the poetic mode and all forms of historical discourse in order to advance the notion of a "poetics of history," for which he proposes a scheme of governing tropes (1973, ix–xii, 1–42). Louis Mink's 1970 essay represents an earlier formulation of the same view, albeit in less elaborated form, of the relation between history and fiction.

4. An explicit and characteristic statement of this continuity is contained in the preface to Sembène Ousmane's novel *Harmattan*, in which he claims an identity between the status and function of the *griot* in traditional culture and the writer in modern Africa. The preface is intended as an explanation of his own practice of fiction either in written form or in that eminently modern mode of narrative: the cinematic. As is well known, Ousmane's films are often complementary to his printed fiction; three of his films, *La noire de. . . . Mandabi*, and *Xala*, are cinematic versions of texts he had previously published. Ousmane's relation to the African narrative tradition, however, remains largely at the level of function rather than of form, for his own writing belongs clearly to a Western tradition of realism. His novel *Les bouts de bois de Dieu (God's Bits of Wood)*, considered one of the best examples of socialist realism, is really an extension of nineteenth-century realism and naturalism; the novel, based on an actual historical event, the stike of the Dakar-Niger railway workers in 1947–1948, derives its inspiration essentially from Emile Zola's *Germinal*.

5. This is no place to go into the details of African oral tradition, but it is important to dispel certain common misconceptions. It is often assumed that orality is incapable of sustaining more than "simple forms," in the sense in which André Jolles, for instance, used this term in his study of legends and other forms of popular expression in Europe (see his *Formes simples*). The terminology that has been habitually applied to the oral tradition suggests a naive and elementary character that bears no relation to a proper conception of literature as complex art. This is a misconception that has arisen from early studies of oral literature in Africa, which concentrated upon the more obvious and more accessible forms and ignored the major and more densely textured texts. For a consideration of the poetic properties of oral literature across cultures, see Zumthor, 1983.

6. Anthropology itself, as a discipline, has come in our own time to self-understanding as a reinscription, in terms of Western science, of the

discourse of myth, of which narratives form a distinct component. This point is illustrated in an arresting way by the retelling in "La geste d'Asdiwal" by Claude Lévi-Strauss of a Native American myth as an essential procedure in his analytical approach to the myth. The implications of the narrative and the scriptive in anthropology have received special emphasis in the theoretical work of scholars of the so-called new anthropology in the United States; see Clifford and Marcus, 1986.

7. Jacques Le Goff sums up the situation when he writes: "In societies without writing, collective memory seems to organize itself around three major interests: the collective identity based on myths, and more particularly, myths of origin, the prestige of leading families that is expressed by genealogies, and the technical knowledge that is transmitted by practical formulas that are deeply imbued with religious magic" (1992, 580); for a comprehensive discussion of the function of myth in articulating structures of knowledge in preliterate and preindustrial societies, see Gusdorf, 1962.

8. From this point of view, the argument of Lévi-Strauss's *La pensée sauvage* can be considered an extension of what he developed in *Le totémisme aujourd'hui*.

9. Paris: Seuil, 1990. All quotations are from this edition.

Chapter 7

1. The phrase is of course an echo of V. S. Naipaul's title for the first of his three books on India. For a comprehensive discussion of the image of Africa in the Western imagination, see Fanoudh-Siefer (1968) and Hammond and Jablow (1992).

2. Achebe's example spawned a cluster of novels in Anglophone Africa focused on the theme of revaluation and cultural conflict. This is especially the case in the work of a group of Igbo writers who may be said to constitute a school deriving its inspiration and method from his work. Among these may be cited, as the most prominent, Flora Nwapa, John Munonye, Onuora Nzekwu, and Elechi Amadi; Buchi Emecheta's work bears an indirect relation to this "school" (see Emenyonu, 1974). The long shadow cast by Achebe over these writers is best illustrated by the insufficient and even scant attention that has been paid to Elechi Amadi's powerful novel, *The Great Ponds*, in my view one of the masterpieces of modern African literature. Further afield, we may cite the case of Ngugi wa Thiong'o, who has acknowledged his debt to Achebe. To recognize the innovative significance of *Things Fall Apart* is, however, far from stating that Achebe "invented" African literature, as Gikandi claims in his 1991 study of Achebe, and repeats in his introduction to the annotated edition published in 1996. Unless the Anglophone area is to be taken as representing the whole field and the novel as the privileged

medium, African literature cannot be said to have begun with the publication of Achebe's novel in 1958. That would discount the whole area of African literature in the indigenous languages, beginning with the oral tradition itself and extending to the written literature in the vernaculars, with the work of Thomas Mfolo and D. O. Fagunwa, for example, as major landmarks. Moreover, as regards African literature in the European languages, even if we set aside the work of African writers of European extraction (considered in my 1990 essay "The African Imagination"), the Francophone writers had established a new tradition of African literary expression before the publication of the significant texts in English. It is of course possible to consider such figures as René Maran and Paul Hazoumé as precursors but not Léopold Sédar Senghor, whose first volume of poems, *Chants d'ombre*, was published in 1945. The volume itself testifies to a conscious project of African literature, explicitly stated in the poem "Lettre à un Poète" dedicated to Aimé Césaire, a poem that presents itself as a veritable manifesto for the creation of a new literature expressive of the African environment. Later, Senghor elaborates this point in the essay "Comme les Lamantins vont boire à la source," which serves as postscript to his 1960 volume, *Ethiopiques*. Indeed, if we seek a precise reference for the "invention" of African literature, this can only be the historic *Anthologie de la nouvelle poésie nègre et malgache*, compiled by Senghor and published in 1948. The point is that African literature in the European languages was a distinct area of modern African expression well before Achebe came on the scene.

3. Achebe himself has sought to clarify this ideological project by presenting it as a vindication, in the face of persistent Western denigration, of the African claim to human achievement. According to him, the novel was motivated by the desire to demonstrate that the precolonial order in Africa was not "one long night of savagery." ("The Novelist as Teacher," *Hopes and Impediments*, 45). Furthermore, he has indicated that, in its elaboration as a work of fiction, *Things Fall Apart* represents his corrective response to the portrayal of Africa in Joyce Cary's *Mister Johnson* and Joseph Conrad's *Heart of Darkness* ("Named for Victoria, Queen of England" and "An Image of Africa," in the same volume, and Achebe's preface to *The African Trilogy*). To these writers must be added H. Rider Haggard, Edgar Wallace, and John Buchan, whose works were staples of the colonial literature in Nigeria and other African territories in the former British empire.

4. *Things Fall Apart*, 1962. All further page references will be indicated in the text.

5. We might note that Achebe's observation about Okonkwo applies equally to Ezeulu, the focus of his third novel, *Arrow of God*; both function as characters in what Biodun Jeyifo (1993) has described as "fictional genealogies of colonialism" in Africa.

6. For an extensive discussion of the relation between Achebe's recreation of Igbo culture in his novels and the ethnographic literature on the Igbo by Western anthropologists (George Basden, P. Amaury Talbot, Charles Kingsley, Meek, and others), see Wren, 1980. Basden's *Among the Ibos of Nigeria* has long been considered the standard work on the subject.

7. I have in mind here Ian Watt's thesis concerning the association between a realistic convention and the modern novel in its genesis, this convention arising from the diversified forms of experience ushered in by the change from an agrarian to an industrial mode of production (Watt, 1957). According to Watt, this made it imperative for the novelist to provide the reader with background information (down to the baking of bread) related to the context of the narrative. The example he cites of the buildup of detail in *Robinson Crusoe* is especially illuminating, insofar as the economic rationale for realism is disguised in this tale of a fantastic, exotic appearance. The same propensity toward realism is evident in the novels of Jane Austen, in which it serves a critical purpose. Despite a homogeneous public (or because of it?) the reproduction of everyday life and manners as part of the fabric of social experience in her time fostered immediate recognition by the reader, a response conducive to the creation by the novelist of the ironic distance necessary for her critical reflection on her characters and situations. The apogee of this realism was attained in the nineteeth-century French novel, which combined the same ironic function with a "documentary" character. For, despite the scorn poured by Roland Barthes in *Le degré zéro de l'écriture* upon the French realistic novel, its immediate connection to history and to the social transformations of the age created a powerful channel of social criticism that provided, according to Richard Terdiman, a challenge to the repressive institutions of an ascendant bourgeoisie (Terdiman, 1985). As a genre, the novel has of course moved beyond this convention of formal realism toward the modernist reflexive model in which we witness a reciprocal relationship between its narrative content and critical reflection on the art through which it is constituted (Boyd, 1983).

8. Arnold Toynbee's observations regarding what he calls "military virtues" are relevant to a consideration of Achebe's world: "If we wish to understand either the value of the military virtues or the sincerity of the admiration which they win, we must take care to look at them in their native social setting. . . . The military virtues are cultivated and admired in a milieu in which social forces are not sharply distinguished in people's minds from the non-human natural forces, and in which it is at the same time taken for granted that natural forces are not amenable to human control" (Toynbee, 1950, 15).

9. The type as represented in Igbo culture reappears in the character of Danda in Nkem Nwakwo's novel of that name; the closest parallel in

Western literature would be perhaps the good soldier Svejk, in Jaroslav Hasek's famous antiwar novel.

10. François Mauriac has remarked upon the procedure he terms *hypertrophie* by which novelists and dramatists tend to exaggerate specific moral or psychological traits in their characters at the expense of others, so that each one of these characters (e.g., Iago, Goriot, or Raskolnikov) strikes us as representative of a singular aspect of life or experience. We observe a similar process in the creation by Achebe of Okonkwo as an outsized character.

11. The expression served as methodological focus for the investigations in social psychology undertaken by Kardiner and Ovesey (Kardiner, 1945; see also Dufrenne, 1953).

12. It is in this light that Lévi-Strauss has interpreted "The Story of Asdiwal" as a dramatization of the tension between the masculine and the feminine principles; the myth thus reflects, according to him, a perception of the dualism of the natural order and its resonances within the imagination (Lévi-Strauss, 1977). The contradiction between the symbolic representation of women and their social position is of course a feature of most traditional cultures; for a discussion as this applies to India, see Kumari, 2000.

13. As a matter of comparative interest, we might note the parallel between Achebe's treatment of the father-son conflict in *Things Fall Apart* and Samuel Butler's treatment of the same theme in *The Way of All Flesh*. The family story in *Things Fall Apart* is taken up again in the sequel, *No Longer at Ease*. We now know that Achebe's original plan was to write a trilogy based upon a family saga, a plan that he abandoned with the writing of *Arrow of God*, the work that is, without question, his masterpiece. The irony of history is explored more fully in this work in a fictional register that incorporates a religious element and is focused on a hero, Ezeulu, who assumes the dimension of a world historical figure and whose tragic stature is underlined by the intertextual resonance of his bitter return, like Shakespeare's Lear, in a raging storm, accompanied by a character who functions as his shadow.

14. For this historical background (not directly considered in Achebe's novel) see Diké, 1956; also Wren, 1980.

15. For a preliminary approach to an explication of the structure of imagery in *Things Fall Apart*, suggestive of the possibility of a Bachelardian analysis, see Muoneke, 1994, 101–2.

16. The first title of the Italian translation (1962) is based on the imagery in this passage: *Le locuste bianche*. The title has since been changed in a more recent translation to *Il crollo* (1994).

17. The notion of "Evil Forest" is not unknown in English, in which the equivalent is "Devil's Dyke."

18. The implications of the historic connection between Christianity and education form the subject of J. F. Ade Ajayi's study, *Christian Missions in Nigeria, 1841–1891: The Making of a New Elite* (1965). As indicated by its subtitle, the study is not merely a historical account of the Christian evangelical effort in Nigeria but also a sociological analysis of its major consequence, the formation of a new Westernized elite in the country. A concrete testimony of this connection is provided by Wole Soyinka's biography of his father in *Isarà*. As with similar elites in other parts of the world, it is to this social group that we owe the national idea in Nigeria. It should be noted that, for this group, an ideology of modernity is inseparable from its anticolonial stance. (Geertz, ed, 1963), the tension between this stance and the movement for cultural revival is discussed in my "Dimensions of African Discourse" (chapter 4 in this volume). Despite the particular circumstances of its rise in the context of British colonial rule and within a multiethnic framework, Nigerian nationalism illustrates the determining influence highlighted by Gellner (1983) and Anderson (1983) of literacy and the role of intellectuals in the emergence of ideas of national identity. (For Nigeria in particular, see Coleman, 1958; Echeruo, 1977; Zachernuk, 2000.)

19. For an extended analysis of Achebe's style and its effect upon the organization of the novel, see Cook, 1977, 75–79. Kwame Appiah, for his part, remarks on Achebe's "mastery of form and language" (1992, ix), while Margaret Lawrence comments in these terms: "a prose plain and spare, informed by his keen sense of irony" (Lawrence, 1968, 107).

20. The logic that underlies the reference here to the potency of the white man's medicine is of a piece with the argument of efficacy advanced by Charles Taylor (1982) and others in favor of the superior epistemological status of Western rationality. See also Wilson, 1970; the three essays in Lukes, 1977, pt. 2, "Rationality and Relativism," 121–74; and especially the comprehensive review of the question by Jürgen Habermas (1984, 8–75).

21. Marjorie Winters's analysis (1981), in which she discerns an evolution of Achebe's style toward the dry prose of official documents, calls to mind Max Weber's observation on the development of institutional bureaucracy and its impersonal character as a sign of the "disenchanted world" of modern society.

22. Barthes associates the "readerly" text expressly with the established classic, which requires hardly any strenuous engagement on the part of the reader, whereas Kermode's phrase draws attention to the inherent complexity of such texts. The recourse to orality gives Achebe's novel what, following Gates, one might call a "speakerly" quality (Gates, 1989).

23. It is well to place Achebe's appraisal of his own society's less flattering aspects against his now-celebrated critique of Joseph Conrad's

Heart of Darkness in his essay "An Image of Africa" (*Hopes and Impediments*, 1–20). Achebe assails Conrad's work as a "racist novel" though he is far from calling for its elimination from the Western canon, as David Denby asserts in his 1995 article, "Jungle Fever." While Achebe does not altogether ignore the antiimperialist thesis of the novella, he seems to equate Conrad's compassion for the Africans to the kind promoted by the ASPCA on behalf of domestic animals. This seems hardly fair to Conrad, but Achebe is not alone in missing the serious moral import of the novella as registered in the epigraph to the first edition ("But the dwarf answered: 'No; something human is dearer to me than the wealth of all the world'—*Grimm's Tales*"). It is regrettable that this epigraph is not always reproduced in current editions of the work, the notable exception being the Norton edition edited by Robert Kimbrough, which also contains Achebe's essay as well as responses to it. On this question, see Hamner, 1990, See also Watts's introduction to the Oxford edition of *Heart of Darkness* and, more recently, Firchow, 2000.

24. It is instructive in this regard to consider the comparison suggested by Michael Valdez Moses between the world depicted in Achebe's novel and the image of early Greek society that emerges from the great classical epics of the Western literary tradition. Moses speaks of the "strikingly Homeric quality of *Things Fall Apart*" and discerns "certain similarities between particular Greek and African civilizations in a way that breaks down the Manichean dualism of the West and its Other." He adds: "In fact, the differences between the ethos of Homer's Mycenaean heroes and that of their Igbo counterparts in Achebe's novels are far less striking than those between either of them and the moral standards and political norms that prevail among contemporary European, American and African intellectuals" (Moses, 1995, 113). Moses might have added that, in both Homer's *Iliad* and Achebe's *Things Fall Apart*, we witness a distancing of the narrator from the hero, which amounts to a questioning of the dominant ethos. In both, we sense a marked distaste for the violence accepted in earlier societies and reflected in epic narratives, which was carried to remarkable heights in the wanton violence and atrocities of the Norse sagas. This narrative distance in the *Iliad* reduces somewhat the analytical value of the distinction so often proposed between epic and novel in terms of the degree of the narrator's investment not only in the action and atmosphere of the narrative but in the moral values of the world it represents.

25. Fredric Jameson has sought to get beyond this privileging of the novel on the part of Georg Lukács by recovering for critical practice a sense of wholeness for all forms of literary expression: "Indeed, no working model of the functioning of language, the nature of communication or of the speech act, and the dynamics of formal and stylistic change is conceivable which does not imply a whole philosophy of history" (Jameson, 1981, 59).

26. This conforms with Hegel's contemptuous dismissal of the literature of earlier societies as creditable historical material, a view given expression at the outset of his philosophy of history: "The historian binds together the fleeting rush of events and deposits it in the temple of Mnemosyne. Myths, folk songs, traditions are not part of original history; they are still obscure modes and peculiar to obscure peoples. Observed and observable reality is a more solid foundation for history than the transience of myths and epics. Once a people has reached firm individuality, such forms cease to be its historical essence" (Hegel, 1953, 3–4).

27. The conception of the historical novel summarized here is that of David Daiches (1956).

28. The point is made even more succinctly and more pointedly by Michel Zéraffa with regard to the novel: "Sont en cause, dans le roman, notre historicité et son sens" (At stake in the novel is our historicity as well as its meaning) (Zéraffa, 1971, 15).

29. For a discussion of the mental landscape that forms the background to Conrad's pessimism, see Jameson, 1981, 251ff.

30. It is always hazardous to move from reading fiction to speculating about the author's opinions in the real world. However, Achebe's nonfictional works confirm his embrace of modernity as a necessary dimension of African renewal. But as his two novels relating to the postindependence period demonstrate—*A Man of the People* and *Anthills of the Savannah*—he takes full cognizance of the problems and dilemmas involved in the process of Africa's accession to modernity. Nevertheless, his commitment has remained firm, despite the frustrations and disappointments that seem indeed to have given him an even sharper edge. The title of his 1988 collection of essays, *Hopes and Impediments*, is sufficiently eloquent to indicate this direction of his sentiments. It seems therefore safe to say that, for Achebe, the African personality is not incompatible with a modern scientific culture. Thus he asks rhetorically, "Why should I start waging war as a Nigerian newspaper editor was doing the other day against 'the soulless efficiency' of Europe's industrial and technological civilization when the very thing my society needs may well be a little technical efficiency" ("The Novelist as Teacher," *Hopes and Impediments*, 43). Add to this the lament at the end of *The Trouble with Nigeria*, that Nigeria has lost the twentieth century and is running the risk of losing the twenty-first as well.

31. In a fine passage written shortly before his death, Irving Howe expanded on Jameson's notion when he defined utopianism as "a necessity of the moral imagination." He continued: "It doesn't necessarily entail a particular politics; it doesn't ensure wisdom in current affairs. What it does provide is a guiding principle, a belief or hope for the future, an understanding that nothing is more mistaken than the common notion that what exists today will continue to exist tomorrow. This kind of uto-

pianism is really another way of appreciating the variety and surprise that history makes possible—possible, nothing more. It is a testimony to the resourcefulness that humanity now and then displays (together with other, far less attractive characteristics). It is a claim for the value of desire, the practicality of yearning—as against the deadliness of acquiescing in the given, simply because it is there" (Howe, 1993, 133).

32. The idea of *Things Fall Apart* as a tragedy in the classical sense was broached in an early essay of mine (Irele, 1965; see also Niven, 1990). Séverac discusses various responses to my classification of Achebe's novel as a tragedy (Séverac, 1997, 506–7).

Chapter 8

1. After taking a degree in history at the University of Cambridge, Brathwaite joined the British Colonial Service and arrived in the former Gold Coast in 1954, on the eve of the country's transition to independent status as the Republic of Ghana. He remained eight years, working as an education officer in various parts of the country, principally in the Akan-speaking areas. He therefore witnessed at first hand the remarkable movement of national resurgence and cultural revival that took place among the people of this African nation during that period. As the analysis that follows indicates, the direct influence of this experience on the composition of *Masks* and on the later development of his poetry and thinking is unmistakable.

2. In addition to the formal criticism cited, Maureen Warner's *E. Kamau Brathwaite's "Masks": Essays and Annotations* (1992) is an indispensable guide to the cultural references and structure of imagery in the volume.

3. In the sleeve note to his Argo recording of *The Arrivants*, Brathwaite provides a striking illustration of these natural connections when he recalls how, while he was living in St. Lucia, he was able to link the seasonal drought on the island with the harmattan he had known in Ghana; the relevant passage of the sleeve note is quoted at the head of his essay "The African Presence in Caribbean Literature," reprinted in *Roots* (1993, 190–258). Brathwaite's sense of the natural and historical bond between the Caribbean and Africa is elaborated in his poetry through the related images of trade winds and sea.

4. Mackey, 1991, 47.

5. *The Arrivants*, 1973, 4. All citations from *Rights of Passage* (1967), *Masks* (1968), and *Islands* (1969) are taken from this edition of the trilogy.

6. For an appraisal of Brathwaite's poetic language in its integration of the aesthetics of orality in *Masks*, see Asein, 1971; Warner, 1992; and Banjo, 1977. These early efforts to relate the language of his poetry more closely to the context of his experience form the basis of what he was

later to call "nation language" (see "History of the Voice," reprinted in *Roots*, 1993, 259–304) and account for the free-ranging idiom of his more recent work. These developments are discussed in Savory, 1995.

7. The historic sites Brathwaite recalls were important centers of the precolonial civilizations of the West African savanna, going back to well before the European Middle Ages.

8. In the first edition of *Masks*, "Adowa" was printed as the second part of "The Forest"; it was separated in later editions presumably to emphasize its specific focus.

9. We might note in passing that this naming is conducive to establishing the specificity of Caribbean humanity in a process of Creolization, a concept for which Brathwaite was the earliest theoretician; see *Contradictory Omens*, 1974. His insights in this long essay are currently being developed in the French-speaking Caribbean, notably by Edouard Glissant (1981) and by the trio of Jean Bernabé, Raphäel Confiant, and Patrick Chamoiseau (1989).

10. Brathwaite, 1987, 49–50. For an illuminating discussion of Brathwaite's second trilogy, see Chamberlin (1993, 189–94).

11. "Sun Song," 1991.

Chapter 9

1. J. P. Clark-Bekederemo, *Collected Plays and Poems*, 1991. All quotations from this edition.

Chapter 10

1. It is impossible for me to go here into a fuller explanation of the term *realism*, which today admits of several interpretations other than the conventional one as it applies to the nineteenth-century European novel. For a discussion of the various possible meanings of the term, see Fischer, 1963, 105–6. An interesting view of realism is also presented by Genette in his essay "Vertige fixe," where he speaks of a "réalisme subjectif" (1969, 73), à propos of Alain Robbe-Grillet's fiction.

2. Kwame Nkrumah gave characteristic expression to African optimism in the early years of independence when he defined the African revolution as that "which heralds the coming of a bright new era for all, a revolution destined to transform radically and completely the entire face of our beloved nation and our human society" (quoted in Post, 1964, 108).

3. Kofi Awoonor, *This Earth My Brother* (London: Heinemann, 1972); pages in text refer to this edition.

4. *Xala*. Paris: Présence Africaine, 1983.

5. *Perpétue ou l'habitude du malheur*. Paris: Buchet Chastel, 1974; pages in text refer to this edition.

6. For a study of Mongo Beti's work in relation to the landscape in which it is rooted, see Melone, 1971.

7. This is Martin Bestman's interpretation of this episode in his 1979 unpublished paper.

8. Soyinka, 1973. Page references are from this edition.

9. "The Cartel" is Soyinka's designation in the novel of that social category in Nigeria best described by C. Wright Mill's term the *power elite*.

10. This recalls the psychic terms of Sorel's conception, in his *Réflexions sur la violence* (1946), of revolutionary action as a form of mass therapy; in this conception, "the general strike" is not so much the harbinger of revolution as its symbolic enactment.

11. See "The Fourth Stage" in Soyinka's *Art, Dialogue and Outrage.* (1988), 21–34.

12. For a discussion, see Irele, "The Season of a Mind," in *The African Experience in Literature and Ideology*, 198–211.

13. Ouologuem, 1968. All quotations are from this edition.

14. Further evidence is provided by Ouologuem's frankly pornographic *Les mille et une bibles du sexe*, 1969.

Bibliography

Abimbola, Wande, ed. and trans. *Ifá Divination Poetry*. New York: NOK, 1977.

Abrams, M. H. *The Mirror and the Lamp: Romantic Theory and The Critical Tradition*. New York: Oxford University Press, 1953.

Achebe, Chinua. *Things Fall Apart*. London: Heinemann, 1958; reprint, 1962.

————. *No Longer at Ease*. London: Heinemann. 1960.

————. *Le locuste bianche* (*Things Fall Apart*), trans. G. De Carlo. Milan: Mondadori, 1962. The title changed in a more recent translation: *Il crollo*, trans. S. A. Cameroni. Milan: Jaca, 1994.

————. *Arrow of God*. London: Heinemann, 1964.

————. "Conversation with Chinua Achebe." Interview with Lewis Nkosi and Wole Soyinka. *Africa Report* (July 1964): 19–21. Reprinted in *Conversations with Chinua Achebe*, ed. Bernth Lindfors, 11–17. Jackson: University of Mississippi Press, 1997.

————. *A Man of the People*. London: Heinemann, 1966.

————. *Beware Soul Brother*. London: Heinemann, 1972.

————. "Chi in Igbo Cosmology," in *Morning Yet on Creation Day*, 159–75 London: Heinemann, 1975; New York: Anchor Press/Doubleday, 1975.

————. *The Trouble with Nigeria*. Enugu: Fourth Dimension, 1983.

————. *Anthills of the Savannah*. London: Heinemann, 1987.

————. *Hopes and Impediments: Selected Essays, 1965–87*. London: Heinemann, 1988.

————. Preface. *The African Trilogy*, ed. Achebe. London: Picador, 1988.

————. Interview. *America*, June 29, 1991.

———. *Home and Exile*. New York: Oxford University Press, 2000.

Adotevi, Stanislas. *Négritude et négrologues*. Paris: Union Générale d'Editions, 1972.

Ajayi, J. F. Ade. *Christian Missions in Nigeria, 1841–1891: The Making of a New Elite*. London: Longman, 1965.

Althusser, Louis, "Ideology and Ideological State Apparatuses," in *Lenin and Philosophy and Other Essays*, trans. Ben Brewster, 121–73 London: New Left Books, 1971.

Amadi, Elechi. *The Great Ponds*. London: Heinemann, 1969.

Anderson, Benedict. *Imagined Communities: Reflections on the Origin and Spread of Nationalism*. London: Verso, 1983.

Andrade, Susan Z. "The Joys of Daughterhood: Gender, Nationalism and the Making of Literary Tradition(s)." in *Cultural Institutions of the Novel*, ed. Deidre Lynch and William B. Warner, 249–75. Durham, N.C: Duke University Press, 1996.

Anozie, Sunday. *Sociologie du roman africain*. Paris: Aubier-Montaigne, 1970.

———. *Christopher Okigbo: Creative Rhetoric*. London: Evans, 1972.

Appadurai, Arjun. *Modernity at Large: Cultural Dimensions of Globalization*. Minneapolis: University of Minnesota Press, 1996.

Appiah, Kwame Anthony. "Soyinka and the Philosophy of Culture," in *Philosophy in Africa: Trends and Perspectives*, ed. P. O. Bodunrin, 250–63. Ile-Ife : University of Ife Press, 1985.

———. Introduction. *Things Fall Apart* by Chinua Achebe. New York: Knopf, 1992.

Armah, Ayi Kwei. *The Beautyful Ones Are Not Yet Born*. London: Heinemann, 1969.

———. *Fragments*. London: Heinemann, 1970.

———. *Two Thousand Seasons*. Nairobi: East African Publishing House, 1973.

Armstrong, Robert Plant. *The Affecting Presence*. Urbana: University of Illinois Press, 1971.

Asante, Molefi. *Afrocentricity*. Trenton, N.J.: Africa World Press, 1988.

———. *The Afrocentric Idea*. Philadelphia, Pa.: Temple University Press, 1987. 2d ed., 1998.

Asein, Samuel Omo. "The Concept of Form: A Study of Some Ancestral Elements in Brathwaite's Trilogy." *African Studies Association of the West Indies Bulletin* 4 (1971): 9–38.

Ashcroft, Bill, Gareth Griffiths, and Helen Tiffin. *The Empire Writes Back: Theory and Practice in Postcolonial Literatures*. London: Routledge, 1989.

Auerbach, Eric. *Mimesis*, trans. by W. R. Trask. Princeton, N.J.: Princeton University Press, 1953.

Avrich, Paul. *The Russian Anarchists*. New York: Norton, 1978.

Awoonor, Kofi. *This Earth My Brother . . . An Allegorical Tale of Africa*. London: Heinemann, 1971

Bâ, Amadou Hampaté. *Kaïdara, récit initiatique, peul*. Paris: Armand Colin, 1969.

———. *L'Etrange destin de Wangrin*. Paris: Union Générale d'Editions, 1973.

———. *Vie et Enseignement de Tierno Bokar, le sage de Bandiagara*. Paris: Editions du Seuil, 1980.

———. "The Living Tradition," in *UNESCO General History of Africa*, ed. Ki-Zerbo, 166–203. Berkeley: University of California Press, 1981.

———. *L'empire peul du Macina*, 2d ed., Abidjan, Ivory Coast: Nouvelles Editions Africaines, 1984.

Bailyn, Bernard. *On the Teaching and Writing of History*. Hanover, N.H.: University Press of New England, 1994.

Baker, Houston A., Jr. *The Journey Back: Issues in Black Literature and Criticism*. Chicago: University of Chicago Press, 1980.

———. *Blues, Ideology and Afro-American Literature: A Vernacular Theory*. Chicago: University of Chicago Press, 1984.

Bakhtin, Mikhail. "Epic and Novel," in *The Dialogic Imagination*, ed. by Michael Holquist, 3–40. Trans. by Caryl Emerson and Michael Holquist. Austin: University of Texas Press, 1981.

Balandier, Georges. "Tradition et modernité," in his *Anthropologie politique*, 3d ed., 186–218. Paris: Presses Universitaires de France, 1984.

———. *Le désordre: Éloge du mouvement*. Paris: Fayard, 1988.

Banjo, Ayo. "A Stylistic Approach to the Poetry of Edward Brathwaite." Unpublished paper, University of Ibadan, 1977.

Barber, Karin. *I Could Speak until Tomorrow: Oriki, Women and the Past in a Yoruba Town*. Washington, D.C.: Smithsonian Institution Press, 1991.

Barraclough, Geoffrey. *An Introduction to Contemporary History*. Harmondsworth, England: Penguin, 1967.

Barthes, Roland. *Le degré zéro de l'écriture*. Paris: Seuil, 1953. Trans. Ann Lavers and Colin Smith as *Writing Degree Zero*. New York: Hill and Wang, 1968.

———. *Sur Racine*. Paris: Seuil, 1963.

———. *S/Z*. Paris: Seuil, 1970. Trans. Richard Miller. New York: Hill and Wang, 1986.

———. "Introduction to the Structural Analysis of Narrative." *New Literary History* 2 (1975): 237–72.

Bascom, William Russell. *Ifa Divination: Communication between Gods and Men in West Africa*. Bloomington: Indiana University Press, 1969.

Basden, George. *Among the Ibos of Nigeria*. London, 1921; reprint, London: Cass, 1966.

Bassir, Olumbe, ed. *West African Verse: An Anthology*. Ibadan: Ibadan University Press, 1957.

Bastide, Roger. *L'Afrique dans l'oeuvre de Castro Soromenho*. Paris: J-P Oswald, 1960.

Bell, Bernard B. *The Afro-American Novel and Its Tradition*. Amherst: University of Massachusetts Press, 1987.

Benjamin, Walter. *Illuminations*. London: Fontana/Collins, 1973.

Bernabé, Jean, Raphaël Confiant, and Patrick Chamoiseau. *Eloge de la créolité*. Paris: Gallimard, 1989.

Bestman, Martin. "Une lecture de *Perpétue* de Mongo Beti." Unpublished paper, University of Ife, 1979.

Beti, Mongo. *Mission terminée*. Paris: Buchet-Chastel, 1957. Trans. Peter Green as *Mission to Kala*. London: Heinemann, 1964.

———. *Le roi miraculé*. Paris: Buchet-Chastel, 1958. Trans. Peter Green as *King Lazarus*. New York: Collier, 1971.

———. *Perpétue ou l'habitude du malheur*. Paris: Éditions Buchet/Chastel, 1974. Trans. John Reed and Clive Wake as *Perpetua and the Habit of Unhappiness*. London: Heinemann, 1978.

———. *Remember Ruben*. Paris: Union Générale d'Editions, 1974. Trans. Gerald Moore, under same title. Ibadan: New Horn Press. 1980.

———. *Main basse sur le Cameroun*. Paris: Maspero, 1978.

———. *La ruine presque cocasse d'un polichinelle*. Paris: Peuples Noirs, Peuples Africains, 1979. Trans. Richard Bjornson as *Lament for an African Pol*. Washington, D.C.: Three Continents, 1980.

Bhabha, Homi. "DissemiNation," in *Nation and Narration*, 291–322. London: Routledge, 1990; reprint *The Location of Culture*, 139–170 London: Routledge, 1994.

———. "Signs Taken for Wonders: Questions of Ambivalence and Authority under a Tree outside of Delhi, May 1817," *The Location of Culture*, 102–122.

Biebuyck, Daniel, and Mateene C. Kahombo, eds. *The Mwindo Epic*. Berkeley: University of California Press, 1971.

Bjornson, Richard. *The African Quest for Freedom and Identity: Cameroonian Writing and the National Experience*. Bloomington: Indiana University Press, 1991.

Black, Michael. "F. R. Leavis: 1895–1978." *New Universities Quarterly*, 32, no. 3 (Summer 1978): 293–304.

Bloomfield, Leonard. *Language*. 1933; reprint, New York: Holt, Rinehart and Winston, 1965.

Blyden, Edward Wilmot. *Christianity, Islam and the Negro Race*. London, 1887; repr., Edinburgh: Edinburgh University Press, 1962.

———. *African Life and Customs*. 1908; reprint, London: African Publication Society, 1969.

Boilat, Abbé. *Esquisses sénégalaises*. 1853; reprint, Dakar: Nouvelles Editions Africaines, 1986.

Booker, Keith. *The African Novel in English: An Introduction*. Portsmouth, N.H.: Heinemann, 1998.

Boyd, Michael. *The Reflexive Novel*. Lewisburg, Pa.: Bucknell University Press, 1983.

Brantlinger, Patrick. *Crusoe's Footprints: Cultural Studies in Britain and America*. New York: Routledge, 1990.

Brathwaite, Edward Kamau. *The Arrivants*, (comprising *Rights of Passage, Masks, and Islands*). London: Oxford University Press, 1973.

———. *Contradictory Omens*. Mona, Kingston, Jamaica: Savacou, 1974.

———. *Other Exiles*. London: Oxford University Press, 1975.

———. *Mother Poem*. Oxford: Oxford University Press, 1977.

———. *X/Self*. Oxford: Oxford University Press, 1987

———. "Sun Song" *Hambone* 9 (Winter 1991): 39–41

———. *Roots*. Ann Arbor: University of Michigan Press, 1993.

Brennan, Timothy. "The National Longing for Form," in *Nation and Narration*, ed. Homi Bhabha, 44–70. London: Routledge, 1990.

Cahoone, Lawrence E. *The Dilemma of Modernity*. Albany: State University of New York Press, 1988.

Calame-Griaule, Geneviève. *Ethnologie et langage*. Paris: Gallimard, 1965.

Callenbach, Ernest. *Ecotopia*. New York: Bantam, 1976.

Césaire, Aimé. *Cahier d'un retour au pays natal*. Paris: Présence Africaine, 1956.

———. *Une tempête*. Paris: Seuil, 1969.

———. *Collected Poems*, trans. Clayton Eshleman and Anette Smith. Berkeley: University of California Press, 1983.

Chadwick, H. Munro, and N. Kershaw Chadwick. *The Growth of Literature*. 3 Vols. Cambridge: Cambridge University Press, 1986.

Chamberlin, J. Edward. *Come Back to Me, My Language*. Urbana: University of Illinois Press, 1993.

Chinweizu, Onwuchekwa Jemie, and Ikechukwu Madubuike. *Toward the Decolonization of African Literature*. Enugu, Nigeria: Fourth Dimension, 1980.

Clark-Bekederemo, J. P. *America, Their America*. New York: Africana Publishing Corporation, 1969.

———. *The Example of Shakespeare*. Evanston: Northwestern University Press, 1970.

———. *The Ozidi Saga*. Ibadan: Oxford University Press: 1977; reprint, Washington, D.C.: Howard University Press, 1992.

———. *Collected Plays and Poetry, 1958–1988*. Washington, D.C.: Howard University Press, 1991.

Clifford, James, and George E. Marcus, eds. *Writing Culture: The Poetics and Politics of Ethnography*. Berkeley: University of California Press, 1986.

Coetzee, J. M. *White Writing: On the Culture of Letters in South Africa*. New Haven, Conn.: Yale University Press, 1988.

———. *The Novel in Africa*. Occasional Papers of the Doreen B. Townsend Center for the Humanities, no. 17. Berkeley: University of California, 1999.

Cohen, William B. *The French Encounter with Africans*. Bloomington: Indiana University Press, 1980.

Coleman, James. *Nigeria: Background to Nationalism*. Los Angeles: University of California Press, 1958.

Conrad, Joseph. *Heart of Darkness*, ed. Robert Kimbrough. New York: Norton, 1988.

Cook, David. *African Literature: A Critical View*. London: Longman, 1977.

Cope, Trevor, ed. *Izibongo—Zulu Praise Poems*. Collected by James Stuart. Oxford: Clarendon, 1968.

Costanzo, Angelo. *Surprizing Narrative: Olaudah Equiano and the Beginnings of Black Autobiography*. Westport, Conn.: Greenwood, 1987.

Coupez, A., and Th. Kamanzi, eds. *Littérature de cour au Rwanda*. Oxford: Clarendon, 1970.

Crummell, Alexander. *The Future of Africa*. New York: Scribner, 1862.

Culler, Jonathan. *Structuralist Poetics: Structuralism, Linguistics and the Study of Literature*. Ithaca, N.Y.: Cornell University Press, 1975.

Daiches, David. *Critical Approaches to Literature*. Englewood Cliffs, N.J.: Prentice-Hall, 1956.

David, Mary. *Wole Soyinka: A Quest for Renewal*. Madras: BI Publications, 1995.

Davis, Carole Boyce. "Motherhood in the Works of Male and Female Igbo Writers: Achebe, Emecheta, Nwapa, and Nzekwu," in *Ngambika: Studies of Women in African Literature*, ed. Carole Boyce Davis and Anne Adams Graves, 241–56. Trenton, N.J.: Africa World Press, 1986.

Davis, Charles T., and Henry Louis Gates, Jr. *The Slave's Narrative*. New York: Oxford University Press, 1985.

Deane, Seamus, ed. *Nationalism, Colonialism and Literature*. Minneapolis: University of Minnesota Press, 1990.

Denby, David. "Jungle Fever." *New Yorker*, Nov. 6, 1995, pp. 118–29.

Diagne, Pathé. *L'Europhilosophie*. Dakar: Sankoré, 1982.

Diké, K. Onwuka. *Trade and Politics in the Niger Delta, 1830–1885*. London: Oxford University Press, 1956.

Diop, Birago. *Les nouveaux contes d'Amadou Koumba*. Paris: Présence Africaine, 1958.

———. *Les contes d'Amadou Koumba*. Paris: Présence Africaine, 1961.

———. *Contes et lavanes*. Paris: Présence Africaine, 1963.

Du Bois, W. E. B. *The Souls of Black Folk*. New York: Modern Library, 1996.

Dufrenne, Michel. *La personnalité de base*. Paris: Presses Universitaires de France, 1953.

Eagleton, Terry. *Criticism and Ideology*. Oxford: Basil Blackwell, 1976.

———. *The Ideology of the Aesthetic*. Oxford: Basil Blackwell, 1990.

Echeruo, Michael J. C. *Joyce Cary and the Novel of Africa*. New York: Africana, 1973.

———. *Victorian Lagos*. London: Macmillan, 1977.

———. *The Conditioned Imagination from Shakespeare to Conrad*. New York: Holmes & Meier, 1978.

———. *Ahamefula: A Matter of Identity*. Owerri: Imo State Ministry of Information, 1979.

Egudu, Romanus. "Chinua Achebe and the Igbo Narrative Tradition." *Research in African Literatures* 12, no. 1 (1981): 43–54.

Eliade, Mircea. *Cosmos and History: The Myth of the Eternal Return*, trans. Willard Trask. New York: Harper and Row, 1954.

Emenyonu, Ernest. *The Rise of the Igbo Novel*. Ibadan: Oxford University Press, 1974.

Equiano, Olaudah. *The Interesting Narrative of the Life of Olaudah Equiano*, ed. Paul Edwards. London, 1789; reprint, London:Dawson, 1969.

———. *Equiano's Travels*, ed. Paul Edwards. London: Heinemann, 1969.

Esslin, Martin. *The Theatre of the Absurd*. Garden City, N.Y.: Doubleday, 1961.

Fanon, Frantz. *Les damnés de la terre*. Paris: Maspéro, 1961. Trans. Constance Farrington as *The Wretched of the Earth*. New York: Grove, 1967.

Fanoudh-Siefer, L. *Le mythe du nègre et de l'Afrique dans la littérature française de 1800 à la deuxième guerre mondiale*. Paris: Klincksieck, 1968.

Ferry, Luc, and Alain Renaut. *French Philosophy in the Sixties*, trans. Mary S. Cattani. Amherst: University of Massachusetts Press, 1989.

Finnegan, Ruth. *Oral Literature in Africa*. London: Oxford University Press, 1970.

———. "Literacy versus Non Literacy: The Great Divide?" in *Modes of Thought*, ed. Robert Horton and Ruth Finnegan, 112–144. London: Faber and Faber, 1973.

———. "Oral Literature and Writing in the South Pacific," in *Oral and Traditional Literatures*, ed. Norman Simms, 22–36. Hamilton, New Zealand: Outrigger, 1982.

Firchow, Peter Edgerly. *Envisioning Africa: Racism and Imperialism in Conrad's "Heart of Darkness."* Lexington: University Press of Kentucky, 2000.

Fischer, Ernst. *The Necessity of Art*. Harmondsworth, England: Penguin, 1963.

Fish, Stanley. *Is There a Text in This Class? The Authority of Interpretive Communities*. Cambridge, Mass.: Harvard University Press, 1980.

Fleming, Bruce E. "What Is the Value of Literary Studies." *New Literary History* 31 (2000): 459–76.

Foley, John Miles. *The Theory of Oral Composition: History and Methodology.* Bloomington: Indiana University Press, 1988.

———. *Oral-Formulaic Theory: A Folklore Casebook.* New York: Garland, 1990.

Foucault, Michel. *L'ordre du discours.* Paris: Gallimard, 1971.

Frobenius, Leo. *Histoire de la civilisation africaine.* Paris: Gallimard, 1952.

Fyfe, Christopher. *Africanus Horton: West African Scientist and Patriot.* New York: Oxford University Press, 1972.

Garrett, Naomi Mills. *The Renaissance of Haitian Poetry.* Paris: Présence Africaine, 1963.

Gates, Henry Louis, Jr. "Being, the Will and the Semantics of Death." *Harvard Educational Review* 51, no. 1 (1981): 163–173.

———. ed. *"Race," Writing and Difference.* Chicago: University of Chicago Press, 1986.

———. ed. *Figures in Black.* New York: Oxford University Press, 1987.

———. General foreword to titles in the *Schomburg Library of Nineteenth-Century Black Women Writers.* New York: Oxford University Press, 1988.

———. *The Signifyin' Monkey.* New York: Oxford University Press, 1989.

Gay, Peter. *The Enlightenment: An Interpretation.* New York: Norton, 1966.

Gayle, Addison, ed. *The Black Aesthetic.* Garden City, N.Y.: Doubleday, 1971.

Geertz, Clifford, ed. *Old Societies and New States: The Quest for Modernity in Asia and Africa.* New York: Free Press, 1963.

Gellner, Ernest. *Thought and Change.* London: Weidenfeld and Nicholson, 1965.

———. *Nations and Nationalism.* Ithaca, N.Y.: Cornell University Press, 1983.

Genette, Gérard. "Vertige fixe," in *Figures 1.* Paris: Seuil, 1969. 145–70.

———. *Figures III.* Paris: Seuil, 1972.

Gérard, Albert. *Four African Literatures.* Berkeley: University of California Press, 1971.

———. *African Language Literature.* Washington, D.C.: Three Continents, 1981.

Gikandi, Simon. *Reading the African Novel.* London: James Currey, 1987.

———. *Reading Chinua Achebe: Language and Ideology in Fiction.* London: James Currey, 1991.

———. "Chinua Achebe and the Invention of African Literature." Introduction to *Things Fall Apart* by Chinua Achebe. Oxford: Heinemann, 1996.

Glissant, Edouard. *Le discours antillais*. Paris: Seuil, 1981. Trans. J. Michael Dash as *Caribbean Discourse: Selected Essays*. Charlottesville: University Press of Virginia, 1989.

Gobineau, Joseph Arthur de. *Essai sur l'inégalité des races humaines*. 3 vols. Paris: Didot, 1853–1855. Trans. A. Collins as *The Inequality of Human Races*. Torrance, Calif.: Noontide, 1983.

Goody, Jack. *The Myth of the Bagre*. Oxford: Clarendon, 1972.

———. *The Domestication of the Savage Mind*. Cambridge: Cambridge University Press, 1977.

———. *The Interface between the Oral and the Written*. Cambridge: Cambridge University Press, 1987.

Gordon, D. *Self-Determination and History in the Third World*. Princeton, N.J.: Princeton University Press, 1971.

Graff, Gerald. *Poetic Statement and Critical Dogma*. Chicago: University of Chicago Press, 1980.

Grégoire, Abbé Henri. *De la littérature des Nègres*. Paris: Maradan, 1808. Trans. D. B. Warden as *An Enquiry Concerning the Intellectual and Moral Faculties and Literature of Negroes*. Brooklyn, 1810. Reprint, College Park, Md.: McGrath, 1967.

Gusdorf, Georges. *Mythe et métaphysique*. Paris: Payot, 1962.

Gyekye, Kwame. *Tradition and Modernity: Philosophical Reflections on the African Experience*. New York : Oxford University Press, 1997.

Habermas, Jürgen. *The Theory of Communicative Action*, vol. 1: *Reason and the Rationalization of Society*, trans. Thomas McCarthy. Boston: Beacon Press, 1984 and 1986.

Hammond, Dorothy, and Alta Jablow. *The Africa That Never Was*. Prospect Heights, Ill.: Waveland, 1992.

Hamner, Robert, ed. *Joseph Conrad: Third World Perspectives*. Washington, D.C.: Three Continents, 1990.

Harlow, Barbara. *Resistance Literature*. London: Methuen, 1987.

Hasek, Jaroslav. *The Good Soldier Svejk*, trans. Cecil Parrott. Harmondsworth, England: Penguin, 1973.

Hazoumé, Paul. *Doguicimi*. 1938. Reprint, Paris: Maisonneuve et Larose, 1978. trans. Richard Bjornson. Washington, D.C.: Three Continents, 1990.

Hegel, G. F. *Reason in History*, trans. Robert S. Hartman. Englewood Cliffs, N.J: Prentice-Hall, 1953.

Hochbruck, Wolfgang. " 'I Have Spoken': Fictional 'Orality' in Indigenous Fiction." *College Literature* 23, no. 2 (June 1996): 132–42.

Hodge, Robert. *Literature as Discourse*. Baltimore, Md.: John Hopkins University Press, 1990.

Hountondji, Paulin. *Sur la "philosophie africaine."* Paris: Maspéro, 1983.

Hove, Chenjerai. *Bones*. Oxford: Heinemann, 1990.

Howe, Irving. *Politics and the Novel.* 1957; reprint, New York: Meridian, 1987.

———. "The Spirit of the Times." *Dissent* (Spring 1993): 133.

Huannou, Adrien. *La Question des littératures nationales.* Abidjan, Ivory Coast: Editions CEDA, 1989.

Innes, C. L. *Chinua Achebe.* Cambridge: Cambridge University Press, 1990.

Innes, Gordon, ed. *Sunjata: Three Mandinka Versions.* London: SOAS, University of London, 1974.

Irele, Abiola. "The Tragic Conflict in Achebe's Novels." *Black Orpheus* 17 (1965): 24–32. Reprint, *Introduction to African Literature: An Anthology of Critical Writing from "Black Orpheus,"* ed. Ulli Beier, 167–78. London: Longman, 1967.

———. "Tradition and the Yoruba Writer." *Odu* 11 (Jan. 1975). Reprint, *The African Experience in Literature and Ideology,* 174–97. London: Heinemann, 1981, and Bloomington: Indiana University Press, 1990.

———. "Studying African Literature," in *The African Experience,* 9–26.

———. "Pan-Africanism and African Nationalism," in *The African Experience,* 117–24.

———. "The Season of a Mind," in *The African Experience,* 198–211.

———. "In Praise of Alienation." Inaugural lecture delivered at the University of Ibadan, 1987. Reprint, *The Surreptitious Speech: Présence Africaine and the Politics of Otherness,* ed. V. Y. Mudimbe, 207–24. Chicago: University of Chicago Press, 1992.

———. "Second Language Literatures: An African Perspective," in *Thresholds: Anglophone African Literature/Seuils: Les littératures africaines anglophones,* ed. Christine Fioupou, 7–22. Special Number of *Anglophonia/Caliban: French Journal of English Studies.* No. 7 (2000). Presses Universitaires de Toulouse-Mirail.

Iyasere, Solomon. "Narrative Techniques in *Things Fall Apart,"* in *Critical Perspectives on Chinua Achebe,* ed. C. L. Innes and Bernth Lindfors, 92–110. Washington, D.C.: Three Continents, 1978.

Izevbaye, D. S. "Soyinka's Black Orpheus," in *Neo-African Literature and Culture,* ed. Bernth Lindfors and Ulla Schild, 147–158. Mainz: Heyman, 1976.

Jahn, Janheinz. *Muntu.* London: Faber and Faber, 1961.

———. A *History of Neo-African Literature.* London: Faber and Faber, 1966.

Jameson, Fredric. *The Political Unconscious: Narrative as a Socially Symbolic Act.* Ithaca, N.Y.: Cornell University Press, 1981.

———. "Third World Literature in the Era of Multinational Capitalism." *Social Text* 5, no. 3 (1986): 65–88.

JanMohamed, Abdul, and David Lloyd, eds. *The Nature and Context of Minority Discourse.* New York: Oxford University Press, 1990.

Jeyifo, Biodun. "Wole Soyinka and the Tropes of Disalienation." Introduction to *Art, Dialogue and Outrage by Wole Soyinka*, viii–xxxi. Ibadan: New Horn, 1988.

———. "The Resilience and the Predicament of Obierika," in *Chinua Achebe: A Celebration*, ed. Kirsten Holst Peterson and Anna Rutherford, 51–70. Oxford: Heinemann, 1990.

———. "Determinations of Remembering: Postcolonial Fictional Genealogies of Colonialism in Africa." *Stanford Literature Review* 10, nos. 1–2 (1993a): 99–116.

———. "Okonkwo and His Mother: *Things Fall Apart* and Issues of Gender in the Constitution of African Postcolonial Discourse." *Callaloo* 16, no. 4 (1993b): 847–58.

Johnson, John William. *The Epic of Son-Jara*. Text by Fa-Digi Sisòkò. Bloomington: Indiana University Press, 1986.

Johnson, Samuel. *The History of the Yoruba*. Lagos, Nigeria: CMS Bookshops, 1921.

Jolles, André. *Formes simples*. Paris: Seuil, 1972.

Julien, Eileen. *African Novels and the Question of Orality*. Bloomington: Indiana. University Press, 1992.

July, Robert. *The Origins of Modern African Thought*. London: Faber and Faber, 1968.

Kadima-Nzuji, Mukala. *La littérature zaïroise de langue française*. Paris: Karthala, 1984.

Kane, Cheikh Hamidou. *L'aventure ambiguë*. Paris: Julliard, 1961.

Kane, Mohammadou. *Roman africain et tradition*. Dakar: Nouvelles Editions Africaines, 1982.

Kardiner, A. *The Psychological Frontiers of Society*. New York: Columbia University Press, 1945.

Khair, Tabish. "Debate." *Wasafiri* 31 (Spring 2000): 82–83.

Ker, David. *The African Novel and the Modernist Tradition*. New York: Lang, 1997.

Kermode, Frank. *The Art of Telling*. Cambridge, Mass.: Harvard University Press, 1983.

Kesteloot, Lilyan. *Les écrivains noirs de langue française: Naissance d'une littérature*. Brussels: Institut Solvay, 1963. Trans. Ellen Conroy Kennedy as *Black Writers in French*. Washington, D.C.: Howard University Press, 1991.

———. "Mythe, epopée et histoire Africaine," in *Littérature africaine et histoire*, 38–45. Paris: Editions Nouvelles du Sud, 1991.

Khatibi, Abdelkebir. *Maghreb Pluriel*. Paris: Denoël, 1983.

Ki-Zerbo, Joseph. Introduction to *UNESCO General History of Africa*, vol. 1: *Methodology and African History*, 1–24. Berkeley: University of California Press, 1981.

Kourouma, Ahmadou. *Les soleils des indépendances*. Paris: Seuil, 1976.

————. *Monnè, outrages et défis*. Paris: Seuil, 1990.

Krieger, Milton. "Education and Development in Western Nigeria: The Legacy of S. O. Awokoya, 1952–1985." *International Journal of African Historical Studies* 20, no. 4 (1987): 647–55.

Krieger, Murray. *The Institution of Theory*. Baltimore: Johns Hopkins University Press, 1994.

Kubayanda, Josaphat. *The Poet's Africa*. Westport, Conn.: Greenwood, 1990.

Kumar, Krishan. *Prophecy and Progress: The Sociology of Post-Industrial Society*. Harmondsworth, England: Penguin, 1978.

Kumari, Vinaya. "Woman Centered Play: A Feminist Reading of Selected Plays of Rabindranath Tagore, Girish Karnad and Vijay Tendulkar." Ph.D. thesis, Mother Teresa Women's University, Kodaikanal, India, 2000.

Kunene, Daniel P. *Heroic Poetry of the Basotho*. Oxford: Clarendon, 1971.

Kunene, Mazisi. *Zulu Poems*. New York: Africana, 1970.

————. *Emperor Shaka the Great*. London: Heinemann, 1979.

Lamming, George. *In the Castle of My Skin*. New York: McGraw-Hill, 1953.

————. *The Pleasures of Exile*. London: Michael Joseph, 1960.

Lawrence, Margaret. *Long Drums and Canons*. London: Macmillan, 1968.

Laye, Camara. *L'enfant noir*. Paris: Plon, 1953; trans. James Kirkup as *The Dark Child*. New York, Farrar, Straus and Giroux, 1971.

————. *Le maître de la parole*. Paris: Plon, 1978. Trans. James Kirkup as *The Guardian of the Word: Kouma Lafôlô Kouma*. New York: Vintage, 1984.

Le Goff, Jacques. *History and Memory*, trans. Steven Randall and Elizabeth Claman. New York: Columbia University Press, 1992.

Leavis, F. R. *The Living Principle*. London: Chatto and Windus, 1975.

Lévi-Strauss, Claude. *La pensée sauvage*. Paris: Plon, 1962.

————. *Le totémisme aujourd'hui*. Paris: Presses Universitaires de France, 1962.

————. "The Story of Asdiwal" (*La geste d'Asdiwal*), in *The Structural Study of Myth and Totemism*, ed. Edmund Leach, 1–47. Trans. Nicholas Mann. London: Tavistock, 1967.

Lévy-Bruhl, Lucien. *Carnets*. Paris: Presses Universitaires de France, 1939. Trans. Peter Rivière as *The Notebooks on Primitive Mentality*. Oxford: Basil Blackwell, 1975.

————. *La metalité primitive*. Paris: Presses Universitaires de France, 1960. Trans. L. Clare as *Primitive Mentality*. New York: AMS Press, 1978.

Lindfors, Bernth. "The Palm Oil with Which Words Are Eaten." *African Literature Today* 1 (1968): 3–18.

————, ed. *Conversations with Chinua Achebe*. Jackson: University Press of Mississippi, 1997.

Lord, Albert. *The Singer of Tales*. Cambridge, Mass.: Harvard University Press, 1960; reprint, 2000.

Lukács, Georg. *The Theory of the Novel*. Cambridge, Mass.: Harvard University Press, 1977.

Lukes, Steve. *Essays in Social Theory*. New York: Columbia University Press, 1977.

Lynch, Hollis. *Edward Wilmot Blyden: Pan-Negro Patriot*. New York: Oxford University Press, 1967.

———, ed. *Selected Letters of Edward Wilmot Blyden*. New York: KTO Press, 1978.

Lyotard, Jean-François. *La condition postmoderne*. Paris: Editions de Minuit, 1979.

Mackey, Nathaniel. "An Interview with Edward Kamau Brathwaite." *Hambone* 9 (Winter 1991): 42–59.

Mahood, Molly. *The Colonial Encounter*. London: Rex Collings, 1977.

Malinowski, Bronislaw. "The Problem of Meaning in Primitive Languages," in *The Meaning of Meaning*, ed. C. K. Ogden and I. A. Richards, 297–336. London, 1923; Reprint, New York: Harcourt Brace Jovanovich, 1989.

Mannheim, Karl. *Essays on Sociology and Social Psychology*, ed. Paul Kecskemeti. London: Routledge and Kegan Paul, 1953.

Manuel, Frank E., and Fritzie P. Manuel. *Utopian Thought in the Western World*. Cambridge, Mass.: Harvard University Press, 1979.

Maran, René. *Batouala, véritable roman nègre*. Paris: Albin Michel, 1921. Trans. Barbara Beck and Alexandre Mboukou as *Batouala: A True Black Novel*. Washington D.C.: Black Orpheus Press, 1972.

———. *Le livre de la brousse*. Paris: Albin Michel, 1934.

Marshall, Paule. *Praisesong for the Widow*. New York: Putnam's, 1983.

Marx, Karl. "The Holy Family," in *Karl Marx/Frederick Engels Collected Works*, 4:1–211. Moscow: Progress, 1975.

Marx, Leo. *The Machine in the Garden*. New York: Oxford University Press, 1970.

Mazrui, Ali. *The African Condition, a Political Diagnosis*. London: Heinemann, 1980.

Mbembe, Achille. *Les Afriques indociles*. Paris: Karthala, 1988.

McLuhan, Marshall. *The Gutenberg Galaxy: The Making of Typographic Man*. Toronto: University of Toronto Press, 1962.

McNeil, Linda D. *Recreating the World/Word: The Mythic Mode as Symbolic Discourse*. Albany: State University of New York Press, 1992.

Meek, Charles Kingsley. *Law and Authority in a Nigerian Tribe*. London: Oxford University Press, 1937.

Melone, Thomas. *Mongo Beti—L'homme et l'oeuvre*. Paris: Présence Africaine, 1971.

————. *Chinua Achebe et la tragédie de l'histoire*. Paris: Présence Africaine, 1973.

Memmi, Albert. *Portrait du colonisé*. Paris: Buchet-Chastel, 1957. Trans. Howard Greenfeld as *The Colonizer and the Colonized*. Boston: Beacon, 1967.

Miller, Christopher. *Blank Darkness: Africanist Discourse in French*. Chicago: University of Chicago Press, 1985.

Mink, Louis. "History and Fiction as Modes of Comprehension." *New Literary History* 1, no. 3 (1970): 541–58.

————. *Historical Understanding*, ed. Brian Fay, Eugene O. Golob, and Richard T. Vann. Ithaca, N.Y.: Cornell University Press, 1987.

Miyoshi, Masao. "Thinking Aloud in Japan." *Raritan* 9, no. 2 (Fall 1989): 29–45.

Mofolo, Thomas. *Chaka*, trans. Daniel Kunene. London: Heinemann, 1981.

Monteil, Vincent. *Islam noir*. Paris: Karthala, 1983.

Moses, Jeremiah. *Alexander Crummel: A Study of Civilization and Discontent*. New York: Oxford University Press, 1989.

Moses, Michael Valdez. *The Novel and the Globalization of Culture*. New York: Oxford University Press, 1995.

Mphahlele, Ezekiel. *Down Second Avenue*. Garden City, N.Y.: Anchor, 1971.

Mpondo, Simon. "Provisional Notes on Literature and Criticism in Africa." *Présence Africaine* 78 (1971): 118–42.

Mudimbe, Valentin. *The Invention of Africa*. Bloomington: Indiana University Press, 1988.

Muoneke, Romanus Okey. *Art, Rebellion and Redemption: A Reading of the Novels of Chinua Achebe*. New York: Lang, 1994.

Naipaul, V. S. *An Area of Darkness*. London: André Deutsch, 1964.

Nda, Paul. *Les intellectuels et le pouvoir en Afrique*. Paris: L'Harmattan, 1987.

Ngugi wa Thiong'o. *Devil on the Cross*. London: Heinemann, 1982.

————. *Decolonizing the Mind*. London: James Currey/Heinemann, 1986.

————. *Matigari*. London: Heinemann, 1989.

Niven, Alastair. "Chinua Achebe and the Possibility of Modern Tragedy," in *Chinua Achebe: A Celebration*, ed. Kirsten Holst Peterson and Anna Rutherford, 41–50. London: Heinemann, 1990.

Nixon, Rob. "Caribbean and African Appropriations of *The Tempest*," *Critical Inquiry* 13, no. 3 (Spring 1987): 557–77.

Nketia, Kwabena. *Funeral Dirges of the Akan People*. Accra: University of the Gold Coast Press, 1958.

Nkrumah, Kwame. *Africa Must Unite*. London: Heinemann, 1964.

————. *Consciencism*. London: Panaf, 1970.

Nora, Pierre. "Between Memory and History: *Les lieux de mémoire*." *Representations* 26 (1989): 7–24.

Nwakwo, Nkem. *Danda*. London: Heinemann, 1964.

Nwoga, Donatus. "The Igbo World of Achebe's *Arrow of God*." *Research in African Literatures* 12, no. 1 (1981): 14–42.

Nyerere, Julius. *Ujamaa: Essays on Socialism*. London: Oxford University Press, 1973.

Obiechina, Emmanuel. *Culture, Society and the West African Novel*. Cambridge: Cambridge University Press, 1975.

———. "Perception of Colonialism in West African Literature," in *Literature and Modern West African Culture*, ed. D. J. Nwoga, 53–67. Benin City: Ethiope, 1978.

———. *Language and Theme: Essays in African Literature*. Washington, D.C.: Howard University Press, 1990.

———. "Narrative Proverbs in the African Novel." *Research in African Literatures* 24, no. 4 (1993): 123–40.

Ogude, Stephen. "Facts into Fiction: Equiano's Narrative Revisited." *Research in African Literatures* 13, no. 1 (1982): 31–43.

Okara, Gabriel. *The Voice*. London: André Deutsch, 1964.

Okigbo, Christopher. *Labyrinths, with Path of Thunder*. New York: Africana, 1971.

Okpweho, Isidore. *The Epic in Africa*. New York: Columbia University Press, 1979.

———, ed. *The Oral Performance in Africa*. Ibadan: Spectrum, 1990.

———. *African Oral Literature: Backgrounds, Character, and Continuity*. Bloomington: Indiana University Press, 1992.

Olney, James. *Tell Me, Africa: An Approach to African Literature*. Princeton: Princeton, N.J.: Princeton University Press, 1973.

Ong, Walter J. *Orality and Literacy: The Technologizing of the Word*. London: Methuen, 1982.

Osofisan, Femi. *Eshu and the Vagabond Minstrels*. Ibadan, Nigeria: New Horn Press, 1987.

Ouologuem, Yambo. *Le devoir de violence*. Paris: Seuil, 1968. Trans. Ralph Mannhein as *Bound to Violence*. New York: Harcourt Brace Jovanovich, 1971.

———. *Les mille et une bibles du sexe*. Paris: Editions du Dauphin, 1969.

Ousmane, Sembène. *Les bouts de bois de Dieu*. Paris: Debresse, 1960. Trans. Francis Price as *God's Bits of Wood*. Garden City, N.Y.: Doubleday, 1962.

———. *Harmattan*. Paris: Présence Africaine, 1962.

———. *Vehi-ciosane ou Blanche-genèse, suivi du Mandat* Paris: Présence Africaine, 1966. Trans. Clive Wake as *The Money Order*, with *White Genesis*. London: Heinemann, 1972

———. *Voltaïques*. Paris: Présence Africaine, 1971. Trans. Len Ortzen as *Tribal Scars and Other Stories*. London: Heinemann, 1974.

————. *Xala*. Paris: Présence Africaine, 1973. Trans. Clive Wake, same title. Westport, Conn.: Lawrence Hill, 1983.

Outlaw, Lucius. "African Philosophy: Deconstructive and Reconstructive Challenges," in *Contemporary Philosophy: A New Survey*, ed. G. Flostad, 5:9–44. Dordrecht: Martinus Nijhoff, 1987.

Oyono, Ferdinand. *Une vie de Boy*. Paris: Julliard, 1956. Trans. John Reed as *Houseboy*. London: Heinemann, 1966.

————. *Le vieux nègre et la médaille*. Paris, Julliard, 1956. Trans. John Reed as *The Old Man and the Medal*. London: Heinemann, 1967.

Phelan, James. "Narrative Discourse, Literary Character and Ideology," in *Reading Narrative*, ed. James Phelan, 132–46. Columbus: Ohio State University Press, 1989.

Poirier, J. "L'Afrique noire: Entre tradition et modernité." *Bulletin des Séances, Académie Royale des Sciences d'Outre-Mer* 40 (Jan. 1994): 17–26.

Pollard, Sidney. *The Idea of Progress*. Harmondsworth, England: Penguin, 1971.

Post, K. *The New States of West Africa*. Harmondsworth, England: Penguin, 1964.

Priebe, Richard. *Myth, Realism and the West African Writer*. Trenton, N.J.: Africa World Press, 1988.

Propp, Vladimir. *Morphology of the Folktale*. Austin: University of Texas Press, 1968.

Ranger, Terence, ed. *The Invention of Tradition*. Cambridge: Cambridge University Press, 1983.

Retamar, Roberto Fernandez. *Caliban and Other Essays*, trans. Edward Baker. Minneapolis: University of Minnesota Press, 1989.

Ricard, Alain. "La ré-appropriation de la signature: Brèves reflexions sur l'oeuvre d'Amadou Hampaté Bâ." Paper presented at the Conference of the Association pour l'Etude la Littérature Africaine (APELA), October 1985.

Roberts, Mary Nooter, and Allen Roberts, eds. "Audacities of Memory." Introduction to *Memory: Luba Art and the Making of History*. New York: Museum for African Art, and Munich: Prestel, 1996.

Rooney, David. *Kwame Nkrumah: The Political Kingdom in the Third World*. New York: St. Martin's, 1988.

Rorty, Richard. *Truth and Progress: Philosophiocal Papers. Volume 3*. Cambridge: Cambridge University Press, 1998.

Said, Edward. *Orientalism*. New York: Random House, 1978.

————. Preface to *Literature and Society*. Baltimore: Johns Hopkins University Press, 1980.

————. *The World, the Text and the Critic*. London: Faber and Faber, 1984.

Savory, Elaine. "Returning to Syrcorax / Prospero's Response: Edward Kamau Brathwaite's Word Journey." in *The Art of Kamau Brathwaite*, ed. Stewart Brown, 208–30. Bridgend: Seren, 1995.

Schwarz-Bart, André. *Le dernier des justes.* 1959; Trans. Stephen Becker as *The Last of the Just*. New York: Atheneum, 1961.

Senghor, Léopold Sédar. *Anthologie de la nouvelle poésie nègre et malgache.* Paris: Presses Universitaires de France, 1948; 2d ed., 1970.

———. *On African Socialism.* New York: Praeger, 1964.

———. *Ethiopiques: Poèmes.* Paris: Seuil, 1964. Trans. Melvin Dixon as *The Collected Poetry*. Charlottesville: University of Virginia Press, 1991.

Séverac, Alain. *Les romans de Chinua Achebe: De l'ordre au chaos.* Villeneuve d'Ascq, France: Presses Universitaires du Septentrion, 1997.

Shi, Edward. *The Simple Life.* New York: Oxford University Press, 1985.

Sim, Stuart. "Lyotard and the Politics of Antifoundationalism." *Radical Philosophy* 44 (Autumn 1986): 8–13.

Sorel, Georges. *Réflexions sur la violence.* Paris: Rivière, 1946.

Sow, Alfa Ibrahim. *Inventaire du fonds Amadou Hampaté Bâ.* Paris: Klincksieck, 1970.

Soyinka, Wole. *The Interpreters.* London: André Deutsch, 1965.

———. "The Writer in a Modern African State." *Transition* 31 (June–July 1967): 11–13.

———. *The Man Died.* London: Rex Collings, 1972.

———. *Season of Anomy.* London: Rex Collings, 1973.

———. *Myth, Literature and the African World.* Cambridge: Cambridge University Press, 1976.

———. *Death and the King's Horseman*, in *Six Plays*. London: Methuen, 1984.

———. *Art, Dialogue and Outrage.* Ibadan: New Horn Press, 1988a.

———. *Isarà.* New York: Random House, 1988b.

Spivak, Gayatri Chakravorty. *In Other Worlds: Essays in Cultural Politics.* London: Routledge, 1988.

Stead, C. K. *The New Poetic.* London: Hutchinson University Library, 1964.

Stratton, Florence. *Contemporary African Literature and the Politics of Gender.* London: Routledge, 1994.

Stimpson, Catherine. "Ad/d Feminam: Women, Literature, and Society," in *Literature and Society*, ed. Said, 174–92. Baltimore: Johns Hopkins University Press, 1980.

Suleri, Sarah. "Naipaul's Arrival." *Yale Journal of Criticism* 2, no. 1 (1988): 25–50.

Tahir, Ibrahim. *The Last Imam.* London: KPI, 1984.

Talbot, P. Amaury. *The Peoples of Southern Nigeria.* 4 vols. London, 1926. Reprint, London, Cass, 1967.

Taylor, Charles. "Rationality," in *Rationality and Relativism*, ed. Martin Hollis and Steven Lukes, 87–105. Oxford: Blackwell, 1982.

Terdiman, Richard. *Discourse/Counter Discourse*. Ithaca, N.Y.: Cornell University Press, 1985.

Tidjani-Serpos, Nouréini. "Evolution de la narration romanesque africaine: *L'étrange destin de Wangrin* d'Amadou Hampaté Bâ." *Présence Francophone* 24 (1984): 107–21.

Tonnies, Ferdinand. *Community and Society: Gemeinschaft und Gesellschaft*, trans. and ed. Charles P. Loomis. East Lansing: Michigan State University Press, 1957.

Towa, Marcien. *Essai sur la problématique philosophique dans l'Afrique actuelle*. Yaoundé, Cameroon: Editions CLE, 1971.

——. *L'idée d'une philosophie africaine*. Yaoundé, Cameroon: Editions CLE, 1980.

Toynbee, Arnold. "Militarism and the Military Virtues," in *War and Civilization*, 12–25. New York: Oxford University Press, 1950.

Trilling, Lionel. *The Liberal Imagination: Essays on Literature and Society*. New York: Anchor, 1957

Trimingham, J. Spencer. *Islam in West Africa*. Oxford: Clarendon, 1959.

Turner, Victor. *The Forest of Symbols: Aspects of Ndembu Ritual*. Ithaca, N.Y.: Cornell University Press, 1967.

Wali, Obi. "The Dead End of African Literature." *Transition* 11 (Sept. 1963): 13–15.

Walicki, Andrzej. *The Slavophile Controversy: History of a Conservative Utopia in Nineteenth-Century Russian Thought*. Oxford: Clarendon, 1975.

Walsh, William. *A Manifold Voice: Studies in Commonwealth Literature*. New York: Barnes and Noble, 1970.

Warner, Maureen. "Odomankoma Kyreme Se." *Caribbean Quarterly* 19, no. 2 (June 1973): 51–59.

——. *E. Kamau Brathwaite's "Masks": Essays and Annotations*. Kingston, Jamaica: Institute of Caribbean Studies, 1992.

Watt, Ian. *The Rise of the Novel: Studies in Defoe, Richardson, and Fielding*. London, 1957. Reprint, London: Hogarth, 1987.

Watts, Cedric. Introduction to *Joseph Conrad: Heart of Darkness and Other Tales*. London: Oxford University Press, 1998.

White, Hayden. *Metahistory: The Historical Imagination in Nineteenth-Century Europe*. Baltimore: Johns Hopkins University Press, 1973.

——. *The Content of the Form: Narrative Discourse and Historical Representation*. Baltimore: Johns Hopkins University Press, 1987.

Williams, Raymond. *George Orwell*. New York: Columbia University Press, 1971.

Wilson, Brian, ed. *Rationality*. Oxford: Blackwell, 1970.

Winters, Marjorie. "An Objective Approach to Achebe's Style." *Research in African Literatures* 12, no. 1 (1981): 55–68.

Wren, Robert. *Achebe's World: The Historical and Cultural Context of the Novels*. Washington, D.C.: Three Continents, 1980.

Wright, Richard. *Black Boy: A Record of Childhood and Youth*. New York: Harper & Brothers, 1945.

Zachernuk, Philip S. *Colonial Subjects: An African Intelligentsia and Atlantic Ideas*. Charlottesville: University Press of Virginia, 2000.

Zahan, Dominique. *La dialectique du verbe chez les Bambara*. Paris: Mouton, 1963.

Zéraffa, Michel. *Roman et société*. Paris: Presses Universitaires de France, 1971.

Zobel. Joseph. *La Rue Cases-Nègres*. Paris: Editions Jean Froissart, 1950. Reprint, Présence Africaine, 1974. Trans. Keith Q. Warner as *Black Shack Alley*. Boulder, Colo.: L. Rienner, 1997.

Zumthor, Paul. *Introduction à la poésie orale*. Paris: Seuil, 1983. Trans. Kathryn Murphy-Judy as *Oral Poetry: An Introduction*. Minneapolis: University of Minnesota Press, 1990.

Index

oral, xvi
Ozidi, 10, 35
Sundiata, 10, 35
Equiano, Olaudah, 46–48, 69
Eshu and the Vagabond Minstrels
(Osofisan), 64
Essentialism, 21, 71
Esslin, Martin, 202
Esu, 21
Ethiopiques (Senghor), 54, 257n2
Ethnolect, black, 21
Etrange destin de Wangrin, L' [*The
Fortunes of Wangrin*] (Bâ)
ambiguity in, 86–87
colonial impact in, 87–92
irony in, 90
oral tradition in, 82–86, 93
structure and style in, 93–97
European-language African literature,
ix, xii-xiii, 67, 142, 169
and discontinuity of experience, 16–
17
and drama, 17
function of, 6–7, 12
and literary tradition, 43, 59–60, 67,
117
and orality, 19, 30
and racial question, 70–71
as vehicle for indictment of Europe,
69–74
See also Clark-Bekederemo, John
Pepper; Ngugi wa Thiong'o
Example of Shakespeare (Clark-
Bekederemo), 175

Fagunwa, D. O., 17, 30, 257n2
Fanon, Frantz, 63, 69, 242
Farah, Nuddin, 64, 248n4
Finnegan, Ruth, 8, 25, 26
Fleming, Bruce E., 248n3
Foley, John Miles, 249n7
folk opera, Nigerian, 13
folktale and orality, xvi, 17–18, 34,
58
in Bâ, 92
in Diop, 40

Fortunes of Wangrin, The (Bâ). *See
Etrange destin de Wangrin, L'*
Foucault, Michel, 69, 81, 253n9
Fragments (Armah), 18, 64, 216
Frobenius, Leo, 54
Fugard, Athol, 15
Fyfe, Christopher, 50

Garrett, Naomi Mills, 252n9
Garuba, Harry, 211
Garvey, Marcus, 70
Gates, Henry Louis, Jr., 21, 46, 49, 72,
251n6
Gayle, Addison, 72
Ge'ez, 30, 251n2
Gellner, Ernest, 78
Genette, Gérard, 127
Gérard, Albert, 11, 30, 44
Gikandi, Simon, 122, 142, 144, 256–
57n2
Glissant, Edouard, 264n9
Gobineau, Arthur, 250n1
God's Bits of Wood [*Les bouts de bois de
Dieu*] (Sembène Ousmane), 221,
255n4
Goethe, 38
Goody, Jack, 24, 35, 47, 140
Gordimer, Nadine, 15, 248n4
Gordon, D., 71
Graff, Gerald, xvii, 119
Great Ponds, The (Amadi), 59, 256n2
Greene, Graham, 14, 178
Grégoire, Abbé, 152n6, 253n10
Griaule, Marcel, 3
Griot, 11, 39, 109, 255n4
Guillén, Nicolas, 20, 154–55, 179
Gurnah, Abdelrazak, 248n4
Gyekye, Kwame, ix, 63

Habermas, Jürgen, 247n1, 260n20
Harlem Renaissance, 20, 252n9
Harlow, Barbara, 116
Harmattan, L' (Sembène Ousmane),
255n4
Hausa literature, 13–14
Havensgate (Okigbo), 186